Teach Yourself
VISUALLY™
WordPress®

Visual

by Janet Majure

WILEY

Wiley Publishing, Inc.

Teach Yourself VISUALLY™ WordPress®

Published by
Wiley Publishing, Inc.
10475 Crosspoint Boulevard
Indianapolis, IN 46256

www.wiley.com

Published simultaneously in Canada

Copyright © 2010 by Wiley Publishing, Inc., Indianapolis, Indiana

No part of this publication may be reproduced, stored in a retrieval system or transmitted in any form or by any means, electronic, mechanical, photocopying, recording, scanning or otherwise, except as permitted under Sections 107 or 108 of the 1976 United States Copyright Act, without either the prior written permission of the Publisher, or authorization through payment of the appropriate per-copy fee to the Copyright Clearance Center, 222 Rosewood Drive, Danvers, MA 01923, 978-750-8400, fax 978-646-8600. Requests to the Publisher for permission should be addressed to the Permissions Department, John Wiley & Sons, Inc., 111 River Street, Hoboken, NJ 07030, 201-748-6011, fax 201-748-6008, or online at www.wiley.com/go/permissions.

Library of Congress Control Number: 2010921234

ISBN: 978-0-470-57092-0

Manufactured in the United States of America

10 9 8 7 6 5 4 3 2

Trademark Acknowledgments

Wiley, the Wiley Publishing logo, Visual, the Visual logo, Teach Yourself VISUALLY, Read Less - Learn More and related trade dress are trademarks or registered trademarks of John Wiley & Sons, Inc. and/or its affiliates. WordPress is a registered trademark of Automattic, Inc. All other trademarks are the property of their respective owners. Wiley Publishing, Inc. is not associated with any product or vendor mentioned in this book.

LIMIT OF LIABILITY/DISCLAIMER OF WARRANTY: THE PUBLISHER AND THE AUTHOR MAKE NO REPRESENTATIONS OR WARRANTIES WITH RESPECT TO THE ACCURACY OR COMPLETENESS OF THE CONTENTS OF THIS WORK AND SPECIFICALLY DISCLAIM ALL WARRANTIES, INCLUDING WITHOUT LIMITATION WARRANTIES OF FITNESS FOR A PARTICULAR PURPOSE. NO WARRANTY MAY BE CREATED OR EXTENDED BY SALES OR PROMOTIONAL MATERIALS. THE ADVICE AND STRATEGIES CONTAINED HEREIN MAY NOT BE SUITABLE FOR EVERY SITUATION. THIS WORK IS SOLD WITH THE UNDERSTANDING THAT THE PUBLISHER IS NOT ENGAGED IN RENDERING LEGAL, ACCOUNTING, OR OTHER PROFESSIONAL SERVICES. IF PROFESSIONAL ASSISTANCE IS REQUIRED, THE SERVICES OF A COMPETENT PROFESSIONAL PERSON SHOULD BE SOUGHT. NEITHER THE PUBLISHER NOR THE AUTHOR SHALL BE LIABLE FOR DAMAGES ARISING HEREFROM. THE FACT THAT AN ORGANIZATION OR WEBSITE IS REFERRED TO IN THIS WORK AS A CITATION AND/OR A POTENTIAL SOURCE OF FURTHER INFORMATION DOES NOT MEAN THAT THE AUTHOR OR THE PUBLISHER ENDORSES THE INFORMATION THE ORGANIZATION OR WEBSITE MAY PROVIDE OR RECOMMENDATIONS IT MAY MAKE. FURTHER, READERS SHOULD BE AWARE THAT INTERNET WEBSITES LISTED IN THIS WORK MAY HAVE CHANGED OR DISAPPEARED BETWEEN WHEN THIS WORK WAS WRITTEN AND WHEN IT IS READ.

FOR PURPOSES OF ILLUSTRATING THE CONCEPTS AND TECHNIQUES DESCRIBED IN THIS BOOK, THE AUTHOR HAS CREATED VARIOUS NAMES, COMPANY NAMES, MAILING, E-MAIL AND INTERNET ADDRESSES, PHONE AND FAX NUMBERS AND SIMILAR INFORMATION, ALL OF WHICH ARE FICTITIOUS. ANY RESEMBLANCE OF THESE FICTITIOUS NAMES, ADDRESSES, PHONE AND FAX NUMBERS AND SIMILAR INFORMATION TO ANY ACTUAL PERSON, COMPANY AND/OR ORGANIZATION IS UNINTENTIONAL AND PURELY COINCIDENTAL.

Contact Us

For general information on our other products and services please contact our Customer Care Department within the U.S. at 877-762-2974, outside the U.S. at 317-572-3993 or fax 317-572-4002.

For technical support please visit www.wiley.com/techsupport.

WILEY

Wiley Publishing, Inc.

Sales

Contact Wiley at (877) 762-2974 or fax (317) 572-4002.

Credits

Acquisitions Editor
Aaron Black

Sr. Project Editor
Sarah Hellert

Technical Editor
Donna L. Baker

Copy Editor
Scott Tullis

Editorial Director
Robyn Siesky

Business Manager
Amy Knies

Sr. Marketing Manager
Sandy Smith

**Vice President and Executive
Group Publisher**
Richard Swadley

**Vice President and Executive
Publisher**
Barry Pruett

Project Coordinator
Patrick Redmond

**Graphics and Production
Specialists**
Beth Brooks
Carrie A. Cesavice
Andrea Hornberger
Jennifer Mayberry

Quality Control Technician
Lindsay Littrell

Proofreader
Jacqui Brownstein

Indexer
Valerie Haynes Perry

Screen Artists
Ana Carrillo
Jill A. Proll

Illustrators
Ronda David-Burroughs
Cheryl Grubbs
Mark Pinto

About the Author

Janet Majure is an author, writer, and editor with more than 30 years in the publishing industry. She writes for three WordPress blogs (her individual blogs HomecookingRevival.com and Foodperson.com plus group blog Ethicurean.com) and has written and edited books, newsletters, articles for daily newspapers, and technical white papers. A former journalist, her topics have been wide ranging, but these days she focuses on food and technology.

Author's Acknowledgments

The author gratefully acknowledges the WordPress community, which has made this amazing software available, as well as the ongoing support of family and friends. In particular, she thanks friend, neighbor, colleague, and agent Neil Salkind.

How to Use This Book

Who Needs This Book?

This book is for the reader who has never used this particular technology or software application. It is also for readers who want to expand their knowledge.

The Conventions in This Book

❶ Steps

This book uses step-by-step instructions to guide you easily through each task. Numbered steps are actions you must do; bulleted steps clarify a point, step, or optional feature; and indented steps give you the result.

❷ Notes

Notes give additional information — special conditions that may occur during an operation, a situation that you want to avoid, or a cross reference to a related area of the book.

❸ Icons and buttons

Icons and buttons show you exactly what you need to click to perform a step.

❹ Tips

Tips offer additional information, including warnings and shortcuts.

❺ Bold

Bold type shows command names and options. It also indicates text and numbers that you must type.

❻ Italics

Italic type introduces and defines a new term.

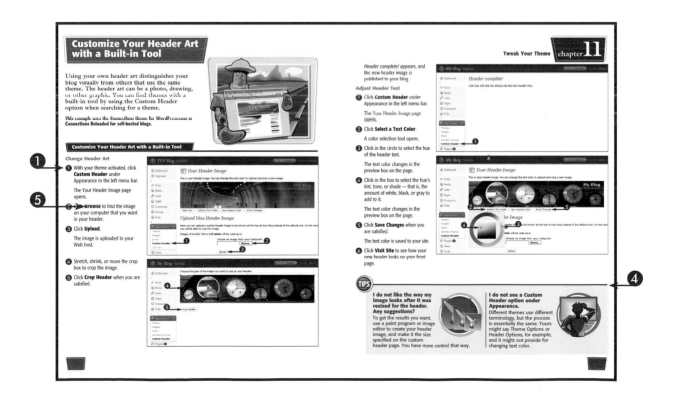

Table of Contents

 **chapter 1**   **Introducing Blogging and WordPress**

Choose a Version of WordPress 4

Choose a Blog Topic 6

Research Blog Titles 8

Buy a Domain Name 10

Plan Your Blog's Content 12

chapter 2   Set Up Your WordPress.com Blog

Sign Up with WordPress.com 16

View Your New Blog 18

Get to Know the WordPress.com Global Dashboard 20

Get to Know Your Blog's Dashboard 22

Create Your WordPress.com Profile 24

Select Your Blog's General Settings 26

Choose and Install a New Theme 28

Consider Premium WordPress.com Options 30

chapter 3 Set Up Your Self-Hosted WordPress.org Blog

Choose a Host for Your Blog. 34

Install WordPress via Your Host's Automatic Installation 36

Get an FTP Application. 38

Download WordPress Software 39

Set Up the MySQL Database 40

Upload the WordPress Files 42

Complete the Configuration and Installation. 44

Troubleshoot Installation Errors 46

chapter 4 Choose Your Self-Hosted Blog's Settings

Log On to the WordPress Dashboard. 50

Review the Dashboard and General Settings. 52

Choose a New Theme 54

Install Your New Theme 56

Choose Among Your Theme's Special Settings 60

Table of Contents

chapter 5 Know Your Blog's Dashboard in Detail

Customize and Navigate the Dashboard 64
Review the Writing Settings. 66
Set Up to Post by E-mail 67
Choose the Discussion Settings. 68
Permalinks for Self-Hosted Blogs 70
WordPress.com Domains Page. 71
About Privacy Settings 72
Select Your Privacy Settings. 73

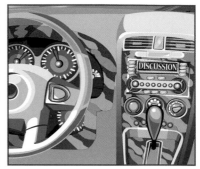

chapter 6 Create Written Blog Content

Get to Know the New Post Page 76
Introducing the WYSIWYG Editor and Toolbar 78
Introducing the HTML Editor and Toolbar 80
Write and Publish Your First Blog Post. 82
Add Formatting to Your Text 84
Recall an Earlier Version of Your Blog Post 86
Write and Publish a Page. 88
Edit or Delete a Post or Page. 90
Quick Edit Posts and Pages 91
Add Text Hyperlinks to Your Post or Page 92
Paste Text from Other Sources 94

Create a Post with Press This. 96

Create a Post via Quick Press 98

Speed Up Posting with Google Gears. 99

Consider Using a Blogging Client 100

Create a Post with Windows Live Writer 101

Import Posts from Another Blogging Platform. 102

Create a Blogroll. 104

chapter 7

Create Visual and Audio Content

Consider Media Issues. 108

Review Media Settings. 109

Prepare Images for Uploading 110

Upload and Insert an Image While Posting 112

Insert Images from Web Sources 114

Image Formatting from Add an Image Window 116

Image Formatting from Edit Image Window 118

Insert Images into Media Library 120

Insert an Image Gallery 122

Add a Slide Show to Your Posts 124

Link to YouTube (and Other) Videos 126

Upload Video Files to Your Host. 128

Link to a Podcast or Sound File from Your Blog 130

Create and Install a Favicon for a Self-Hosted Blog. 132

Create and Install a Favicon at WordPress.com. 134

Table of Contents

Introducing Widgets and Plugins 138

Choose and Insert Widgets 140

Rearrange and Remove Widgets. 142

Add Sidebar Items Using HTML in a Text Widget 144

Get a Key and Activate Akismet 146

Find Plugins 148

Consider These Popular Plugins 150

Install and Activate a Plugin. 152

Edit What You Write. 156

Use Typography to Enhance Posts 158

Use Images to Enhance Posts 160

Use the More Option to Break Your Posts in Two 162

Understanding Categories and Tags. 164

Create Categories. 166

Create Tags. 168

Apply Categories and Tags to Posts 170

Convert Categories and Tags. 172

chapter 10 Build Traffic to Your Blog

Create a Comment Policy 176

Comment on Someone Else's Blog 178

What to Say on Someone Else's Blog 179

Moderate Comments 180

Edit a Comment 182

Respond to Comments on Your Blog 184

Deal with Comment Spam 186

Allow Threaded Comments 188

Understanding Trackbacks and Pingbacks 190

Understanding and Joining RSS Feeds 192

Add a Feed to Your Sidebar 194

Use FeedBurner to Track Feed Traffic 196

Offer FeedBurner E-mail Subscriptions 198

Connect with Twitter 200

Promote Your Blog via Social Media 202

Optimize Your Blog for Search Engines 204

Use Surveys and Polls 206

chapter 11 Tweak Your Theme

Customize Your Header Art with a Built-in Tool 210

Understanding the Theme Editor 212

Add Copyright Information to the Footer 214

Change the Title on Your Blogroll 216

Create and Use a Page Template 218

Introducing CSS 220

Try CSS with the Web Developer Toolbar 222

Add a Category RSS Feed Link 224

Table of Contents

chapter 12 Use WordPress for Content Management

Understanding User Capabilities. 228

Add Authors and Contributors 230

Create a Member Community. 232

Add a Forum to Your Blog. 234

Manage Documents. 236

Use a Static Page as Your Home Page 238

Add a Blog to an Existing Static Web Site. 240

Create a Portfolio of Your Photos or Art. 242

Considerations for Your Portfolio 243

Place Ads on Your Blog 244

Add Google Ads to Your Site. 246

Add Amazon Affiliate Ads to Your Site 248

Use Sticky Posts to Control Page Content 250

chapter **13** **Maintain Your WordPress Blog**

Understanding WordPress Backups 254

Get to Know WordPress Support Options 256

Upgrade WordPress Automatically 258

Automatic Upgrade Troubleshooting 259

Upgrade WordPress Manually 260

Clean Out Outdated Drafts 264

Check Your Site for Outdated Links 266

Sign Up for a Statistics Tracker 268

Understanding Your Statistics 270

Install Plugin Upgrades 272

Read Blogs that Focus on WordPress 273

Use WordPress.com in Languages Besides English 274

Self-Hosted WordPress Blogs in Languages Besides English 275

Make a Suggestion 276

Steps to Take When Your Blog Breaks 278

Introducing Blogging and WordPress

Creating a blog is a great way to get your message across once you have decided you have something to share with the world. WordPress blogging software lets you deliver that message for free even while giving you complete control over your site.

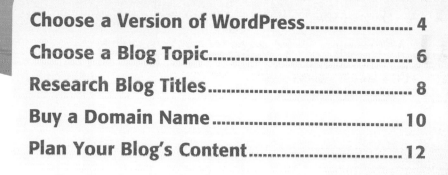

Choose a Version of WordPress........................... 4

Choose a Blog Topic... 6

Research Blog Titles... 8

Buy a Domain Name... 10

Plan Your Blog's Content.................................... 12

Choose a Version of WordPress

WordPress is available in three different varieties. WordPress.com provides hosting service for blogs and standard configurations. WordPress.org offers blogging software for self-hosted blogs plus WordPress MU (multi-user), a relatively complex program that allows you to run thousands of blogs.

This book does not teach how to set up a WordPress MU blogging network, although if you are a blogger on a WordPress MU blog network, such as through a school system or a local newspaper, your experience is similar to that of people with WordPress.com blogs. Whichever WordPress software option you choose, you can change it later. If you choose WordPress.com now and want to go to a WordPress.org blog, it is an easy transition. The reverse is also true.

About WordPress

WordPress is *open-source* software, meaning anyone can download it, use it, and change it for free. It has been around since 2003 as a program for self-hosted blogs, and this book uses versions 2.8.4-2.9.1. The organization that developed around it, WordPress.org, later started WordPress.com for people who did not want to host their own blogs.

Why WordPress?

With other free blogging platforms available, you may wonder why you should choose WordPress. The answer largely comes down to control. With WordPress you own your content, and you can customize to your heart's content. Also, WordPress allows use of static *pages*, which look and act like ordinary Web pages instead of showing content in chronological order as is typical for most blogs.

Hosted WordPress Blogs

WordPress.com is a blog host. Sign up with WordPress.com, and you can start blogging within minutes. The user interface is simple and similar to that of self-hosted WordPress blogs. WordPress.com blogs, however, limit your options in terms of your blog's template and performance.

Self-Hosted WordPress Blogs

Options for customizing your blog are nearly limitless when you have a self-hosted, or independent, WordPress.org blog. The tradeoff is that your independent blog takes a little more effort to get up and running, and keeping the software up-to-date is your job, not the host's.

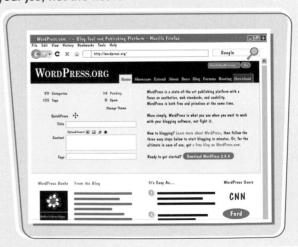

Key Differences: Appearance

WordPress.com offers more than 60 layout designs, called *themes*, but they are good ones. If you want to customize your theme by editing the *cascading style sheet*, or *CSS*, you must pay an annual fee. With a self-hosted WordPress blog, you can choose among countless free themes or purchased themes, or create your own.

Key Differences: Plugins

Plugins are program-like extensions that work with WordPress to add functionality. You can have as many as you want on your independent WordPress blog. WordPress.com does not let you add plugins, although many of the WordPress.com widgets provide plugin functions. A *widget* allows you to arrange sidebar information without writing code.

Key Differences: Ads

With a self-hosted WordPress blog, you can have zero to endless amounts of advertising. At WordPress.com, the blog host itself occasionally posts ads on your blog, unless you pay a no-ad fee. Also, WordPress.com does not allow certain types of ads.

Key Differences: Cost

The blogging software is free, whether you host your own blog or put it on WordPress.com. If you self-host, you must pay for space on a Web server, although that can be as little as a few dollars a month. If you go with WordPress.com, you may wind up paying fees to edit the CSS, eliminate ads, or post videos, costs absent for independent blogs.

Key Differences: Support

WordPress.com has a clearly written support section plus forums and a contact form for support. The support documentation for WordPress.org blogs is called the *codex.* It is written by WordPress volunteers, and its quality is inconsistent. There is no support contact except for the WordPress.org forums, but they are excellent.

Choose a Blog Topic

You can choose anything as your blog topic, but doing a little research may help you identify the topic that you will love to write about and that readers will come looking for.

Expertise

If you are an expert in some field, your knowledge could make an excellent blog topic. By writing about your area of experience you will have plenty of content and confidence, and you may be able to use your blog to attract business and advertising.

Hobby

Perhaps you have a hobby that you avidly pursue and continue to learn more about. This, too, is a good subject for a blog. Fellow hobbyists may look to you for ideas and advice, and they can offer ideas and advice in return.

Business

A blog is a great way to keep in touch with your customers and to attract more customers. It is like a newsletter, only easier. Again, you surely have plenty of content to offer readers, whether it is news about products, special offers, or holiday hours.

Scattershot

One option is not to choose a topic at all and simply to write your blog as you might write a diary. This is a fine approach as long as you are content to attract a small audience. Only a few people, by virtue of their fascinating lives or captivating writing styles, can write a scattershot blog and attract a large number of readers.

Focused

The more focused your topic, the easier it will be for search engines to find it. A focused blog also has greater potential to generate advertising revenues later, if that is one of your goals.

Useful and Entertaining

Whatever topic you choose, you will get more readers if your blog is useful or entertaining — or both. As you narrow your list of possible topics, think about which ones give you the greatest opportunity to be helpful or engaging. Those may be your best bets.

Competition

If you are unconcerned about developing an audience or if you want your blog to focus on your personal life, you need not worry about competition. For other subjects, however, check out the competition before you settle on a blog topic.

Research the Competition

You can get clues as to what is being written about and what is popular at these Web sites:

- http://wordpress.com: See the most popular recent *tags,* which are like keywords, on WordPress.com blogs.

- www.alexa.com: Search for blogs on your topic, and Alexa lists them and their traffic ratings.

- www.technorati.com/pop: This page lists the 100 most popular blogs among Technorati users.

- www.stumbleupon.com: Sign up with this service, select your topic of interest, and then *stumble,* which takes you to blog post after blog post on that subject.

- http://blogsearch.google.com: Search on a topic to find existing blogs and blog posts on the topic.

Research Blog Titles

If you do not take care in naming your blog, you may find down the road that your choice does not serve you well. It may duplicate the name of an existing blog, or you may decide you want to get a domain name but a Web site with your blog's desired domain name already exists.

Blog Title versus Domain

Your *blog title* generally appears across the top of your blog's front page. A *domain name* is the part of a Web address that includes *.com* or *.net* or one of the other domain name extensions. You can read about buying a domain name in the next section, "Buy a Domain Name."

Self-Hosted Blog Names

On a self-hosted blog, it is helpful for the blog title and domain name to match, or at least to correspond, so that people can find you more easily. If you want to name your blog *In My Opinion*, it would be wise to see whether a domain such as *inmyopinion.net* or *imo.com* is available.

WordPress.com Names

At WordPress.com, the username you choose when you sign up becomes part of your blog's Internet address. If your username is *example*, your blog's Web address will be *example.wordpress*.com unless you buy a domain name. The Web address is separate from the blog's title, but it is good for the two to correspond.

Consider the Long Term

If you are going to keep your blog private or are certain that you do not want to develop a significant audience, the blog title makes no difference. Most people start blogs, though, because they want to be heard. If you are one of those people, then consider the steps on these pages.

Brainstorm Names

Your blog topic is the place to start your search for blog titles. Write as many words and phrases as you can think of associated with your topic. If it is a personal blog, you may simply want to use your real name. Even your real name may not be as unique as you think, however, so write down many options.

Narrow the Options

Settle on a handful of blog titles, and then find out whether another site has that name. You may have to try lots of options before you find one not in use. See "Try for a Unique Name" on this page to find out how to check what is being used.

All the Good Names Are Taken!

So many sites are on the Web these days that it may seem that all the good names are taken, but forge onward. You can try alternate spellings, whimsical expressions, or combinations of your name and your interest. If you can make the title memorable and easy to spell, all the better.

If someone else has a Web site or blog with your preferred title, you can still use that title, but it is a bad idea. Besides the potential for legal conflict if someone decides to trademark the title, the bigger issue is that readers may get your blog and the other site confused.

Try for a Unique Name

Take these steps to increase your odds of having a unique blog title:

- Type your proposed blog title into a Google search box along with the word *blog*. Review the search results to see blogs that use your title in full or in part.

- Type your proposed blog title in your browser's address box followed by wordpress.com. For example, you could type **mythoughts.wordpress.com**, and any WordPress.com blogs by that name will pop up in your browser.

- Type the proposed title in the address box followed by blogspot.com, as in **mythoughts.blogspot.com**.

- Do the same thing but use the domain typepad.com.

Buy a Domain Name

If you are self-hosting your blog, you likely will want to buy a domain name to make it easier for readers to find you. You may want to buy one for a WordPress.com blog too.

You can buy a domain name from any number of *registrars*. Web hosts often give their customers a price break on domain registrations, so if you are planning an independent blog, you may want to choose a Web host before registering your domain.

Buy a Domain Name

① Go to http://domain-suggestions. domaintools.com/ in your Web browser.

Note: *This site is one of many where you can search for domains. Your Web host may give you a discounted price.*

② Type the name of your proposed domain in the box.

③ Click **Get Suggestions** or press **Enter**.

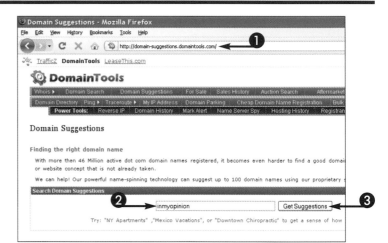

● Domains with the name you searched appear on the top line of the results. Those already registered appear with gray dots under the domain extensions.

● Suggested alternative domain names appear on the successive lines.

If none of the available or suggested domain names satisfies you, repeat steps **2** and **3** until you find one that will work.

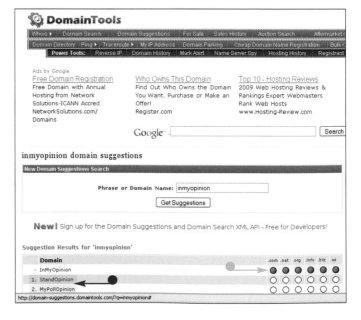

④ Click the domain name you want to register (○ changes to ◉).

● The domain also appears on the right side of the screen under Shopping Cart. You may select multiple domains.

⑤ When you have selected all the domains you want to register, click **Buy This** or **Buy All These Domains** if you selected several.

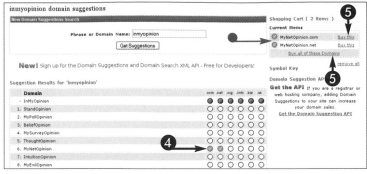

⑥ Review the information on the confirmation page.

⑦ When you are satisfied with your selection or selections, click **Add and Proceed to Checkout**.

Clicking takes you to a new, secure page at a different domain.

⑧ Provide the necessary information to complete your registration. Click **Continue**.

Proceed through the remaining screens until your registration purchase is complete.

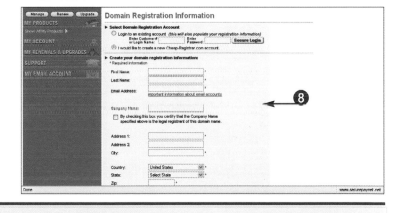

Do I have to buy a domain name?

No. If you do not, however, your URL will be your Web host's domain and directory listing, such as www. webhost.com/myweblog or it could be a subdomain such as myweblog.wordpress.com.

Is the process the same for a WordPress.com blog?

It can be, or you can buy your domain name through WordPress.com. Doing so eliminates a few steps in setup.

Plan Your Blog's Content

Your blog will be easier to create and maintain and easier for readers to follow if you plan your content before you start blogging. By planning ahead, you can give your blog a consistent approach that works for you, your content, and your readers.

Words, Pictures, or Both?

Your choice of having content that is word heavy, picture heavy, or an even balance of words and pictures affects not only the appearance of your blog, but how you spend your time preparing your posts. Give thought now as to what medium best expresses the ideas you want to share.

Consider Post Length

Although there is no general ideal length, there may be an ideal length for you and your blog. Having a somewhat predictable post length enables you to know how long it may take to write a post, and lets regular readers know how much time to allow for reading. You can break up long subjects into a series of posts.

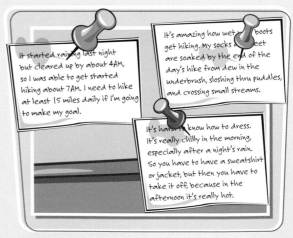

Consider Post Frequency

Some bloggers post multiple times a day; others post once a week. Your blog's topic and your time constraints may dictate how often you can post, and that is fine. *More* is not necessarily better, but *predictable* is definitely better!

Make Your Blog Stand Out

After you have studied other blogs in your subject area, ask what will make your blog unique, aside from its being written by you. If your topic is broad — cars, perhaps — yours will stand out better and be easier to plan if you narrow the subject to, say, restoring Chevrolets from the 1950s, or reviewing late-model two-seat sports cars.

Make Your Blog Accurate

Even if you are an authority in your subject area, you need to check your facts and, where possible, link to your sources. Yes, you can find popular sites, particularly on politics, that use dubious information, but if you want credibility with most readers, you need to get your facts straight. Include fact-checking as part of your content plan.

Suit the Content to the Subject

If your blog is about sculpture or carpentry or any other highly visual subject, you need to have pictures! Podcasts would be desirable on an interview blog. Make sure you have the equipment you need for the media you plan to use. If your blog is about grammar or creative writing, you can probably skip buying a top-flight digital camera.

Set Up Your WordPress.com Blog

Once you have decided to run your blog on WordPress.com, getting set up is a snap. In this chapter you sign up with WordPress.com, get familiar with its workings, choose among settings, and select a visual *theme* for your new blog's appearance.

Sign Up with WordPress.com............................16

View Your New Blog 18

Get to Know the WordPress.com
    Global Dashboard.....................................20

Get to Know Your Blog's Dashboard 22

Create Your WordPress.com Profile..............24

Select Your Blog's General Settings...............26

Choose and Install a New Theme...................28

Consider Premium WordPress.com
    Options...30

Sign Up with WordPress.com

With just a few simple steps, you can sign up with WordPress.com. When you do, you can start communicating, customizing, and getting in touch with the world as soon as you like.

1 Navigate to http://wordpress.com in your Web browser.

2 Click **Sign up now**.

3 Type your proposed username in the Username box.

Note: Keep in mind that the default for your blog's URL is username/wordpress.com.

4 Type a password in the Password box.

5 Retype the password in the Confirm box.

● The Password Strength indicator tells you how secure your password is.

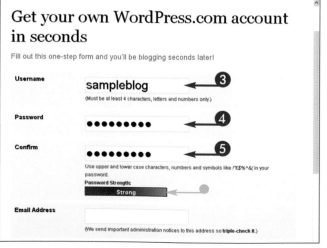

chapter 2

⑥ Type the e-mail address where you want to receive WordPress.com notices in the Email Address box.

● Read the information at the Fascinating Terms of Service link.

⑦ Click the **Legal flotsam** check box (☐ changes to ☑).

⑧ Click **Gimme a blog!** (○ changes to ◉).

⑨ Click **Next**.

The next screen explains that you will receive a confirmation e-mail at the address you provided.

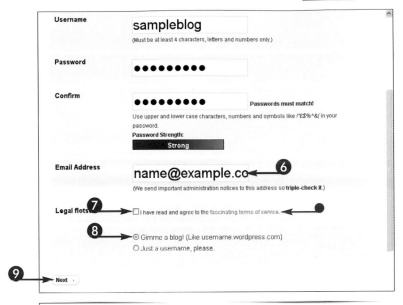

⑩ Click the link in the e-mail you receive to confirm your account.

A new window opens in your browser confirming your account is now active. Click **View your site** to see your new blog.

Note: WordPress sends you a second confirmation e-mail. Keep a copy of it because it contains your username and password as well as an API key that you will need later.

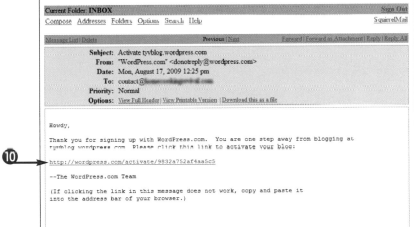

TIP

Can I just sign up without starting a blog?
Yes. Doing so will let you look around the WordPress site and comment on the blogs you find there. You can add your own blog later. To sign up without starting a blog, click **Just a username** (instead of **Gimme a blog!**) on the signup page.

View Your New Blog

Now it is time to learn the parts and pieces that make up your new blog. That general understanding will help you to make decisions as to your blog's appearance and content.

Header

The header, which runs across the top of the screen, displays the blog title and tagline.

Blog Post Title

The post title is the headline for an individual post.

Blog Post Date

Note the format of the date; it can be changed.

Blog Post Author's Name

The default name is your username. Unless you want to remain anonymous, you may want to change this to your nickname or real name when you create your WordPress. com profile later in this chapter.

TYV Blog
Just another WordPress.com weblog

Hello world!
August 17, 2009 by tyvblog

Welcome to WordPress.com. This is your first post. Edit or delete it and start blogging!

Posted in Uncategorized | Edit | 1 Comment »

search this site

Pages
» About

Archives
» August 2009

Categories
» Uncategorized (1)

Blogroll
» WordPress.com
» WordPress.org

Meta
» Site Admin
» Log out
» Valid XHTML
» XFN
» WordPress

Blog at WordPress.com.
Entries (RSS) and Comments (RSS).

Blog Post

The main text section of your blog entry is known as a *post*.

Sidebar

Most themes include sidebars, and you get to choose items that appear in them.

Blog Post Category

You have the option of selecting categories for your blog. Categories, as explained in "Understanding Categories and Tags" in Chapter 9, are useful for organizing your blog's content.

Edit Link

This link appears only when you are logged in, and only on your own blog. It takes you "behind the scenes" to where you create your blog.

Blog Post Comments Link

This link takes you to comments on the post and shows how many comments are recorded.

Footer

The information at the bottom of the page may vary depending on what theme you choose.

The Kubrick Theme

The default blog is in a *theme*, a visual template, known as Kubrick. It is pretty plain, although you can change the color or even the background of the header. The Kubrick theme is a *two-column* theme, with the blog posts appearing in one column and the sidebar serving as the second column. Other themes offer one to four columns.

A Complete Package

Every link you see on the default blog goes to the other pages that are automatically created in your WordPress blog, which include sample text. Just about every element can be changed, too.

A Practice Run

Spend a few moments clicking the various links to see what a default WordPress.com blog looks like and how to navigate through it. Doing so will help you make decisions about your blog's content and appearance.

Sidebar Terms

The sidebar of most themes contains two terms unfamiliar to blog newbies. They are *Blogroll*, which is simply a list of blogs that you favor, and *Meta*. *Meta* refers to *metadata*, or information about your blog and its contents. The links in the Meta section enable you to manage your site.

Get to Know the WordPress.com Global Dashboard

The WordPress.com Global Dashboard gives you ready access to information about your blog as well as links to blogs across the WordPress.com community. It is also a good place to practice using the WordPress interface.

The Global Dashboard provides links to such handy information as statistics about your blog and links to new posts elsewhere on WordPress.com. If you are in a hurry to get blogging, though, you can visit the Global Dashboard later.

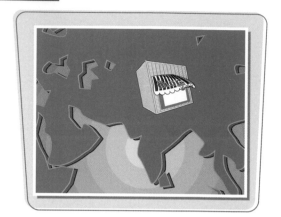

① On the WordPress.com home page, click **My Account**.

Note: WordPress.com uses cookies, so it remembers you from one visit to another.

② Click **Global Dashboard** from the drop-down menu.

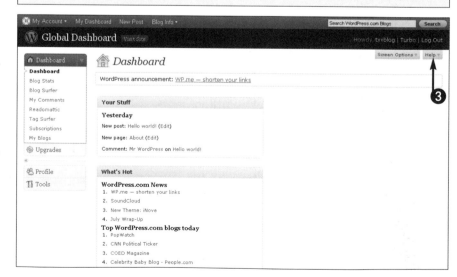

The Global Dashboard opens.

③ After scanning the page to get a sense of what is there, click **Help**.

The Help box opens. It explains how to rearrange the Global Dashboard page and provides links to other kinds of help. Click **Help** again to close the Help box.

④ Position the mouse over the What's Hot box (↖ turns to ✛).

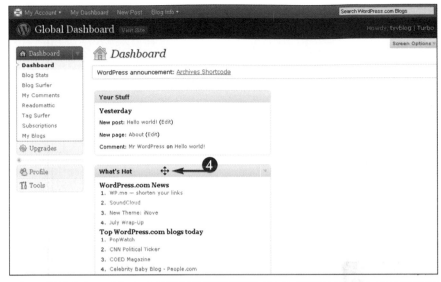

⑤ Click and drag the **What's Hot** box to the right and up until it is beside the Your Stuff box. Release the mouse button.

TIP

What is the difference between the Global Dashboard and My Dashboard in the WordPress menu bar?

Both Dashboards include the Your Stuff and What's Hot boxes by default, but My Dashboard includes additional information boxes and menus specific to your blog. The Global Dashboard is the place to go for a snapshot of what is happening on your blog and on WordPress.com without getting bogged down in details. If you like all your information in one place, though, you may never feel the need to use the Global Dashboard.

Get to Know Your Blog's Dashboard

Your blog's Dashboard is information central. From the Dashboard, you not only can get an overview of current and past activity on your blog, but you also can add to your blog's content.

You can access your Dashboard by clicking My Dashboard on the WordPress.com menu bar. You can rearrange the content by clicking a box's title bar and dragging it to the desired location, and you can expand or collapse boxes on the page by clicking a box's title bar.

Left Menu Bar

Contains navigation links for working on your WordPress.com blog. Most of the items expand when you click them to reveal more options.

Right Now

Provides the facts on how many posts, pages, and other content items your blog has.

QuickPress

Lets you type up a blog post when you are in a hurry and do not need to do anything fancy.

Screen Options Expand Button

Opens a box that lets you choose which content modules appear on your Dashboard.

Recent Comments

Reveals the names of recent commenters along with the name of the post that they commented on and the first line or two of the comment.

Recent Drafts

Shows the headline and opening words of posts that you have written or started but not published. Click the title to edit the draft or resume writing.

Show on Screen

Indicates with a checked box (☑) that the content item appears on your Dashboard.

Screen Layout

Shows with a selected radio button (◉) how many columns WordPress uses to display your Dashboard information.

Screen Options Collapse Button

Collapses the Screen Options box.

Incoming Links

Lists other blogs that link to your site.

Stats

Gives a snapshot of how many times people are viewing your blog and which blog posts are getting the most interest.

Global Dashboard Items

Display the same information that appears on the Global Dashboard.

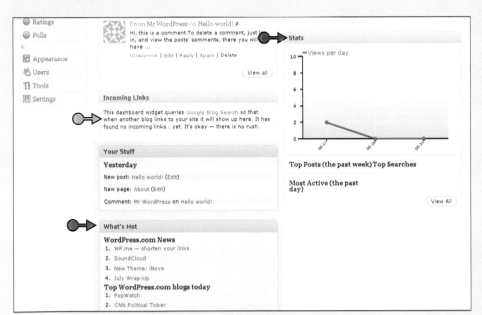

Create Your WordPress.com Profile

Editing your profile lets you choose how you interact with WordPress.com and also what kind of first impression readers get of you.

You can get to the Profile page by clicking your username in the WordPress.com blog title bar or by clicking the Users bar in the left menu bar and choosing Profile.

Create Your WordPress.com Profile

① If you access WordPress.com over an unencrypted connection, click the check box (☐ changes to ☑) next to Browser Connection.

② If you want your blog interface to be in a language besides English, click the Interface Language dropdown menu and choose your preferred language.

③ Click **Change your Gravatar** to select or upload an image to appear with comments on your own and other WordPress.com blogs.

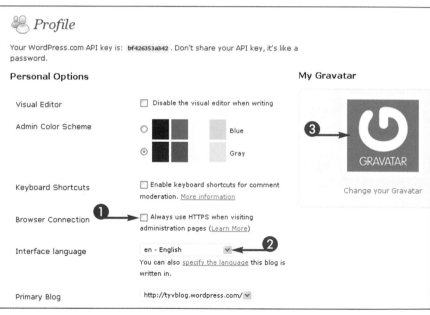

④ Type your first name in the First Name box to have your real name to appear as the author's name.

⑤ Type your last name in the Last Name box to have your real name appear as the author's name.

⑥ If you choose, type a nickname in the Nickname box that is different from your username, which is the default.

Note: Including a nickname gives you another option for how you are identified publicly.

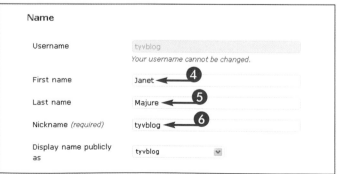

24

⑦ Choose the way you want your name to appear when you are the author of a blog post or comment.

● The default e-mail is the one you provided when you signed up with WordPress.com. You can change it; WordPress e-mails you to confirm the change.

Note: *When you leave comments on other WordPress.com blogs, the blog owner has access to your e-mail address.*

⑧ Type your Web site URL, either for your blog or some other site, in the Website box to associate it with your name.

Note: *By listing your URL here, people are able to click your name on your blog or on your WordPress.com comments and go directly to your Web page.*

⑨ Click **Update Profile** to save your changes.

Display name publicly as   tyvblog   ⑦

Contact Info

E-mail *(required)*   myname@webhost.com

Website   ⑧

AIM

Yahoo IM

Jabber / Google Talk

About Yourself

About Yourself

Biographical Info

Share a little biographical information to fill out your profile. This may be shown publicly.

New Password

If you would like to change the password type a new one. Otherwise leave this blank.

Type your new password again.

Strength indicator

Hint: The password should be at least seven characters long. To make it stronger, use upper and lower case letters, numbers and symbols like ! " ? $ % ^ &).

Update Profile   ⑨

TIPS

What is a Gravatar?
A Gravatar, or *globally recognized avatar*, is an image associated with your e-mail address and blog posts. On blogs with themes that use Gravatars, your image appears with any post or comment you leave.

Why not fill in the other information on this page?
At this writing, WordPress makes no use of this information. There is no harm in completing it, but there is no use to it either.

Select Your Blog's General Settings

In the General Settings, you can let WordPress know basic information such as the name of your blog, where you get e-mail, and what time zone you are in. Nothing in these settings is permanent, though. If you change your mind later, you can change your settings.

Select Your Blog's General Settings

① On the Dashboard, click **Settings** to open the settings list.

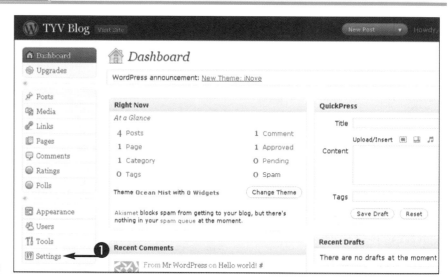

When you do this, WordPress also goes directly to the General Settings screen.

② Type your blog's name in the Blog Title box.

③ Type your blog's tagline in the Tagline box, which by default contains the standard tagline, "Just another WordPress.com weblog."

Note: *The tagline is like a subtitle; it provides a little additional information about your blog and appears on the home page of most WordPress blogs. If you prefer, you can delete the standard tagline and leave the space blank.*

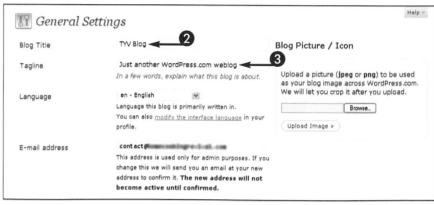

④ In the Language box, choose the language in which you plan to write your blog's posts. The default is English.

⑤ In the E-mail Address box, type the e-mail address where you want to receive notices from WordPress.

⑥ In the Timezone box, select from the drop-down list your location's time relative to UTC, or *coordinated universal time*, as indicated in the tip.

Note: *You must manually reset the zone for daylight savings time.*

⑦ Click a date format (○ changes to ◉).

⑧ Click a time format (○ changes to ◉).

Note: *You can also create a custom format.*

⑨ Select a day in the Week Starts On drop-down list to specify which day of the week any WordPress display calendars start on.

⑩ Click **Save Changes**.

WordPress saves your settings.

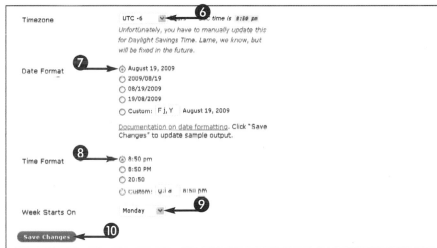

How do I know what the UTC is in my location?
If you are in the United States, you can use this list:

Local Time	UTC	Local Time	UTC
Atlantic Standard	UTC -4	Mountain Daylight	UTC -6
Atlantic Daylight	UTC -3	Pacific Standard	UTC -8
Eastern Standard	UTC -5	Pacific Daylight	UTC -7
Eastern Daylight	UTC -4	Alaskan Standard	UTC -9
Central Standard	UTC -6	Alaskan Daylight	UTC -8
Central Daylight	UTC -5	Hawaii-Aleutian Standard	UTC -10
Mountain Standard	UTC -7	Hawaii-Aleutian Daylight	UTC -9

You can give your blog a personal look by choosing a theme that corresponds with your purpose or personality. WordPress.com gives you many options, including themes for photo galleries and for social networking blogs, and you can customize those options further.

Choose and Install a New Theme

① On My Dashboard, click **Change Theme**.

WordPress opens the Manage Themes page.

● The Manage Themes page lists the current theme at the top.

● Fifteen random themes appear at the bottom of the page.

● WordPress gives you three ways to browse themes.

② Scroll down to view the currently displayed themes.

Each theme bears a brief description and *tags*, which are like keywords. Clicking a tag displays all themes that bear that tag.

③ Click **Feature Filters** to search by particular theme elements.

The Theme Filters box opens.

④ Click theme characteristics that interest you (☐ changes to ☑).

Note: *The selected options are cumulative. If you select, for example, **Green** and **Orange**, the search finds only themes that use both the Green and Orange tags.*

⑤ Click **Apply Filters**.

WordPress presents the first 15 themes that meet your criteria. Try them out by clicking **Preview**.

⑥ When you find a theme you like, click **Activate**.

WordPress presents a nearly blank window, but you can click **Visit Site** near the top of the screen to see your site, now in its new theme. To see your theme's options, click **Appearance** on the Dashboard.

What do all those theme filters mean?
Here is a guide to popular options whose meaning may be unclear.

Theme Filter	What It Is
Fixed Width	Keeps column widths the same no matter how big the window in which they are viewed.
Flexible Width	Lets columns grow wider or narrower to accommodate the screen size of the viewer.
Blavatar	Works like a logo for your blog. It appears in the address bar of browsers that support *favicons*, those tiny icons you may see on some sites.
Front Page Posting	Lets you post as you would on a social networking site, without going to the Dashboard.
Microformats	Allows use of Microformats. Read more at Microformats.org.
Sticky Post	Allows you to keep a particular post at the top of your home page.
RTL Language Support	Supports use of right-to-left languages, such as Arabic and Hebrew.

You can customize WordPress.com more when you choose some of its premium features. These let you use your own domain name, do a custom *cascading style sheet*, or CSS, and more.

Premium Features

Our free features are what makes WordPress.com such a great community, but we offer these optional upgrades to *really* help you stand out from the pack.

Be the master of your domain
Your WordPress.com blog address is a sure sign of style, but what happens when you really get serious about controlling your online identity? It's easy to add your own domain name, like example.com, to your existing WordPress.com blog. Or if you already have your own domain name, it's easy to transfer it to your WordPress.com blog. Registering a domain name with us is only $14.97/year, and mapping an existing domain name is $9.97/year.

http:// mygreatnewblog.com

Extra Storage
If you find yourself running out of space, it's easy to add more storage to your blog. You can add 5, 15, or 25 gigabytes to your blog, so you'll have all the room you need to host tons of photos, videos, and music. Add 5 GB for $19.97/year, 15 GB for $49.97/year, or 25 GB for $89.97/year.

3 + 5 GB GB   15 GB   25 GB

Custom CSS
If you know your way around a cascading style sheet, you can really put a personal touch on your WordPress.com blog. Or use the Custom CSS upgrade with our Sandbox theme to create an entirely new design. All yours for just $14.97/year.

The Lorem
Just another WordPress weblog

Suspendisse non est
DECEMBER 17, 2006

Suspendisse non est. Vivam: feugiat egestas. Pellentesqui ante. Phasellus tincidunt ero justo iaculis ipsum. Donec a turpis. Nullam ut nibh. Done adipiscing viverra erat. In sit

VideoPress
Sometimes, you just have to say it with video. It's a great way to add a little liveliness to your blog. With VideoPress, it's simple—just upload your video and we'll convert it to the right formats for sharing on the web (including an HD option for high definition video). We'll present your videos in great style, with a minimalist player design that won't get in the way or clash with your blog's design. Adding VideoPress to your blog will instantly turn your blog's RSS feed into a Podcast that you can drop right in to any Podcast player like Miro or iTunes.

To the right: an example of VideoPress in action. Turn on HD for the full experience!

Go Ad-Free
From time to time, we display text ads on your blog to logged-out users who aren't regular visitors. Doing this allows us to keep bringing you the free features you love. However, if you'd prefer your readers didn't see ads, you have the control to turn them off.

Unlimited users
The free limit of 35 users per private blog is enough for most people, but if you're building a private site that will have a large community or you're a large organization, buying this upgrade is the

Gifts

Feeling magnanimo got friends or family WordPress.com blo can spread the love them credits that work like a gift ca purchase any of the premium featu

The Premium Features page, at http://en.wordpress.com/products/, provides information about premium features:

- Using your own domain name (see Chapter 1).
- Using your own CSS.
- Buying more storage space.
- Using WordPress.com's VideoPress service.
- Blocking WordPress.com's occasional ads from your blog.
- Allowing more than 35 registered users.

Custom CSS

Cascading Style Sheets, or CSS, provide preconfigured settings for the size, typeface, indention, and color of your blog's type — from headings to footers, posts to comments. CSS also gives the default style settings for images. To change them, you need custom CSS. You can experiment with CSS changes by clicking **Appearance** in the left menu bar and clicking **Edit CSS** before deciding if you want to upgrade to use your own custom CSS.

Adding Storage Space

Your free WordPress.com blog account includes 3 gigabytes of storage. You could blog for years and not use it up unless you use many big images. Because audio and video use a lot of storage, however, WordPress.com requires space upgrades if you want to use audio or video on your blog. You must purchase the VideoPress service to use video.

VideoPress

VideoPress is the most expensive upgrade apart from the 25 gigabyte space upgrade. It is a slick feature if you plan to use video, because it lets you host the video on your blog rather than on a separate site such as YouTube, and it makes your videos available as podcasts.

Buying Upgrades

You must go to the Upgrades page to buy any premium feature. It can be reached by clicking **Upgrades** under Dashboard in the left menu bar. Click **Buy Now** next to any upgrade you want to buy, which takes you to a payment page. You can buy only one upgrade at a time. When you are finished, click **Return to WordPress**.

3

Set Up Your Self-Hosted WordPress.org Blog

Your self-hosted WordPress blog requires a little more effort, but the payoff is in total control of the look and function of your blog.

Choose a Host for Your Blog 34

Install WordPress via Your Host's
    Automatic Installation 36

Get an FTP Application 38

Download WordPress Software 39

Set Up the MySQL Database 40

Upload the WordPress Files 42

Complete the Configuration and
    Installation 44

Troubleshoot Installation Errors 46

Choose a Host for Your Blog

When you choose a reliable and accessible Web host, you can count on your WordPress blog staying online and available. You might even get some technical support for WordPress.

What Web Hosts Do

A Web host provides a computer server that stores your blog's files and databases and makes them available over the Internet. Web hosts usually offer a control panel to help you manage your files and low-cost domain registration options.

WordPress Requirements

Running WordPress requires that the Web host provide two basic software packages: PHP version 4.3 or greater and MySQL version 4.0 or greater. PHP is a scripting language, and MySQL is database software. WordPress also recommends, but does not require, Apache or Nginx as the server software.

Your Requirements

You also need to consider your blog's specific requirements, such as the amount of traffic you expect or hope for, and the type and quantity of media you expect to use. When you start from scratch, this information can be hard to determine, so make your best guess and, when contacting potential hosts, find out how they handle a surge in traffic or changing host packages if your needs change.

Shared or Dedicated Server?

A *shared* server means that the computer on which your Web site resides is also home to other Web sites. A *dedicated* server means it is reserved for your site alone, which naturally is more expensive. A shared server is usually adequate for most small blogs.

Options to Consider

Countless Web hosts are available. Among them are your Internet service provider, or *ISP*; a WordPress-recommended Web host; and all the other Web hosts out there. Your own ISP may — or may not — be the least expensive alternative. Most WordPress-recommended hosts, which you can find at WordPress.org/hosting, provide one-click WordPress installations. For other Web host recommendations, ask friends and read detailed reviews at http://b2evolution.net.

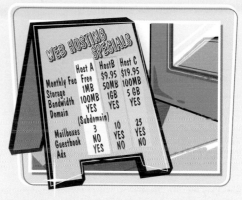

Checking Them Out

Once you have two or three Web hosts to consider, check them out by reading reviews on http://b2evolution.net and by calling the host's support line — not the sales line — to see whether you are likely to be able to get help when you need it. It is easy to get someone to talk on the sales line, but a 10-minute wait when you call support may not be acceptable to you.

Take a Tour

Once you have made a decision and signed up for Web hosting, get familiar with your host's control panel. It makes managing your blog easier and most likely also provides access to site data that you will find helpful.

Install WordPress via Your Host's Automatic Installation

If you chose a Web host with automatic WordPress installation, you can have all the necessary WordPress files installed in the right spot on your host's Web directory in a minute or less. If you have trouble, the Web host is there to help.

Install WordPress via Your Host's Automatic Installation

① After you log on to your Web host and go to its control panel, click its link for WordPress.

● If a WordPress link is not evident, you can call your Web host for help, look on the host's support pages, or click Fantastico or SimpleScripts in the control panel to see if they have a WordPress option.

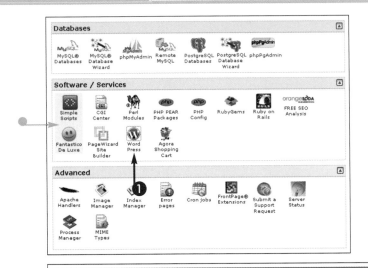

The WordPress installation window opens. In this example, SimpleScripts makes the installation.

② Click **Install**.

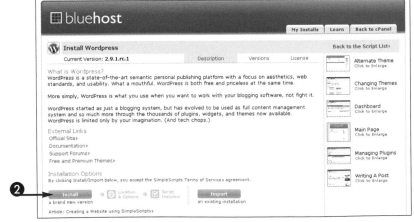

The Installing WordPress window opens.

3 Leave the WordPress version at the default setting, which is the newest stable version.

4 From the drop-down list, choose where you want WordPress installed.

5 Click the link to display Advanced Options and make any desired changes.

Note: SimpleScripts sets admin as your logon name and gives you a random password.

6 After you have reviewed the license agreement, click the check box to agree (☐ changes to ☑), and then click **Complete**.

The SimpleScripts Status window opens and shows the installation progress.

● SimpleScripts alerts you when installation is complete.

● SimpleScripts displays site information including the URL for your new blog and the URL where you go to log on plus your username and password.

7 Click the site URL to see your new blog.

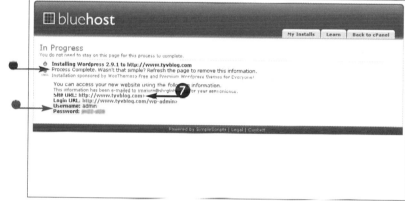

How do I know where to install WordPress?

Your Web host assigns you a home directory where it stores files for your Web site. Among them is a *root directory*, where your WordPress files go. It often is called *public_html* or *Web root* or something on that order. If you are not sure which folder is your root directory, contact your Web host and ask.

An *FTP program*, or file transfer protocol program, lets you easily move files from your computer to your Web host. You will need it to do a manual WordPress installation. Your host may provide an FTP utility through its control panel, but using an FTP *client*, a program on your computer, may be faster.

FileZilla Client is a free, open-source FTP program that works with Windows, Macintosh, and Linux computers.

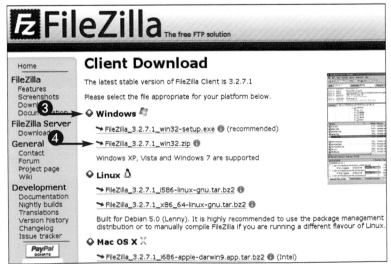

① After starting your Web browser, go to http://filezilla-project.org.

② Click **Download FileZilla Client**.

The FileZilla Client Download window opens.

③ Review the download options to find the version for your computer's operating system.

④ Click the link to the version you need.

A download window opens. Follow the usual steps for your computer for program installation to install FileZilla Client.

Note: You will use your FTP client to upload files to your Web host by way of your FTP address. Your FTP address is probably ftp://yourdomain.com where yourdomain.com stands in place of your regular Web address. Check with your Web host if you are not sure.

Before you can upload WordPress to your Web host for a
manual installation, you first must download the software
from WordPress.org. After this simple process, you will be
ready to complete your manual WordPress installation.

① In your browser, go to http://
wordpress.org/download.

② Click **Download WordPress**. At
this writing, the latest version is
WordPress 2.9.1.

Follow the usual steps to
download a file to your computer.

③ Extract the WordPress files.

Note: *Because WordPress software runs on your
Web host, not on your local computer, it does not
matter whether your computer is a PC or a
Macintosh.*

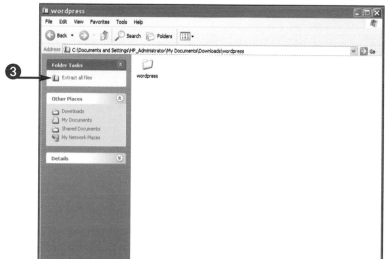

Set Up the MySQL Database

You need a MySQL database to store all the content of your blog. No database, no blog, so you need to set up the database before you load your WordPress software for a manual installation.

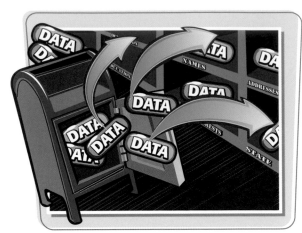

Go to your Web host and log on to its control panel to get started. This example shows the widely used cPanel control panel, but every Web host has an equivalent. Yours may look different, but it does the same thing. Check with technical support at your host if you cannot find the appropriate link.

Set Up the MySQL Database

① In the MySQL Database Wizard, type a name for your database.

You can reach the wizard by clicking **MySQL Database Wizard** in cPanel.

② Click **Next Step**.

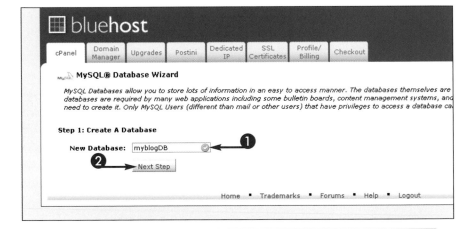

③ Type a username.

④ Type a password.

⑤ Retype the password.

Note: *Be absolutely sure to record the username and password.*

⑥ Click **Next Step**.

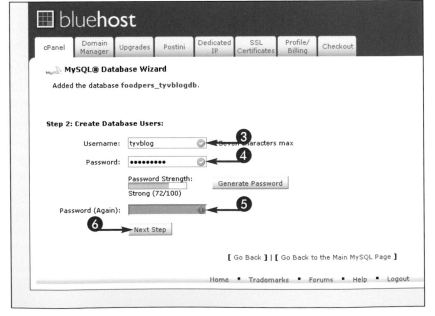

● The next window confirms the name and password.

⑦ To give the user you created — that is you, the administrator — all the privileges you require to set up and operate the database, click **All Privileges** (☐ changes to ☑).

⑧ Click **Next Step**.

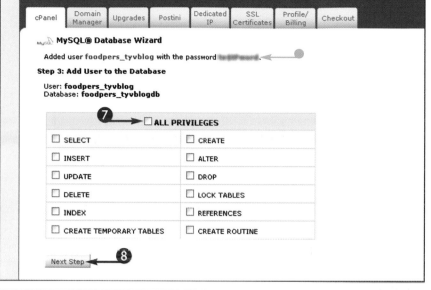

⑨ Review the information on the confirmation screen.

⑩ Click **Return to Home**.

You are back at the cPanel home.

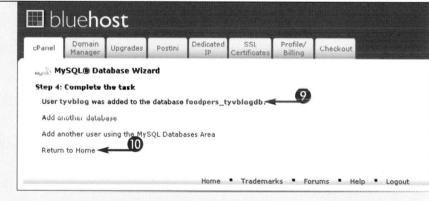

 TIPS

What should I name my database?
Give it a name that you readily associate with your blog so that you will recognize it now and in the future. You may find it helpful if you write it down for the installation process.

Can I use my same username and password?
If you want. The important things are that you can remember them when you want to install your WordPress files.

Upload the WordPress Files

Uploading the WordPress files to your Web host gives you all the files you need for your manual WordPress installation. Here is where you put your FTP client to use.

① After you open your FTP client, FileZilla in this example, type the host name in the Host box.

The host is your blog's URL, such as *myblog.com* unless you want to install your blog somewhere besides the root folder.

② Type the username for your Web host in the Username box.

This is the name that your host requires when you log on to its site or your control panel there.

③ Type your password at your Web host into the Password box.

④ Click **Quickconnect**.

● The files on your local computer appear in the lower left panel.

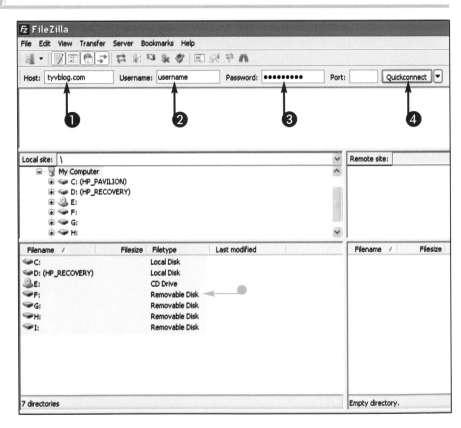

- FileZilla shows the progress of the connection.

- When the connection is made, the files on your Web host appear in the lower right panel.

⑤ Navigate in the left panel until you find the folder containing the WordPress files you downloaded and extracted, and open that folder.

⑥ Select all the files and documents within the WordPress folder.

- Those files include the three folders, or *directories*, starting *wp-* and numerous other files.

⑦ Drag all files to your blog's root directory, which you can find in the public_html directory on your Web host.

FileZilla uploads the files to your Web host. You can watch the progress in the bottom pane of the FileZilla window. This process probably will take several minutes, because the upload is more than 220 megabytes.

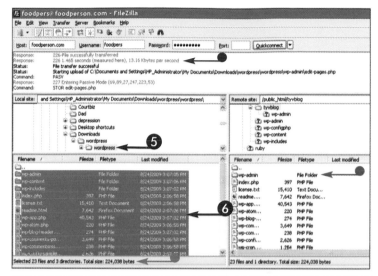

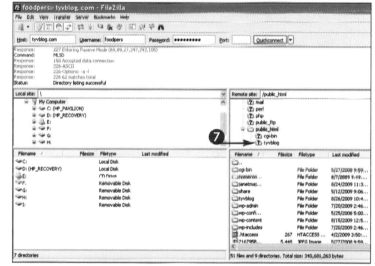

TIPS

Can I just use the FTP utility on my Web host's control panel?

You may. Go to your Web host's control panel and look for something referring to FTP. cPanel has a Web-based utility called File Manager that you can use as well as a Java applet called Unlimited FTP. Some people think that client FTP programs are easier to use.

How do I know what my blog's root directory is?

If you have purchased your own domain, it is the folder, or directory, with the domain name inside the directory for Web files. If you do not know it or cannot figure it out, ask your Web host.

Complete the Configuration and Installation

Completing the configuration of your manual WordPress installation allows your MySQL database and WordPress files to communicate with each other.

① Type your blog's URL in your Web browser address bar and press **Enter**.

● A WordPress error message appears, telling you that WordPress does not find the necessary wp-config.php file.

② Click **Create a Configuration File**.

A WordPress window opens and reminds you of the information you need to create your configuration file.

③ Review the list of needed information, and make sure you have it all available.

● This example covers an individual blog installation, so you may ignore item 5 on the list.

④ Click **Let's go**.

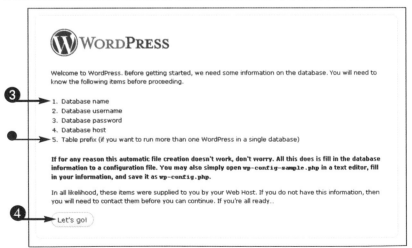

The Setup Configuration File window opens.

5 Type your MySQL database name in the Database Name box.

6 Type your database username in the User Name box.

7 Type your database user password.

8 Click **Submit**.

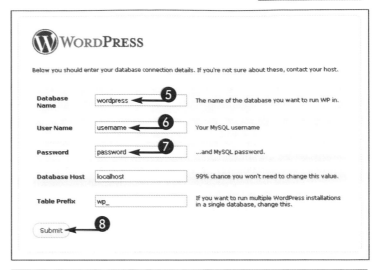

The Welcome window opens.

9 Type your blog title in the Blog Title box.

10 Type your e-mail address in the Your E-mail box.

11 Unless you intend your blog to be private, click the check box to allow your blog to be visible to search engines (☐ changes to ☑).

12 Click **Install WordPress**.

The Success window opens and shows your automatically assigned WordPress username and password. You need them to log on to your WordPress site. Click **Log In** if you are ready.

Note: *WordPress e-mails your username and password to the e-mail address you provided.*

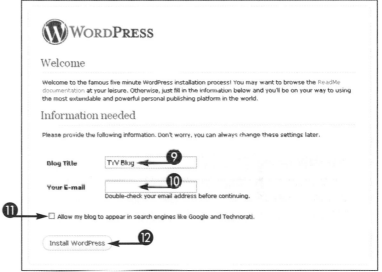

What if my installation did not work?

It all depends on what aspect did not work. Although even the manual installation is fairly simple, there are various places where things can go wrong. The error message or messages you see will guide you. See the next section of this chapter for troubleshooting.

Troubleshoot Installation Errors

Things do not always go as planned, of course. When this happens, a little troubleshooting can address typical problems with manual installation. You can easily overcome most problems.

Trouble Uploading Files

If your Internet connection is slow, you may have trouble uploading the WordPress files to your host. If so, and your Web host uses cPanel, you can upload the WordPress ZIP file and then extract it using the cPanel File Manager. If you do not have cPanel, you can download an inexpensive program called ZipDeploy for Windows and Linux systems, which also lets you extract ZIP files at your Web host.

Cannot Get to First Base

If you have uploaded your files and typed your site's URL and you get a window saying the site cannot be found or is under construction, you may have uploaded the WordPress *folder* instead of its *contents*. If so, just move the files out of the folder using FileZilla or your host's file management utility.

Error Messages

If you get an error message, the first step is to read it. Really. In its short life, WordPress has become very easy to install, and its error messages are one reason why. They provide brief but explicit information to help you fix the problem.

Error Establishing a Database Connection

This error message means you probably made a mistake in typing your database name, username, and user password in the Setup Configuration File window. These names are associated with the MySQL database that you created, as distinct from the username and password you may use to log on to your Web host's control panel. Go back and confirm you entered these correctly.

Cannot Select Database

If WordPress says it cannot select a database, it means you probably erred when typing your database name in the Setup Configuration File window. If you did not make a typing error, check your hosting control panel for the complete and accurate database name, and enter it correctly in the database name box.

A Less Automated Installation

If you are more computer savvy and would prefer to do a fully manual configuration, you may do so. The process involves entering your user information into the configuration file and running the installation script. For details, go to http://codex.wordpress.org/Installing_WordPress.

Forgotten Database Details

You misplaced your database details? The easiest solution is to simply create another empty database and this time keep track of your username and password. The database name is always available via your host control panel.

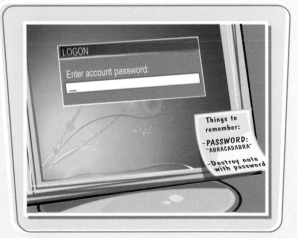

CHAPTER 4

Choose Your Self-Hosted Blog's Settings

Now that you have installed your self-hosted WordPress blog, it is time to get familiar with its many options. These options get you started in exercising the WordPress blogging muscle.

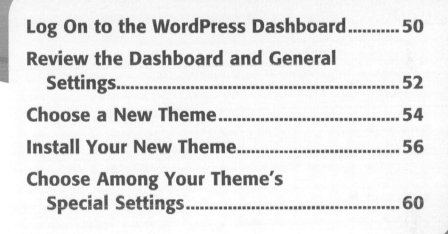

Log On to the WordPress Dashboard 50

Review the Dashboard and General Settings 52

Choose a New Theme 54

Install Your New Theme 56

Choose Among Your Theme's Special Settings 60

Log On to the WordPress Dashboard

Once you are logged onto your WordPress administrative interface, whose main page is called the Dashboard, you can do just about anything you want or need to do with your blog.

You do not need to log on to your Web host to log on to your self-hosted WordPress Dashboard.

Log On to the WordPress Dashboard

From the URL

① After you start your browser, type your blog's URL, followed by **/wp-admin** into the address bar, and press **Enter**.

WordPress takes you to the Log In page.

② Type your WordPress username in the Username box.

③ Type your WordPress password in the Password box.

● If you want WordPress to remember your computer so that you do not have to log on again, click the **Remember Me** check box (☐ changes to ☑).

Note: *It is smart not to use Remember Me if other people have access to your computer.*

④ Click **Log In**.

The Dashboard opens.

From Your Blog

1 Type your blog's URL in the address bar of your browser, and press **Enter** to open your blog's home page.

2 Click the **Log in** link.

WordPress takes you to the Log In page, where you enter your information as above, and then the Dashboard opens.

Note: If you later change the appearance of your blog, you may not necessarily have a Log In link, but you still can log on from the URL.

What do I do if I cannot remember my password?

Click **Lost Your Password?** on the logon screen. The Lost Password window opens, where you type the e-mail address you used when you set up your blog, and then click **Get New Password**. Thus, it is important that you keep track of the information you used when creating your blog. WordPress sends your password to your e-mail address.

When the Dashboard opens, it has a red box across the top. How do I get rid of it?

Simply choose whether to keep the randomly generated password you previously used or choose another password. Click the appropriate link, and the red box disappears.

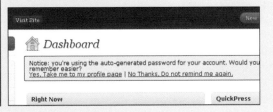

Review the Dashboard and General Settings

You can get an overview of your blog on the Dashboard and start presenting your blog's public face in the General Settings.

The Dashboard of your self-hosted WordPress blog works like My Dashboard at WordPress.com. You can read about it in "Get to Know Your Blog's Dashboard," in Chapter 2. The self-hosted General Settings have some important differences.

Review the Dashboard and General Settings

① After logging into your self-hosted WordPress Dashboard, review the Dashboard to get familiar with it, and then click **Settings**.

The General Settings window opens. See "Select Your Blog's General Settings" in Chapter 2 for settings not mentioned in this section.

② Type or review your blog's URL in the WordPress Address (URL) box. Be sure to type the **http://** portion of the address.

● You can store your self-hosted WordPress blog's files and WordPress software files on different directories on your server. To do so, click the link after the Blog Address (URL) box for instructions.

● See Chapter 12 for information about Membership and New User Default Role.

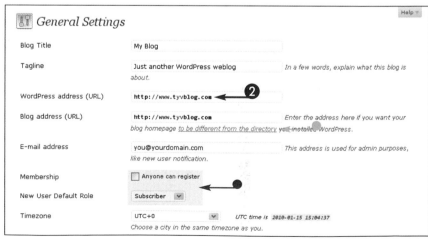

③ Choose a city in your time zone from the drop-down list.

Note: If you choose a UTC time instead of a city, you must manually adjust for daylight savings time.

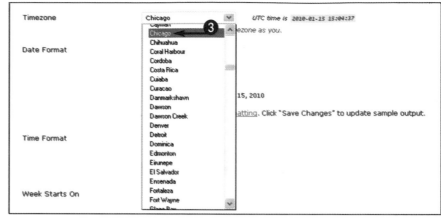

④ Click **Save Changes**.

TIP

How do I create a custom time or date format?

Type the following letters in any order you choose in the custom box. Other characters, such as hyphens or commas, appear exactly as you type them. Here are the most frequently used date and time codes.

Date codes	
l (lowercase *L*)	Full name for day of the week
F	Full name for the month
j	The numbered day of the month
S	The ordinal number suffix for the day of the month, such as *st* for 1st
Y	The year in four digits
y	The year's last two digits

Time codes	
a	Lowercase am or pm
A	Uppercase AM or PM
G	24-hour format of an hour without leading zeros 0 through 23
h	12-hour format of an hour with leading zeros 01 through 12
H	24-hour format of an hour with leading zeros 00 through 23
i	Minutes, with leading zeros 00 to 59
s	Seconds, with leading zeros 00 through 59

Choose a New Theme

Self-hosted WordPress blogs have nearly limitless options when it comes to themes, or visual templates. As a result, you probably can find one that looks and behaves exactly as you want it.

Importance of Appearance

Before anyone reads a word on your blog, a reader first notices its overall appearance. Also, once people associate a certain look with your site, the look helps build the blog's identity. These are two reasons why it is worthwhile to choose your theme carefully, keeping in mind what kind of first impression you want your blog to make.

Theme Organization

Consider the purpose and content of your blog. A standard, latest-post-at-the-top blog can use any basic theme that pleases you. If, however, you want to show off artwork, you might search for *portfolio* themes. If you want to highlight multiple posts on your blog's front page, consider *magazine* or *news* themes. Social-network-type blogs need a front-page posting option.

Free Themes

Perhaps the best way to review hundreds of free themes is to go to the Themes Directory of WordPress.org, at http://wordpress.org/extend/themes/. The directory includes users' ratings and comments, notes about the themes, and theme preview. You can also search from your WordPress installation just as you can in WordPress.com. (See "Choose and Install a New Theme" in Chapter 2.)

Commercial Themes

Commercial or *premium* themes refer to themes you pay for. The expected advantage of premium themes is that, unlike most free themes, they include ongoing support for theme users and they keep their themes aligned with updated WordPress versions. You can find links to such themes at http://wordpress.org/extend/themes/commercial/ or by doing a Google search on *premium themes*.

Custom Themes

In addition to free and premium themes, you also can pay someone to design a theme entirely to your specifications. If you want a custom theme, it is a good idea to get a designer experienced with WordPress themes. It also is a good idea to get a clear understanding up front as to what you get and what it costs.

Customizing Themes

Many, if not most, free and premium themes allow you to make limited adjustments to them simply by making selections in the theme's options panel within the Dashboard's Appearance menu. Those adjustments often include color changes or custom header images. Chapter 11 discusses making additional changes.

Trying Out Your Theme

As exciting as it is to get your blog running, you probably will not have a lot of readers at first. That situation lets you try out a theme or two without upsetting your audience. In this initial phase, get a few posts up and ask people whose opinion you value to comment on your blog's theme.

Install Your New Theme

You can install and activate most free themes more easily than you can change your clothes. Installing commercial themes is only slightly more involved. With your new theme, you are ready to make your first impression.

This section assumes you already chose a theme by following the guidance in the preceding section.

Themes Available from the Manage Themes Search

- After clicking **Change Theme** on the Dashboard, the Manage Themes panel opens and displays the two standard WordPress themes.

- Kubrick is installed by default.

- WordPress Classic is also available.

① Click **Add New Themes**.

The Install Themes panel opens.

② Type the name of your chosen theme in the Search box.

③ Click **Search**.

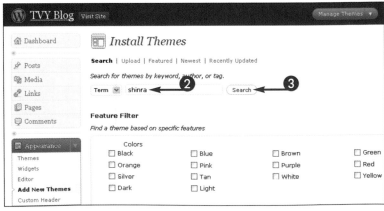

The Install Theme panel displays the designated theme.

④ Click **Install**.

⑤ A confirmation window opens, and you click **Install Now** to confirm.

WordPress displays installation progress as it installs the theme.

⑥ Click **Activate** to make the theme active.

WordPress activates the theme and returns you to the Manage Themes panel.

How many themes can I install?

You can install as many as you like, although they do take up space on your site. Only one theme can be active at a time, however. You may want to experiment a little when you start, and when you settle on one, delete other themes.

Do I have to delete a theme to get rid of it?

No. All you need to do is activate a different theme. Again, after you settle on a theme, it is good practice to delete themes you are not using.

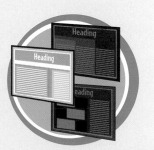

Install Your
New Theme *(continued)*

Numerous attractive themes are available beyond those listed at WordPress.org. One of them may be closer to the look you want, but it may require different installation directions.

Install Your New Theme *(continued)*

Themes Not Available from Manage Themes Search

1. Download the theme you have chosen, and save it to your computer.

   Note: Do not extract it; leave it as a ZIP file.

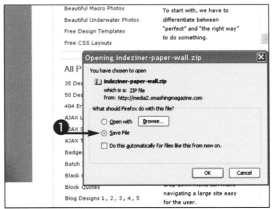

2. On the Install Themes panel — which you reach by clicking **Appearance** in the Dashboard's left menu and clicking **Add New Themes** — click **Upload**.

   A new version of the Install Themes panel opens.

3. Click **Browse**, and find the theme on your computer.

4. Your browser's File Upload window, or the equivalent, opens. When you locate the theme's ZIP file, click **Open**.

5. Click **Install Now**.

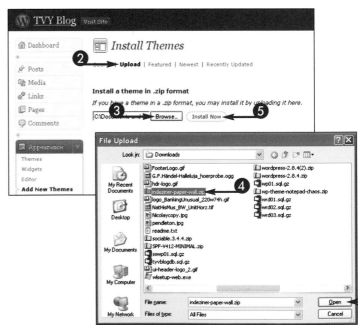

WordPress lists the progress of your installation.

⑥ When the theme is successfully installed, click **Activate**.

● You may get an error message when you upload a theme, but the theme may still work.

The Manage Themes panel opens with the new theme activated.

When Uploading from Install Themes Panel Does Not Work

① After downloading your theme, extract the file, and upload the extracted folder with your FTP software to the themes folder inside the wp-content folder at your Web host.

Note: Check inside the extracted theme folder for a ReadMe.txt file, which may have additional installation instructions.

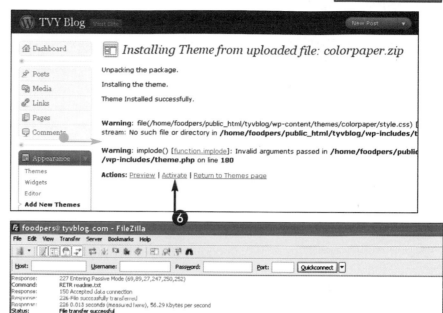

What if I have questions about how my theme works?

The first place to check is on the theme designer's Web site. Designers almost always include a link to their site in the footer of their themes. If you have no luck there, you can also try the WordPress Codex or the forums at WordPress.org, which Chapter 13 discusses.

How can I tell if my cost-free theme is also problem-free?

Alas, virtually no theme, including paid ones, guarantees flawless performance. The ratings and comments on the WordPress.org themes pages can help identify potential problem themes. For other themes, review the theme's home page to see whether it provides significant support information or a forum where users can post questions. Try to get a sense of whether the theme developers respond to questions.

Choose Among Your Theme's Special Settings

Even with a ready made theme, you can customize the look and function of your theme with its special settings. These may include a wide range of options.

The special settings vary with each theme, and just two examples appear on these pages. Most theme settings are accessible under Appearance in the left menu bar of the Dashboard or at the bottom of the left menu bar.

Choose Among Your Theme's Special Settings

With the Default Theme

1 After clicking **Custom Header** on the Appearance menu, click **Upper Color** on the Custom Header panel for the default theme.

A palette of colors opens.

2 Click a color you want to try.

The top part of the header background changes.

3 When you find a color you like, click **Update Header**.

WordPress confirms that the changes have been saved.

4 Change other settings on this panel until you are satisfied with the results, making sure to click **Update Header** when you are done.

5 Click **Visit Site** to see your blog in its new color scheme.

A Theme with Many Options

1 With the Arras theme active, click the **Arras Theme** menu in the left menu bar.

● The Arras Theme Options window opens and reveals multiple tabs, which control the theme's news-style functions.

● A link to Community Forums gives you easy access to additional information about using the theme.

● A Quick Guide explains how to insert thumbnail photos for Arras.

2 Click the **Design** tab.

The Arras Theme Options Overall Design panel opens.

3 Click the Overall Layout drop-down menu to choose the number and placement of columns.

4 If you have a custom style sheet, choose it from the Default Style drop-down menu.

5 Try other settings on other menus, and when you are done, click **Save Changes** at the bottom of the Arras Theme Options panel.

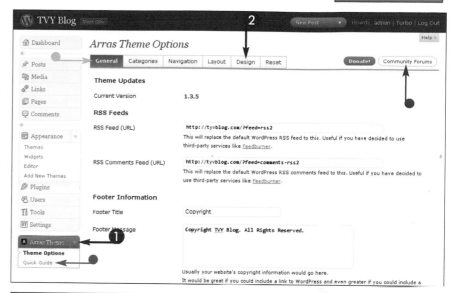

TIPS

My theme allows a custom image in the header. How do I get it there?

Such a theme takes care of the placement and configuration for you. Click the **Upload Image** or **Change Image** button (the name varies with the theme), and locate and select your image. Follow any on-screen instructions for cropping or placing the image. The header images are stored in the theme's folder.

The Dashboard says my theme is widget-ready and I need to configure them. How do I do that?

You can click the link provided and give it a shot, or read about it in Chapter 8. If you do nothing, the theme presents its default sidebar widgets, which may include content such as a search box or list of recent posts.

5

Know Your Blog's Dashboard in Detail

Whether you have a self-hosted WordPress.org blog or a blog hosted at WordPress.com, it is time to get to know the Dashboard and the many settings available to you — for reading, writing, discussion, media, and privacy. You can leave them at their defaults, but your blog will be more to your liking if you get to know your options.

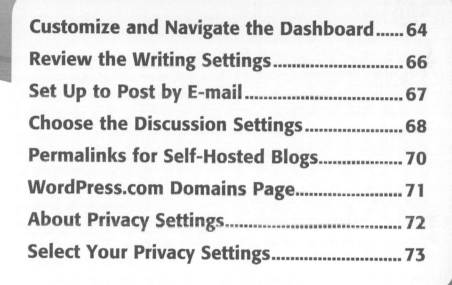

Customize and Navigate the Dashboard...... 64

Review the Writing Settings............................. 66

Set Up to Post by E-mail.................................. 67

Choose the Discussion Settings..................... 68

Permalinks for Self-Hosted Blogs................. 70

WordPress.com Domains Page....................... 71

About Privacy Settings.................................... 72

Select Your Privacy Settings........................... 73

Customize and Navigate the Dashboard

You can change the content and the way it looks on the Dashboard as well as navigate behind the scenes at your site. Making adjustments and learning to navigate give you the information you want in the way that you want it.

See Chapter 2 for an overview of My Dashboard, whose primary parts are identical to the self-hosted WordPress Dashboard.

Customize and Navigate the Dashboard

① On the Dashboard (or My Dashboard), position the mouse over the top of an information module's title bar to reveal a downward pointing triangle (▼).

If the module is collapsed, clicking the arrow expands the module. If the module is expanded, clicking the arrow collapses it.

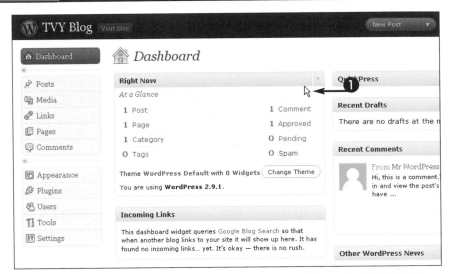

② On the Dashboard (but not on My Dashboard), position the mouse over the title bar of the Incoming Links module to reveal a Configure link and click it.

● The module expands, revealing the URL that sends excerpts to the Dashboard when other blogs link to yours, and the link changes to Cancel.

③ After you change any settings you want, click **Submit** to complete the change and return to the regular module display. Or, click **Cancel** if you want no changes.

Note: The WordPress News and WordPress Development Blog modules also have configuration links.

④ When ☇ changes to ↔ over the lines separating blocks in the left menu bar, click to toggle between a collapsed or expanded menu bar.

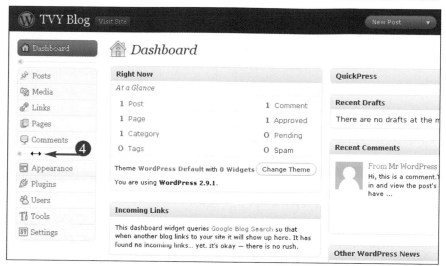

● The menu bar collapses.

⑤ Click the downward arrow (▾) next to New Post to expand the title bar drop-down menu.

The menu expands. You may select an item from the menu, or move your mouse away, and the menu retracts.

Note: The contents of this menu vary depending on which WordPress administrative panel you are viewing.

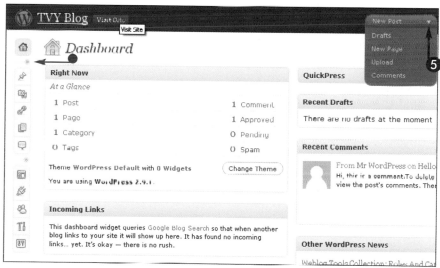

Why does my WordPress Dashboard not include statistics and other items on the WordPress.com My Dashboard?

Because the standard WordPress.org blog installation does not include a statistics feature. However, you have many statistics options, which Chapter 13 discusses.

Can I get the WordPress Development Blog to appear on my WordPress.com My Dashboard?

Not yet. You can, however, sign up for an RSS reader, which is a good idea anyway, and read the blog there. Chapter 10 discusses RSS feeds and readers.

Review the Writing Settings

The writing settings you choose affect the mechanics of how you write your blog posts, whether you write directly into your WordPress interface or post by e-mail or other means. Your writing settings also set your default blog post category.

The Writing Settings page is accessible by clicking Writing under the Settings menu in the left menu bar of the WordPress interface.

Size of the Post Box

Sets the number of lines of text visible on the New Post page, where you probably write most of your blog posts. Ten is the default number; many people prefer more lines.

Formatting

Lets you select whether WordPress automatically inserts graphic emoticons as you type, such as replacing :) with 🙂. Also lets you decide whether WordPress automatically corrects certain XHTML errors. XHTML is a Web page programming language. Selecting this is a good idea.

Default Post Category

Lets you choose what category to assign your posts to when you do not specify at the time you write the post. Until you create your own categories, the only option is Uncategorized.

Default Link Category

Lets you choose what link category your favorite links go to. The default and only option is Blogroll until you create more on the Link Categories page.

Remote Publishing

Lets you use software besides the WordPress interface (for self-hosted blogs only) to write and publish new posts.

Post via E-mail (or Post by E-mail at WordPress.com)

Leads you through the steps to be able to post straight to your blog from e-mail.

Help ▼

🎛 Writing Settings

Size of the post box —— 10 lines

Formatting —— ☑ Convert emoticons like :-) and :-P to graphics on display
☐ WordPress should correct invalidly nested XHTML automatically

Default Post Category —— Uncategorized ▾

Default Link Category —— Blogroll ▾

Remote Publishing ◀●

To post to WordPress from a desktop blogging client or remote website that uses the Atom Publishing Protocol or one of the XML-RPC publishing interfaces you must enable them below.

Atom Publishing Protocol ☐ Enable the Atom Publishing Protocol.

XML-RPC ☐ Enable the WordPress, Movable Type, MetaWeblog and Blogger XML-RPC publishing protocols.

Post via e-mail ◀●

To post to WordPress by e-mail you must set up a secret e-mail account with POP3 access. Any mail received at this address will be posted, so it's a good idea to keep this address very secret. Here are three random strings you could use: J1VSvHHS , 3RQlcLwE , QgLyhkdW .

Mail Server mail.example.com Port 110

Login Name login@example.com

Posting to your blog by e-mail lets you use your familiar e-mail program to create and publish new blog posts, which can be handy when you have a smart phone for sending e-mail.

For a self-hosted blog, first create a special, hard-to-guess e-mail address with your Web host or Internet service provider to use exclusively for blog posts.

Set Up to Post by E-mail

On a Self-Hosted Blog

① On the Writing Settings page under Post via e-mail, type the mail server information from the provider of your special blog-posting e-mail address.

② Type your special e-mail address in the Login Name box.

③ Type the e-mail password in the Password box.

④ Click **Save Changes**.

When you send an e-mail to your special address, WordPress publishes it to your blog.

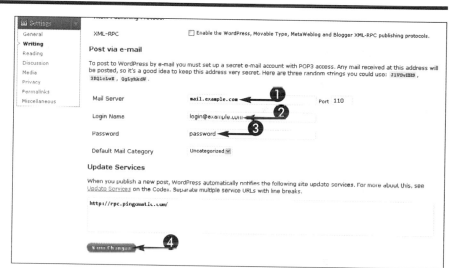

On WordPress.com

① After clicking **My Blogs** on the Writing Settings page or Dashboard menu, click **Enable** under Post by Email.

An e-mail address replaces the Enable button. Send e-mail there to post to blog.

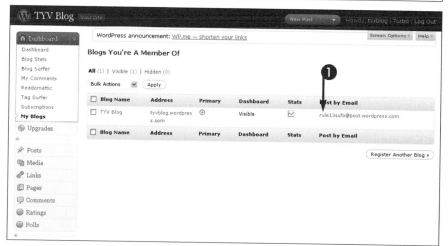

Choose the Discussion Settings

A great thing about blogs is the opportunity to interact with readers. The Discussion Settings let you decide how that interaction operates. Approving, or *moderating*, comments lets you avoid comment spam and block inflammatory comments.

Default Article Settings

Lets you make the default choice as to whether WordPress notifies blogs you link to, accepts notice of links to your site from other blogs, and allows readers to comment.

Threaded Comments

Allows readers and you to respond directly to other comments.

Comment Display Order

Lets you choose whether readers see the newest comment first — or last.

Other Comment Settings

Sets rules for conditions under which you allow comments.

E-mail Me Whenever

Specifies whether you receive e-mail notification of comments posted or held for moderation.

Discussion Settings

Help ▾

Default article settings
- ☑ Attempt to notify any blogs linked to from the article (slows down posting.)
- ☑ Allow link notifications from other blogs (pingbacks and trackbacks.)
- ☑ Allow people to post comments on new articles

(These settings may be overridden for individual articles.)

Other comment settings
- ☑ Comment author must fill out name and e-mail
- ☐ Users must be registered and logged in to comment
- ☐ Automatically close comments on articles older than `14` days
- ☐ Enable threaded (nested) comments `5` ▾ levels deep
- ☑ Break comments into pages with `50` comments per page and the `last` ▾ page displayed by default
- Comments should be displayed with the `older` ▾ comments at the top of each page

E-mail me whenever
- ☑ Anyone posts a comment
- ☑ A comment is held for moderation

Before a comment appears
- ☐ An administrator must always approve the comment
- ☑ Comment author must have a previously approved comment

Comment Moderation

Hold a comment in the queue if it contains `2` or more links. (A common characteristic of comment spam is a large number of hyperlinks.)

When a comment contains any of these words in its content, name, URL, e-mail, or IP, it will be held in the moderation queue. One word or IP per line. It will match inside words, so "press" will match "WordPress".

Before a Comment Appears

Lets you choose to review all comments or automatically accept comments from a previously approved commenter.

Comment Moderation

Sets parameters under which comments are held for your review before posting. Options include a box to specify the minimum number of links that provoke moderation and a box in which you can list terms that may be signs of spam comments. A second box, Comment Blacklist, lets you list terms that automatically identify comments as spam. WordPress.com also lets you choose to respond to comments via e-mail and whether to allow visitors to *subscribe to comments*, a feature that notifies them when a comment is added to a particular blog post.

Avatar Display

Indicates whether or not to show *avatars*, which are like personal logos that you can associate with commenters.

Maximum Rating

Lets you choose which avatar ratings you allow, using the ratings that users indicate when they create avatars at Gravatar.com, the avatar service that WordPress uses.

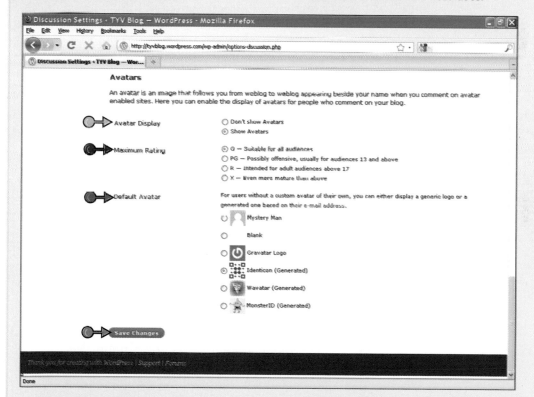

Default Avatar

Allows you to pick a default image for commenters who do not have an avatar. The *generated* options change slightly from one person to the next.

Save Changes

Must be clicked to retain choices on the Comment Settings page.

Permalinks for Self-Hosted Blogs

Your choice of permalink structure affects how well your blog performs and how easily you can remember a post's URL. Making a good choice on the Permalinks Settings page avoids problems later.

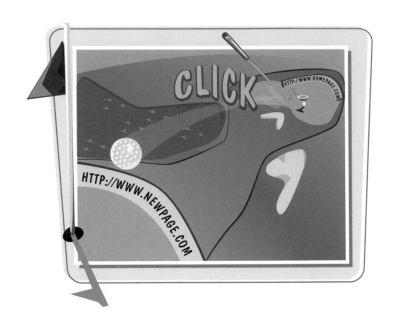

What Is a Permalink?

Permalinks are the unique URLs that WordPress assigns to each post. Permalinks allow you or others to link directly to a particular post, rather than to your blog's home page. WordPress also assigns permalinks to pages that list posts by category and by tag. Changing your permalink structure is a bad idea, so choose a structure you can live with.

Why Permalink Structure Matters

Permalinks that include your post title or category may improve your blog's ranking in search-engine searches. However, WordPress blogs function better when the first part of the URL after the domain name is a number. Unless you have read the WordPress Codex carefully, choose one of the four standard options listed on the Permalinks Settings page.

If you decided to purchase a domain, the Domains page — found under Settings in the left menu bar — is the place to go to change *mynewblog.wordpress.com* to *mynewblog.com*.

The Easiest Way

The easiest way to make your WordPress.com blog appear under your own domain name is to buy the domain name through WordPress.com, under Upgrades near the top of the left menu bar. Then, go to the Domains page under Settings and follow the instructions there.

Another Good Way

If you buy your domain elsewhere and map it to WordPress.com, you must pay the WordPress.com domain mapping fee in addition to your registration fee at the registrar. You also need to give your domain name service the WordPress.com *nameservers* so that it directs traffic from *mynewblog.com* to your WordPress.com blog.

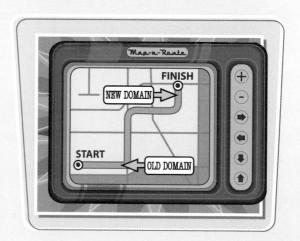

About Privacy Settings

The Internet may not be the place for you if you want to keep your thoughts secret. Still, there are ways you can limit what and where your blog posts are broadcast.

Self-Hosted Blog Privacy

On self-hosted WordPress blogs, only two settings are available, to allow or disallow search engines such as Google to find your blog. Whichever one you choose, anyone with the right URL can find it. If you do not link to other Web sites and do not give out your URL, however, your blog is not easily found.

WordPress.com Blog Privacy

WordPress.com offers the same privacy settings as self-hosted blogs as well as a third option, letting you specify a select group of people who can see your blog. The free WordPress.com hosting allows up to 35 users to be listed. The users must be registered at WordPress.com. WordPress.com employees can read your blog regardless of the settings.

Other Kinds of Privacy

If you are concerned about being identified as the writer of your blog, be sure to read the privacy policy of your Web host (or of WordPress.com if it hosts your blog). Additional privacy settings called *Visibility* are available on a per-post basis. These are discussed in the next section.

You get to choose whether you want the world beating a path to your blog, or whether you would rather keep it to a select few viewers. Your blog's privacy settings let you decide.

Select Your Privacy Settings

For Total Visibility or to Hide Blog from Search Engines

① After going to the Privacy Settings page under the Settings list in the left menu bar, click to choose visibility to search engines (○ changes to ◉).

② Click **Save Changes**.

To Create Viewer List at WordPress.com Blog

③ Click the radio button next to **I would like my blog to be visible only to users I choose** (○ changes to ◉).

Note: Not available on self-hosted blogs.

④ Click **Save Changes**.

⑤ Type the WordPress.com usernames of the individuals you want to see your blog in the Username box.

Note: If you want to add friends who are not WordPress.com members, they have to sign up. They do not have to have a blog.

⑥ Click **Add User**.

● The user appears on a line below the Username box. Repeat for each user you want to add.

⑦ Click **Save Changes**.

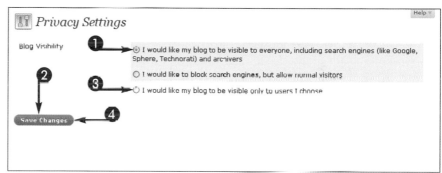

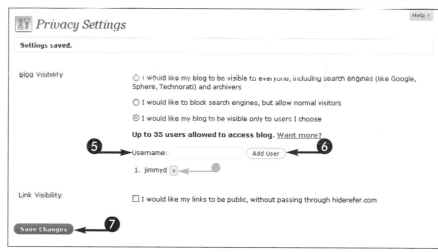

Create Written Blog Content

It is time to get in there and produce content! For most blogs, that means writing, and WordPress offers multiple ways to produce written content. One of them will be ideal for you.

Get to Know the New Post Page 76

Introducing the WYSIWYG Editor and Toolbar 78

Introducing the HTML Editor and Toolbar 80

Write and Publish Your First Blog Post 82

Add Formatting to Your Text 84

Recall an Earlier Version of Your Blog Post 86

Write and Publish a Page 88

Edit or Delete a Post or Page 90

Quick Edit Posts and Pages 91

Add Text Hyperlinks to Your Post or Page 92

Paste Text from Other Sources 94

Create a Post with Press This 96

Create a Post via Quick Press 98

Speed Up Posting with Google Gears 99

Consider Using a Blogging Client 100

Create a Post with Windows Live Writer ... 101

Import Posts from Another Blogging Platform 102

Create a Blogroll 104

Get to Know the New Post Page

The Add New Post page provides the primary location for creating new posts. You can find everything you need to write, edit, and format your written content on the Add New Post page.

Find the Add New Post page by clicking New Post from the drop-down menu near the top right of the WordPress interface screens or by clicking Posts in the left menu bar and then Add New when the Posts menu expands.

Headline Box

Where you type your post's headline.

Media Tools

Lets you upload or insert photos (▣), videos (▤), and music files (♫). The last icon, ✳, lets you upload and add links to PDFs, text files, and other documents. WordPress.com has another icon (◉) for adding a poll.

Toolbar

Provides tools to use as you write, edit, and format your post.

Post Box

Gives you room to type your prose.

Excerpt Box

Provides a space to write abstracts or teasers for your post that may appear in search results, RSS feeds, and on the front page of some themes.

Save Button

Saves your post.

Preview Button

Opens a new window or tab in your browser, which displays how your draft post would look if published.

Add New Post

Screen Options ▾   Help ▾

Upload/Insert ▣ ▤ ♫ ✳   Visual HTML

B *I* ABC

Path: p
Word count: 0

Excerpt

Excerpts are optional hand-crafted summaries of your content that can be used in your theme. Learn more about manual excerpts.

Publish

Save Draft   Preview

Status: **Draft** Edit
Visibility: **Public** Edit
📅 Publish **immediately** Edit

Publish

Post Tags

Add new tag   Add

Separate tags with commas.

Choose from the most used tags in Post Tags

Categories

All Categories   Most Used

☐ Uncategorized

Publish Button

Publishes your post to the Internet.

Tag Box

Lets you assign tags to your posts.

Categories Box

Lets you assign your post to a category of your blog.

Send Trackbacks

Lets you notify non-WordPress blogs when your post has linked to them.

Custom Fields

Allows you to add extra information to your post. That information may be data to help search engines find your post or to make a special feature of your theme work. (Not available at WordPress.com.)

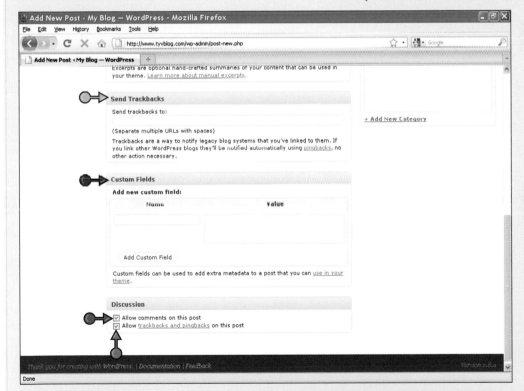

Allow Comments

Lets you choose whether to allow comments on an individual post. Overrides default selection under Discussion Settings.

Allow Trackbacks and Pingbacks

Lets you choose whether to allow trackbacks and pingbacks on an individual post. Overrides default selection under Discussion Settings. Note that allowing trackbacks and pingbacks means other blogs' links to your post will appear as comments on your blog.

Introducing the WYSIWYG Editor and Toolbar

You can write your blog posts almost as though you were using a word processor when you use the WordPress WYSIWYG — *what you see is what you get* — editor.

The official name of the WYSIWYG, or visual, blog post interface is TinyMCE, which Moxiecode Systems AB created.

Visual Tab

Is dark gray when active, which means you can use the WYSIWYG editor and post box.

Text Formats

Change text you select in the post box to bold, italic, or strikeout, as shown on the formatting buttons.

Paragraph Formats

Assigns special paragraph formats as indicated on the buttons: bulleted list, numbered list, and *block quote*, a style format intended for use when quoting others.

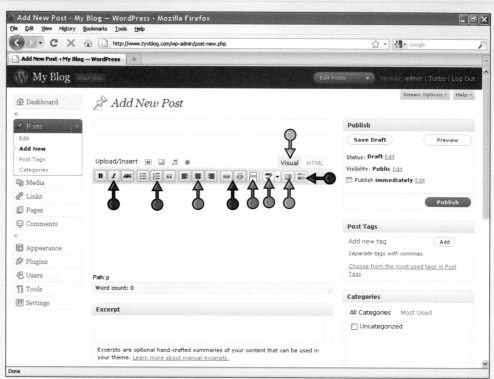

Text Alignment

Causes selected text to be aligned left, centered, or right.

Links

Lets you insert or remove links to other Web locations.

Post Break

Inserts a *More* tag in a spot you choose within your blog post so that only part of the post appears on the front page of your blog.

Spell Checker

Checks the spelling on the post.

Full Screen

Toggles your post box to and from a full screen to make it easy to see more or less of your post.

Extra Buttons

Shows or hides an additional row of buttons.

Styles Menu

Lets you assign an HTML tag to selected text. Read more about HTML in "Introducing the HTML Editor and Toolbar," later in this chapter.

More Formats

Adds underlined text and justified alignment as WYSIWYG formats.

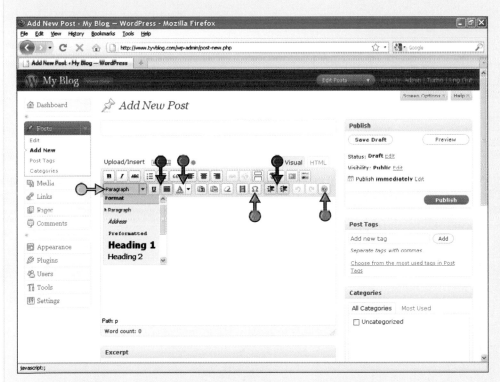

Text Color

Provides the option to add color to text you select.

Special Characters

Opens a pop-up window in which you can choose special characters such as mathematical operators, bullets, letters with accents, or *diacritics*, and dashes.

More Indentions

Changes the indention on paragraphs you select but does not add bullets or block quote formats.

Help

Provides added information about the visual post box, including keyboard shortcuts for various options.

Introducing the HTML Editor and Toolbar

If you are a veteran HTML user, you may prefer to write in the HTML editor window of the post box. Even if you are not an HTML vet, you need to know about it when things do not go as expected with the WYSIWYG editor.

You can find the HTML editor on the New Post Page by clicking the HTML tab at the top of the post box.

What Is HTML?

HTML, which is short for *Hypertext Markup Language*, allows properly marked-up text to be displayed as Web pages. The text contains HTML *tags*, which instruct browsers on how to display text and other content on a Web page.

Benefit of the HTML Editor

As handy as the WordPress WYSIWYG editor is, it sometimes makes mistakes, particularly when you make a lot of formatting changes or paste text from other applications. The HTML editor helps you to clean up the problems. Also, you may need the HTML editor to insert special advertising links at some stage.

Quicktag Buttons

Inserts HTML tags individually or as opening and closing HTML tags if you select text before clicking a button.

Post Box

Displays post text with its HTML tags, rather than as it appears in a Web browser. Note that HTML tags usually are enclosed by angle brackets and have a starting tag and an ending tag for each instruction.

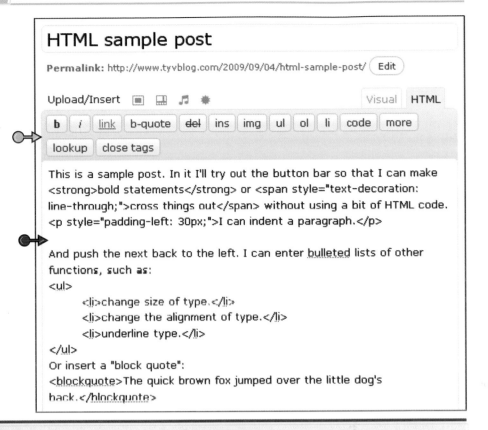

HTML sample post

Permalink: http://www.tyvblog.com/2009/09/04/html-sample-post/ (Edit)

Upload/Insert ▣ ⊞ ♫ ✴ | Visual **HTML**

b | *i* | link | b-quote | del | ins | img | ul | ol | li | code | more
lookup | close tags

This is a sample post. In it I'll try out the button bar so that I can make `<strong>bold statements</strong>` or `<span style="text-decoration: line-through;">cross things out</span>` without using a bit of HTML code. `<p style="padding-left: 30px;">I can indent a paragraph.</p>`

And push the next back to the left. I can enter bulleted lists of other functions, such as:
`<ul>`
`<li>change size of type.</li>`
`<li>change the alignment of type.</li>`
`<li>underline type.</li>`
`</ul>`
Or insert a "block quote":
`<blockquote>The quick brown fox jumped over the little dog's back.</blockquote>`

Getting the Hang of the Editor

You do not have to be an HTML pro to use the HTML editor, but take a moment to get a little familiar with HTML conventions. When you write your first few blog posts, compare the WYSIWYG versions and the HTML versions simply by clicking the Visual and the HTML tabs at the top of the post box.

Advanced HTML

If, on the other hand, you *are* an HTML whiz, you may love the HTML editor because you can use any HTML tags that you want and thereby do more with your posts than what the visual editor allows.

Write and Publish Your First Blog Post

Time to put your words of wisdom on the Web! When you write and publish your first blog post, you are a real blogger. No better time to start than now. There is more than one way to do it, but this lesson covers the basic way.

Write and Publish Your First Blog Post

① Click in the headline box and start typing.

● WordPress displays your post's permalink. If your permalink structure uses the blog post headline (as all WordPress.com blogs do), WordPress inserts hyphens between the words.

● WordPress saves your post as a draft and displays the time saved.

② Press **Tab** to move to the post box.

③ Click **Save Draft** periodically as you work and when you are done.

● WordPress shows the word count.

④ Click **Preview** to see how your post will look when published.

⑤ Return to the Add New Post window, and review the permalink. To change it, click **Edit**.

A box displays the part of your permalink that you can change.

⑥ Make any changes you want.

⑦ Click **Save**.

WordPress saves the edited permalink and closes the edit permalink box.

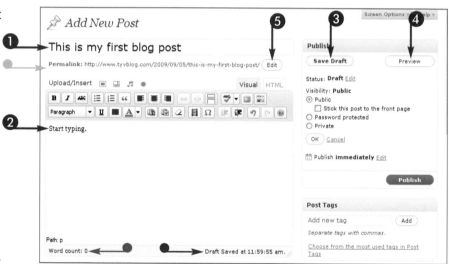

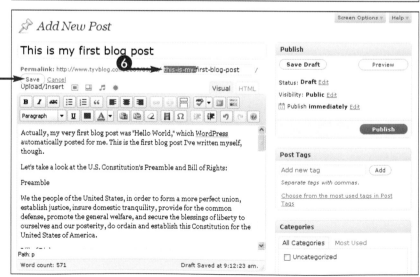

Publish Now

1. If you are satisfied with your post and are ready to publish to the Internet, click **Publish**.

   WordPress publishes your post, and notifies you of that fact. You can click **View Post** next to the permalink display to see your newly published blog post.

Publish Later

2. To schedule your post to publish at a different time, click **Edit**.

   The current date and time appear.

3. Change the date and time to when you want the post to publish to the Web.

4. Click **OK**.

   WordPress displays the Publish box showing the scheduled time. The Publish button now reads Schedule, which you click to confirm that you want the post to be published at the specified time.

TIPS

What is the Get Shortlink button on WordPress. com blogs that appears next to the permalink in the New Post window?

Clicking that button opens a little window that displays a short, alternate link that you may copy for use in places such as Twitter where a long link might not work well. It does not change the actual permalink.

Can you explain the Visibility settings that appear when you click Edit next to Visibility in the Publish box?

The settings determine who can see a particular post. The default is *Public*, so anyone can read the post. You also may make Public posts *sticky,* which means that post always appears at the top of your home page. *Password Protected* lets you assign a password to the post so only people with the password can read its content. *Private* posts are visible only to you and anyone else you have made an editor or administrator on your site. (More on that in Chapter 12.)

Visibility: **Public**
- ◉ Public
  - ☐ Stick this post to the front page
- ○ Password protected
- ○ Private

(OK) Cancel

Add Formatting to Your Text

When you add formatting to your text, you transform your post from one with a rather monotonous appearance to one that looks more inviting and may be easier to scan.

If you previously saved your post as a draft or published it, you can find it by clicking Edit under the Posts menu in the left menu bar.

Add Formatting to Your Text

Add Subheads in the Visual Editor

1. Select the text whose format you want to change.

2. Click the arrow beside Paragraph to reveal the drop-down formatting menu.

3. Click the format you want to apply.

   WordPress applies the formatting to the selected text.

Note: In HTML, the smaller the heading number, the bigger the type as a general rule.

Change the Appearance of Type

1. Select the text whose format you want to change.

2. Click the toolbar button that corresponds to the change you want to make.

   WordPress changes the text as you directed.

Note: B (**B**) is for bold, I (*I*) for italic, ABC (ABC) for strikethrough, and U (U) for underline.

Change Paragraph Formatting

1 Click anywhere within the paragraph you want to change.

Note: Click and drag to select multiple paragraphs.

2 Click a paragraph formatting button to apply.

WordPress changes the paragraph format as you specified. In this example, it indented a paragraph.

3 Click **Update Post** to save changes.

4 Click **View Post** to see how your changes look.

WordPress opens the blog post.

View Your Changes

● Examples of a Heading 2.

● An example of a Heading 3.

● An example of an Indented paragraph.

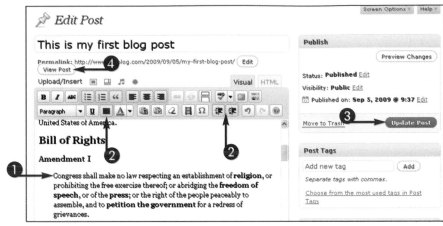

How do I change the text color?

Select the text you want to change, click the color formatting button (●), and then click the color of your choice.

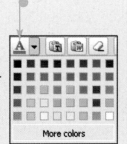

Is there any quicker way to change the formatting?

Yes. Pressing **Ctrl** on a PC (**⌘** on a Mac) plus the following letters changes the text using key strokes only:

B	Bold	**2**	Header 2
I	Italic	**3**	Header 3
U	Underline	**4**	Header 4
1	Header 1		

Recall an Earlier Version of Your Blog Post

Uh-oh. You have writer's remorse and wish you could change your post back to the way you wrote it earlier. Post Revisions to the rescue! This revision-saving feature of WordPress lets you view and restore earlier versions of a post. What a relief.

Once you have saved your post, even if you have not published it, a simple *undo* command does not undo the changes.

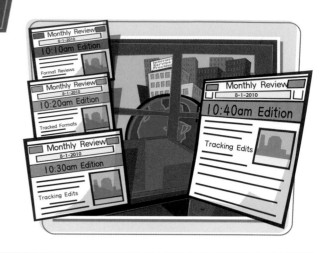

Recall an Earlier Version of Your Blog Post

① Scroll to the bottom of your New Post page (or Edit Post page).

A list of post revisions appears.

② Click the version that you think you would like to restore.

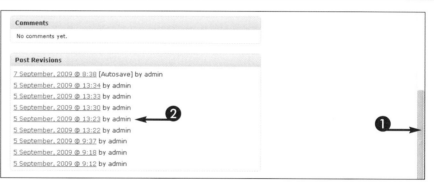

WordPress opens a new page that displays that version, in the HTML format and, at the bottom of that page, the list of revisions that you can compare.

③ Click a radio button beside the revisions that you want to compare (○ changes to ◉).

Note: *One button must be in the left column of buttons, and the other must be in the right column.*

④ Click **Compare Revisions**.

WordPress displays the two versions side by side, and it highlights places in which the two versions are different.

5 When you are satisfied that you have identified the desired previous version, click **Restore** next to it in the list.

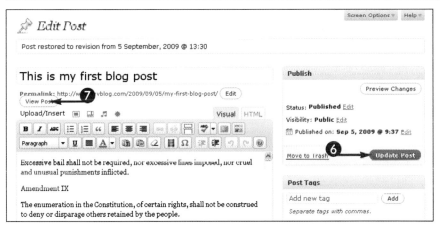

Post Revisions

(Compare Revisions)

	Date Created	Author	Actions
○ ⊙	5 September, 2009 @ 14:00 [Current Revision]	admin	
○ ○	7 September, 2009 @ 8:53 [Autosave]	admin	Restore
○ ○	5 September, 2009 @ 13:34	admin	Restore
○ ○	5 September, 2009 @ 13:33	admin	Restore
⊙ ○	5 September, 2009 @ 13:30	admin	Restore
○ ○	5 September, 2009 @ 13:23	admin	Restore

WordPress restores the desired version and returns you to the New Post (or Edit Post) page.

6 Make any changes you want, and then click **Update Post** if the post already has been published (or **Save Draft** if the post has not been published).

7 If desired, click **View Post** to see the restored post on your blog.

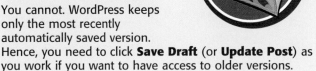

Screen Options ▾   Help ▾

🔖 *Edit Post*

Post restored to revision from 5 September, 2009 @ 13:30

This is my first blog post

Permalink: http://www.myblog.com/2009/09/05/my-first-blog-post/ (Edit)
(View Post)

Upload/Insert 🖼 🖽 ♫ ✳   Visual | HTML

B *I* ABC ☰ ☰ ❝ ▤ ▤ ▤ ∞ ⬚ ⬚ 🎨 ▾ ▣ ▦
Paragraph ▾ **U** ▬ **A** ▾ 🖼 🖼 ② ▤ Ω ⬚ ⬚ ↺ ↻ ⓘ

Excessive bail shall not be required, nor excessive fines imposed, nor cruel and unusual punishments inflicted.

Amendment IX

The enumeration in the Constitution, of certain rights, shall not be construed to deny or disparage others retained by the people.

Publish

(Preview Changes)

Status: **Published** Edit
Visibility: **Public** Edit
🗓 Published on: **Sep 5, 2009 @ 9:37** Edit

Move to Trash   (**Update Post**)

Post Tags

Add new tag   (Add)
Separate tags with commas.

Can I compare one old version with another old version?

Yes. Just click the radio buttons beside the versions you want to compare.

I relied on WordPress automatically saving my post as I worked, but I see only one Autosave version in the list. How can I get an earlier Autosave version?

You cannot. WordPress keeps only the most recently automatically saved version.
Hence, you need to click **Save Draft** (or **Update Post**) as you work if you want to have access to older versions.

Write and Publish a Page

Unlike most blog platforms, WordPress allows you to write and publish *pages*. Pages are *static*, meaning they do not change as you add posts. Most themes make pages always accessible from your blog's home page.

The initial installation of the WordPress software (or blog registration at WordPress.com) by default includes one page, called *About*. WordPress also lets you make *child* or *subpages* of pages.

Write and Publish a Page

① Under Pages, click **Add New**.

② On the Add New page, type a headline or label in the headline box.

Note: If your theme displays your pages as tabs on your home page, use a short label.

③ Type your text in the page text box.

Note: If desired, add formatting as described in "Add Formatting to Your Text."

④ If desired, edit the permalink.

Note: Unlike post permalinks, page default permalinks have no reference to dates or numbers.

⑤ Click **Save Draft** periodically as you work and when you are done.

⑥ Click **Preview** to see how your page will appear on your Web site.

⑦ After returning to the New Post page, click the arrow next to Main Page (no parent).

⑧ Click **About** to make the About page the *parent* of the new page you just made. If you prefer to keep your page as a main page rather than a subpage, simply collapse the menu and proceed.

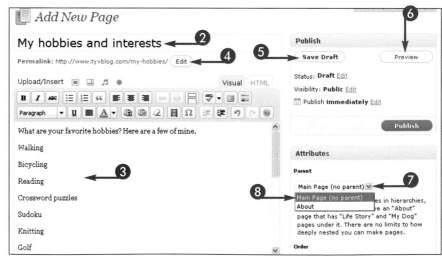

- Some themes include more than one page template, or standard page layouts. Those themes have a Template section in the Attributes module, and you may choose your preferred template from this list. If you do not see a Template section, your theme does not have multiple page templates.

- Pages usually appear in alphabetical order, but the Order box lets you assign each page a number to specify the order in which your home page lists your other pages.

9 Review the discussion settings and change them if you want.

10 When you are done, be sure to click **Update Page** at the top of the page.

11 When you are ready to publish your page to your Web site, click **Publish**.

Note: The Publish module works just the same for pages as it does for posts. See "Write and Publish Your First Blog Post" earlier in this chapter for more information.

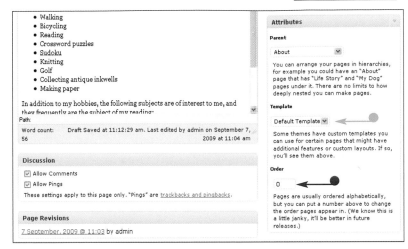

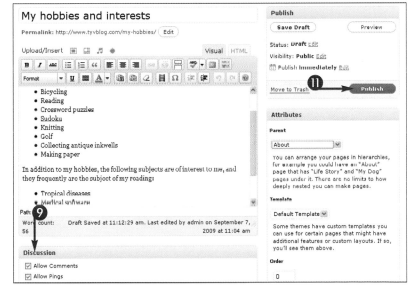

What can I use pages for?

You can use one as the home page for your blog by selecting it in the Reading Settings. You can use a page or pages to display products or family photos or link lists. Essentially, you can use them for just about anything you would use a Web page for. See Chapter 12 for more ideas.

Can I make my own page templates?

Yes. You can learn how in Chapter 11.

Edit or Delete a Post or Page

Knowing how to edit or delete a post or a page after you have published it or saved it as a draft lets you keep your content current. It also lets you write and edit when it is convenient for you and then return to finish later.

The editing process is the same for posts and pages. This section uses a post as an example.

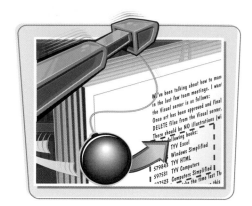

Basic Editing

① Click **Posts** (or **Pages**).

The Edit Posts (or Edit Pages) page opens, and related submenus open in the menu bar under Posts (or Pages). You can:

● Filter posts by date or category or both.

● Search posts.

● View posts in a list, as shown, or with the headline and *excerpt*, which is either the excerpt you wrote on the New Post page or the first 55 words of your post if you did not write an excerpt.

② Click the post (or page) you want to edit.

The Edit Post (or Edit Page) window opens. Except for the page title, this page is the same as the New Post page. You can edit and update as you did when you first wrote a new post or page.

Quick Edit Posts or Pages

① Position the mouse over the post (or page) you want to edit.

A set of four options appears.

② Click **Quick Edit**.

The Quick Edit panel opens.

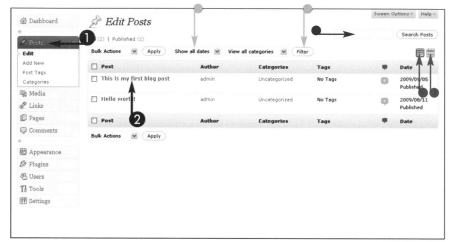

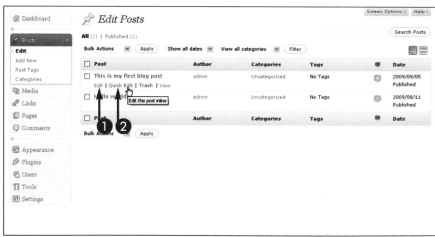

Quick Edit Posts and Pages

The Quick Edit panels let you change almost everything about your draft or published pages or posts — except the main text — without leaving the Edit Posts (or Edit Pages) page.

The Quick Edit Posts Panel

- The Title box shows the headline.
- The Slug shows the editable part of the permalink.
- Date shows the publication date and time, or the date and time the post was last saved.

- Password-protect the post.
- Make the post private.
- Designate or eliminate category classifications.

- Add or delete tags.
- Discussion settings.
- Change the publishing status or make the post sticky.

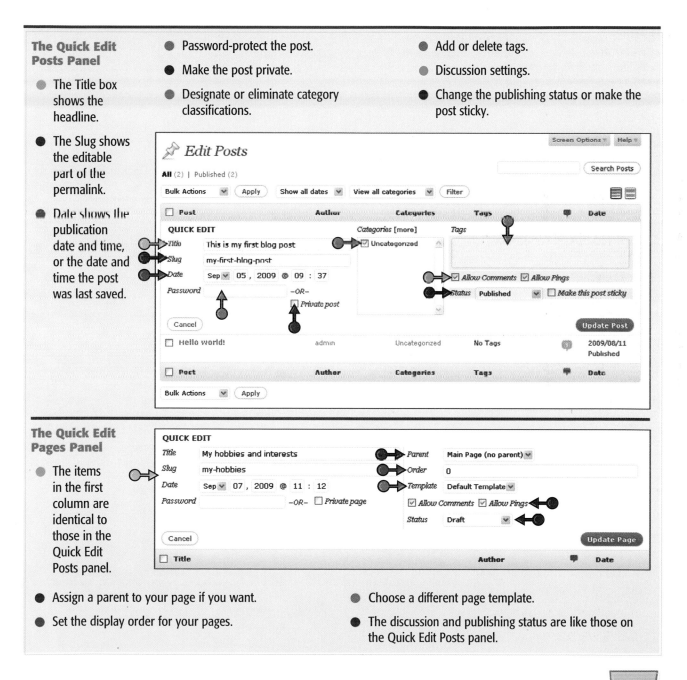

The Quick Edit Pages Panel

- The items in the first column are identical to those in the Quick Edit Posts panel.

- Assign a parent to your page if you want.
- Set the display order for your pages.

- Choose a different page template.
- The discussion and publishing status are like those on the Quick Edit Posts panel.

Add Text Hyperlinks to Your Post or Page

When you add hyperlinks, you can give others credit for ideas you mention or quote, lead readers to additional pertinent information, and reach out to fellow bloggers, who love it when you link to them.

A hyperlink is a reference to another location on the Web — including elsewhere on your site.

Add Text Hyperlinks to Your Post or Page

① Select the URL on the page you want to link to and copy it.

Note: *With most browsers, you can copy the URL by pressing* **Ctrl** + **C** *(*⌘ + **C** *on a Mac). Or, you can select* **Copy** *from the Edit menu.*

② Click the text that you want to make into a hyperlink within your post or page.

③ Click the link icon (⊕) on the toolbar.

④ In the Insert/Edit Link window, paste the URL you copied in the Link URL box.

Press **Tab** twice to advance to the Title box.

Note: The URL needs to include the protocol, or http:// portion, of the Web address, and WordPress automatically includes it.

⑤ Type the name of the page or a description.

Note: The Title text is optional. It is what readers see when they position their mouse over a link. If you do not type anything in the Title box, readers see the URL.

⑥ Click **Update**.

WordPress returns to the Edit Post page.

● The Title text of the link appears on the Edit Post page when you position your mouse over the link. The link is not active on this page, however. It is active when you preview the page or publish it.

⑦ Click **Update Post**.

The link is saved to your site.

TIPS

How do I link to another page on my site?

You do it the same way you would link to another site: Copy the URL (the permalink), and paste it in the Insert/edit link window.

Can I get the link to open in a new window instead of the same window as my blog?

Click the Target drop-down menu in the Insert/edit link window, and select **Open link in a new window** (●). If not specified, WordPress opens links in the same window.

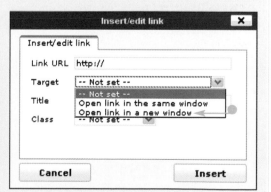

Paste Text from Other Sources

You can write blog posts in Microsoft Word — even do considerable formatting — and then paste them into your WordPress post (or page text) box and keep the formatting, as long as you know how. You also can remove unwanted formatting with WordPress's special pasting tools.

Paste from Word Documents

1. After copying the text in a Word document that you want to use in your blog, go to the New Post or Edit Post page where you want to paste the text in WordPress. Click the **Word Paste** button (⊞).

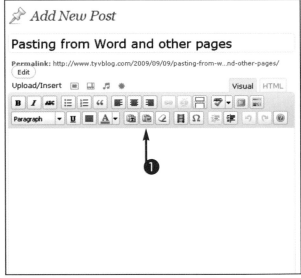

The Paste from Word window opens.

2. Press Ctrl + V (⌘ + V on Mac) to insert the copied Word text.

3. Click **Insert**.

Your copy, as written in Word, appears in the post (or page text) box.

WordPress pastes the text without extraneous coding, but it does not hurt to check the HTML window to make sure.

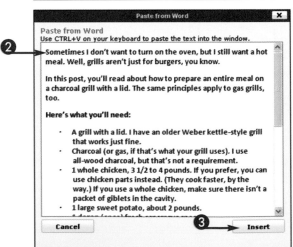

Paste Formatted Type as Text

① After copying the text, such as from another Web page, that you want to put in your post or page, click the **Paste Text** button (🖺).

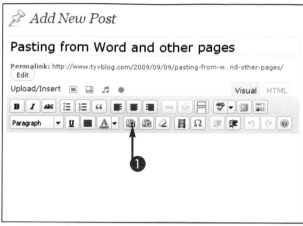

The Paste as Plain Text window opens.

② Press **Ctrl** + **V** (**⌘** + **V** on Mac) to insert the copied text.

WordPress pastes the text without formatting.

● You may choose not to retain line breaks by clearing the **Keep linebreaks** check box (☑ changes to ☐).

③ Click **Insert**.

Your copy appears as plain text in the post (or page text) box.

 TIPS

Why would I want to paste text without formatting?

It often is easier to paste copied material from other Web sites as plain text and then add whatever formatting you want than it is to remove and reformat text that you copied. If you are skeptical, paste something from another Web page straight into the Visual blog post window. Then, click the **HTML** tab to see the coding. Chances are you will see a *lot* of code, even though it may not appear to change things much in the Visual editor.

I pasted a table from Word, which looks fine, but I cannot seem to type anything below it. What should I do?

Click the **HTML** tab at the top of the post or page text entry window. You will see `</table>` at the end of the table. Click after that HTML tag and start typing. Then, return to the Visual editor and proceed as usual. Similar problems can occur when the Visual editor mistakenly puts your insertion point where it does not belong between HTML tags. The same remedy can solve those problems.

Create a Post with Press This

You can blog about a Web site you are reading without leaving that site. The Press This *bookmarklet* lets you go straight to a stripped-down post writing and editing window.

Create a Post with Press This

1 On the Tools page in the WordPress administrative panel, right-click **Press This** (or click and hold on Mac).

2 Select **Bookmark This Link**.

Your browser presents options for adding Press This to your browser's list of bookmarks or favorites. After you have made your selections, the bookmarklet is added to your list.

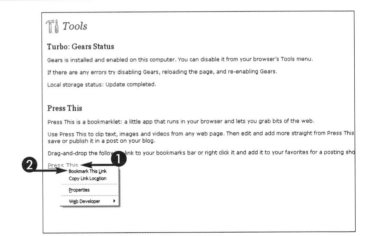

3 When you are on a Web page that you want to blog about, you can click **Press This** in your bookmarks list, which opens a logon window for your blog.

4 Type your username in the Username box.

5 Type your password in the Password box.

6 Click **Log In**.

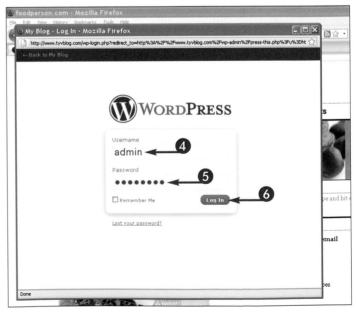

The Press This window opens, showing a link to that page in the post box and headline box.

7 Type your blog entry.

Note: If you want to add formatting beyond that provided by the tool buttons, go to the main Edit Post window.

● You can go to your Word Press administrative panel by clicking **My Blog > Press This**.

8 Click **Publish** when you finish.

Your blog post is published, your writing disappears from the Press This window, and the Press This window gives more options:

● Choose **View post**, and your browser goes to the new post on your blog.

● Click **Edit post**, and your browser goes to the Edit Post page of your blog.

● The **Close Window** option returns you to the Web page where you started.

The Press This window closes.

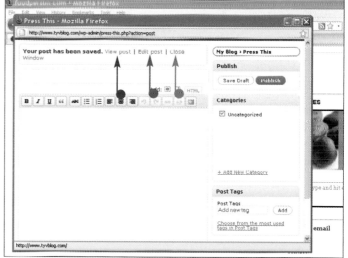

 TIPS

What if I click Save Draft instead of Publish?

Just as with the publishing option, the words you just wrote disappear, and the Press This window presents three options, for viewing or editing the post, or simply closing the Press This window. In addition, WordPress saves the post as a draft. If you choose the view option in Press This, you see a preview. The other two options are the same as with a published post.

How can I use Press This if I have more than one blog?

Blogs hosted at WordPress.com have an extra pane in the Press This window. You can choose which of your blogs you want to publish the item to. If you have more than one self-hosted WordPress blog, add a bookmarklet from the Tools page of each of your blogs, and give each bookmarklet a name alluding to the pertinent blog.

If you do not want to do anything fancy, you can get your blog post up and on the Web in a flash with Quick Press, available from the Dashboard.

1 On the Dashboard (or My Dashboard in WordPress.com blogs), in the Quick Press module type your post's headline in the Title box.

2 Type your message in the Content box.

Note: *You may use HTML tags in the Quick Press content box. If your message exceeds the tiny Content box, a scroll bar appears on the right side of the window.*

3 List any topic tags you want. (Find out more about tags in Chapter 9.)

4 Click **Publish**.

WordPress publishes and clears the QuickPress boxes.

5 Click **View Post** to see your new post.

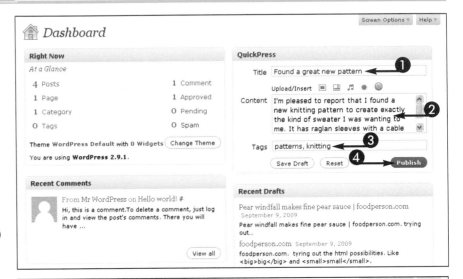

Speed Up Posting with Google Gears

If you sometimes find your blog posting bogs down as you wait for information to upload, you can speed things along with Google Gears. Gears, a browser extension like Flash, lets you store your WordPress files on your local computer and then add them to your site only when you publish.

Once Gears is installed and enabled, you do not have to do anything to *use* it!

① After you click **Install Now** on the Tools page in your WordPress administrative panel and the Gears window opens, click **Install Gears**.

A user agreement opens, which you need to read and approve before proceeding to install Gears as you would install any program on your computer.

Note: You should install Gears only on your personal computer, not a public computer.

② After the installation process finishes and you click **Enable Gears** on the Tools page, click the **I trust this site** check box (☐ changes to ☑) in the Gears Security Warning box.

③ Click **Allow**.

WordPress displays the status of the files being downloaded to your computer and advises you when the update is complete.

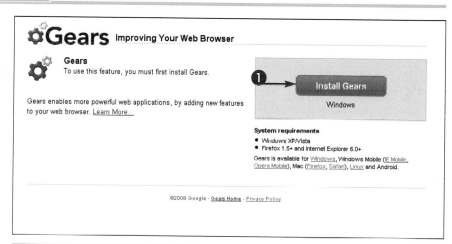

Consider Using a Blogging Client

You can download programs, called *clients*, that let you write your blog post offline. These programs mean you do not have to be connected to the Internet to write your posts, and many have more user friendly interfaces than the WordPress Dashboard.

Advantages of Blogging Clients

Advantages vary, but a couple are fairly consistent among blog clients. One is that you can write posts without having to go online and then post them, formatted and with images if you want, in fewer steps. Also, many clients allow you to use keyboard shortcuts when typing and provide easy ways to do fancier formatting, including inserting tables.

Available Blogging Clients

Windows Live Writer, which is for PCs, is among the most popular clients, but several others are available, including clients for Macintosh and Linux. You can find lists at http://codex.wordpress.org/Weblog_Client or http://support.wordpress.com/xml-rpc for WordPress.com blogs.

How Blog Clients Work

When you use a blog client, you write in the interface provided and you supply the logon information that you use for your blog. You then create your blog posts, and when you are ready to publish, the client publishes your post. Some clients can publish to multiple blogs.

A popular blogging client, is Windows Live Writer, it is free, and you will recognize many functions if you are familiar with Microsoft Word. It is a good blog client for PC users.

To start, you need to download the writer from http://windowslivewriter. spaces.live.com/ and install it on your computer. Then, start up the program and provide the requested information on the configuration screens.

Create a Post with Windows Live Writer

1 While logged into your blog, go to the Writing Settings page and check the box beside XML-RPC (☐ changes to ☑).

Be sure to save your changes at the bottom of the Writing Settings page.

Note: *WordPress.com blogs always have this setting enabled.*

2 In Windows Live Writer, type a headline in the box provided.

Note: *The headline box outline disappears after you click outside the box.*

3 Type your message in the space below the headline.

4 Click the **Preview** tab to see how your post will look on your site.

5 Click **Save** under the File menu, or press Ctrl + S (⌘ + S on Mac) to save your work.

6 When you are finished with your post, click **Publish**.

Windows Live Writer uploads your post to your blog and publishes it.

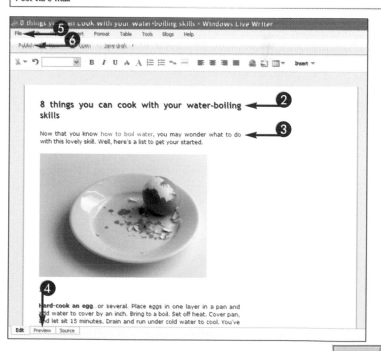

Import Posts from Another Blogging Platform

If you have come to WordPress because you are frustrated with a different blogging platform, WordPress makes it easy to import your posts. Then, your new WordPress blog will have all the posts from your old blog, too.

Start by clicking Tools in the left menu bar, and then click Import.

Import Posts from Another Blogging Platform

① On the Import page, click your blogging platform.

This example uses Blogger.

● If you are moving from another blog platform, click your blog platform and follow the directions.

Note: You can import posts from more sources into a self-hosted blog than into a WordPress.com blog.

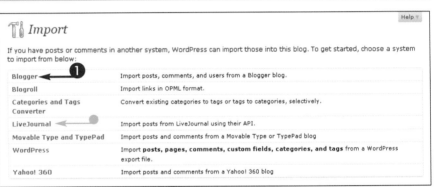

② Click **Authorize** to allow Google, which owns Blogger, to send your Blogger data.

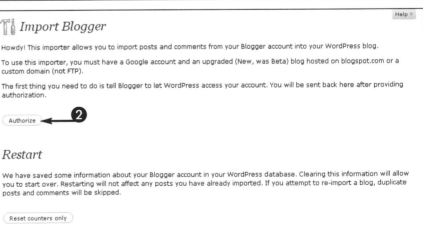

The Google Accounts window opens.

3 Click **Grant access**.

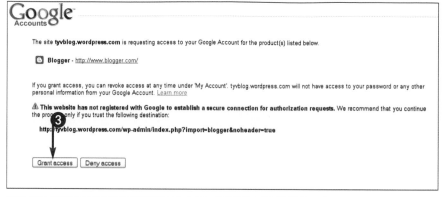

A Blogger Blogs window opens that displays all Blogger blogs associated with your Google account.

4 Click **Import** next to the blog you want to import.

● The Posts and Comments columns indicate the progress of your import. If your previous blog was large, the import process may take a while. WordPress allows you to go to other pages and check back periodically if you want.

When the import is finished, all your previous posts and comments appear on your WordPress blog.

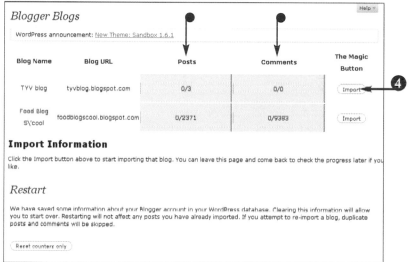

Can I import my blogroll too?

Most likely. You just need to save your blogroll as an OPML file. To do so, Blogger users can go to Google Reader, a feed reader that automatically stores Blogger blogroll links, click **Settings**, click **Import/Export** and, at the bottom of the page, click **Export your subscriptions as an OPML file**. TypePad users can click the **TypeLists** tab, click their blog list, and click **Import/Export** and **Export to OPML**.

Back at WordPress, click **Blogroll** on the Imports page, and follow the directions.

Create a Blogroll

You can share the love by including other Web sites and blogs in your *blogroll*. Adding them to your blogroll also lets them know that your blog exists. Everybody wins!

① Click **Links** in the Dashboard's left menu bar.

The Edit Links window opens.

Note: Every new blog comes with a few links already listed. They vary according to the theme.

② Click **Add New**.

The Add New Link window opens.

③ In the Name box, type the name of the link as you want it to appear in your blogroll.

④ Type the complete address of the site in the Web Address box.

⑤ If you want, type a brief — as in four or five words — description of the site in the Description box.

⑥ Click the **Blogroll** check box (☐ changes to ☑).

⑦ Scroll down to the Target box.

8 Click the **_blank** radio button
(○ changes to ◉).

9 If desired, complete the
relationship information.

10 Return to the top of the page and
click **Add Link**.

WordPress saves the link and
returns a new Add New Link
screen.

Target

○ **_blank** - new window or tab.
○ **_top** - current window or tab, with no frames.
○ **_none** - same window or tab.

Choose the target frame for your link.

Link Relationship (XFN)

rel:

identity   ☐ another web address of mine

friendship   ○ contact ○ acquaintance ○ friend ◉
                                  none

physical   ☐ met

professional   ☐ co-worker ☐ colleague

● A confirmation that the link has
been added appears.

● You can type the name of your
next link, and proceed as before
to add more blogroll links.

When you are done, you can view
your blogroll by going to your
site's front page.

🔗 *Add New Link*

Link added.

Name

Example: Nifty blogging software

Web Address

Example: http://wordpress.org/ — don't forget the http://

Description

This will be shown when someone hovers over the link in the blogroll, or optionally
below the link.

TIPS

**How do I get rid of the links
supplied with my theme?**
You can click the **Delete** link visible
when you position the mouse over
the link on the Edit Links page. Or,
you can click the check boxes next
to all the links you want to remove,
and then click **Delete** in the Bulk
Actions drop-down menu (●), and
click **Apply** to complete the action.

🔗 *Edit Links*

Bulk Actions ▼ (Apply)
Bulk Actions
Delete ◀———

☐ **Development Blog**

**How do I organize my links into
link categories?**
You can add link categories on the
Add New Link, Edit Link, or Link
Categories pages. Then, when you
edit individual links, you can select
under which category or categories
you want the link to appear.

Create Visual and Audio Content

Just because the program is called *Word*Press does not mean pictures and sounds are not welcome. In fact, WordPress provides all the tools you need to use images, audio, and video files with your blog.

Consider Media Issues 108

Review Media Settings 109

Prepare Images for Uploading 110

Upload and Insert an Image
    While Posting...112

Insert Images from Web Sources..................114

Image Formatting from Add an
    Image Window...116

Image Formatting from Edit
    Image Window...118

Insert Images into Media Library 120

Insert an Image Gallery...................................122

Add a Slide Show to Your Posts 124

Link to YouTube (and Other) Videos 126

Upload Video Files to Your Host...................128

Link to a Podcast or Sound File
    from Your Blog...130

Create and Install a Favicon
    for a Self-Hosted Blog................................132

Create and Install a Favicon
    at WordPress.com...134

Consider Media Issues

It is the rare blog that includes words and only words. You, too, can enrich your readers' blog experience by including images, sounds, and even video on your blog.

Images and Dimensions

Web browsers display images according to the number of pixels set aside for them. If you upload an image 1600 pixels wide, but you have room only for a 500-pixel image, the browser reduces the image to display it. The large image causes the page to load more slowly and uses more memory than a 500-pixel image would have.

Media Selection

Well-chosen media enhances a blog, but too much or poorly chosen media can be a distraction. Well-chosen media includes a map that shows a location you recommend, a photograph that illustrates a point you have made, or a video clip that demonstrates a process you describe. A poor choice might include a fuzzy photo that fails to make the desired point.

Media and Memory

One picture may be worth *more* than a thousand words in terms of computer memory. Sound and video files use even more memory. In fact, WordPress.com requires you to pay for increased memory if you want to use these media. If your blog is self-hosted, make sure you have enough space with your host to accumulate sound and video files.

Review Media Settings

The default settings may be fine for you, but you need to review them to make sure they do what you want them to do. They let you set standard images sizes for a consistent look and keep track of where you store media files online.

Review Media Settings

① Click **Media** under the Settings menu in the left menu bar.

The Media Settings window opens.

② Review the dimensions listed next to Thumbnail size, Medium size, and Large size to make sure they are appropriate for your blog.

Note: See Chapter 11 for tips on determining your blog theme's dimensions.

③ Clear the **Crop thumbnail** check box (☑ changes to ☐) unless you want thumbnails to display to an exact size that you specify. (This option is unavailable at WordPress.com.)

④ Click **Save Changes**.

⑤ Click **Miscellaneous** under the Settings menu in the left menu bar. (This menu does not exist at WordPress.com.)

The Miscellaneous Settings page opens. Leave the default setting for the upload folder.

⑥ Click the **Organize my uploads** check box (☐ changes to ☑).

⑦ Click **Save Changes**.

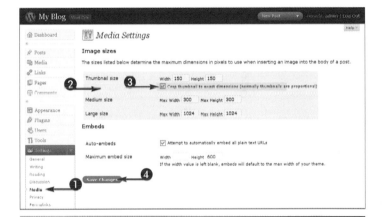

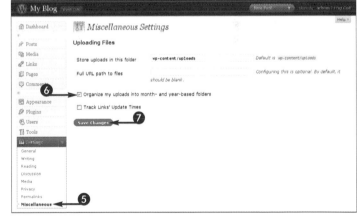

Prepare Images for Uploading

When you take the time to edit and resize images before you post them on your blog, you assure that your images look their best and do not slow down your site.

Although WordPress provides some online editing tools, you will do better with an image editor to prepare your photos and other images. It can be a simple and free program, such as GIMP or Picasa, or the do-it-all Adobe Photoshop. If you have a digital camera, it may provide a basic editing program, too.

Crop to Focus Interest

Crop is the term that editors use for trimming images. Use your editor's cropping tool to eliminate distracting activity, objects, or blank areas or to zero in on the item of particular interest. Save an unedited version of the photo, although your editor may do so automatically, in case you change your mind.

Adjust the Image

Take advantage of the editor's tools to eliminate "red eye" in flash photos, to straighten out sloping horizons, and to correct poorly rendered color, contrast, and other image flaws. You want people to see the image, not be put off by its shortcomings.

Annotate the Image

Add arrows, labels, and other notations to your image if they would help readers. For example, a simple "start here" and an arrow can make a map much more meaningful to your readers than a large amount of text. Similarly, clear labels on graphs aid in understanding.

Save the Image

After you have finished editing, you need to save your image in a file format that Web browsers can display properly. The acceptable formats are JPEG, which stands for Joint Photographic Experts Group, GIF, or Graphics Interchange Format, and PNG, for Portable Network Graphics.

Choose a File Format

GIF is best for images with few colors because it retains quality and creates a small file. GIF often is good for logos. JPEG supports millions of colors and thus is good for photographs, but it creates bigger files unless you increase compression, which reduces JPEG image quality. PNG is the newest format and shares many GIF advantages, but some older browsers do not support it.

Resize the Image

Unless you got your image from another Web site, chances are it is bigger than you want on your blog. View it at 100 percent size in your image editor to see how big the image *really* is. Use your editor's resizing tools to reduce it to the largest size you would want it to appear on your site.

Upload and Insert an Image While Posting

By using the tools that WordPress provides, you can upload your images from your computer in a batch or one at a time. Then, you can insert them into your blog posts to add some visual pizzazz to your site.

You can upload images and insert images as part of your post-writing process or as a separate operation.

Upload and Insert an Image While Posting

① From the New Post or Edit Post page, click in your blog post at the location where you want to insert your image.

② Click the **Add an Image** button (🖼).

The Add an Image window opens.

Note: *When you upload an image, WordPress also makes the image available for a gallery on your post and stores it in your site's Media Library.*

③ Click **Select Files**.

A window for browsing for files opens.

④ When you find the file you want to upload, select it.

⑤ Click **Open**.

The Add an Image window displays a bar that says "Crunching" as WordPress uploads your file.

When it finishes, the Add an Image window changes and displays your uploaded image.

● If WordPress tells you that your upload failed, the lower portion of this window does not appear. Click **Browser uploader** and try again.

⑥ In the Title box, type the words that you want to appear on the Web page when a viewer positions the mouse over the picture.

Note: The default title is the image's file name.

⑦ Click **Insert into Post** at the bottom of the page.

● The Add an Image window disappears, and the Edit Post window displays the image where your cursor was.

⑧ Click **Update Post** to save the change.

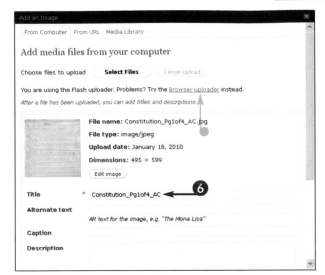

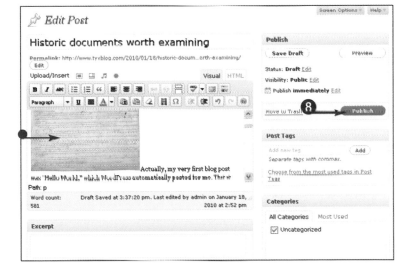

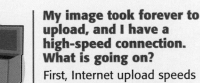

TIPS

Do I have to do something with all the boxes presented in Add an Image after I upload my image?

No. The only box that requires information is Title, which defaults to the image file name. In fact, you can simply click **Insert File** after you have uploaded the image if you want.

My image took forever to upload, and I have a high-speed connection. What is going on?

First, Internet upload speeds typically are slower than download speeds. The bigger issue, however, probably is that your image file is too large. Try to keep it less than 150 kilobytes or so.

Insert Images from Web Sources

You can save storage space on your Web host when you insert images based on other Web sites. You do not have to download or upload the image files; you embed, or *hotlink*, them with a URL. Sometimes, though, this can slow your page loading time or set the stage for a future broken link.

Get permission from the image owner to use the image, unless the image is in the public domain or the Web site gives copyright permission.

Insert Images from Web Sources

① Right-click the image you want to link to (or click and hold the mouse button on Mac).

② Click **Copy Image Location**.

The link is saved to your computer's clipboard.

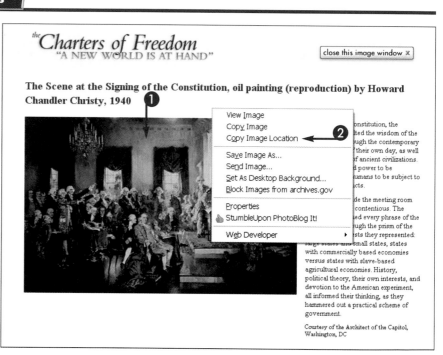

③ Click the **Add an Image** button (⬛) at the top of the New Post or Edit Post window.

④ Click **From URL** at the top of the Add an Image window.

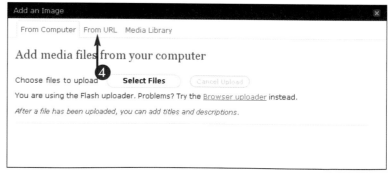

The Add Media File from URL window opens.

⑤ Type or paste a copied image URL in the Image URL box.

⑥ Type a title, which a reader sees when positioning the mouse over the image, in the Image Title box.

⑦ Click **Insert into Post**.

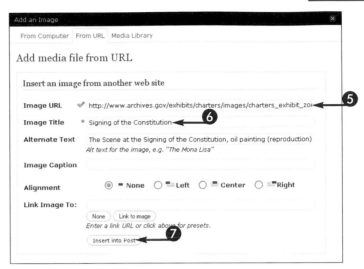

● The Add an Image window disappears, and the Edit Post window displays the image where your cursor was.

⑧ Click **Save Draft**.

⑨ Click **Preview** to see how the image looks on your Web site.

TIPS

Where can I find images in the public domain?

A favorite location for finding images is Wikimedia Commons, at http://commons.wikimedia.org. Also, images on U.S. government Web sites almost always are available copyright-free.

I found photos that say they are subject to the Creative Commons Share Alike license. What does that mean?

Numerous licensing and copyright options exist. The most common seem to be standard copyrights, which means you must get permission before using the photo, and Creative Commons licenses, of which there are several versions. For more information about the Creative Commons licenses, go to http://creativecommons.org/about/licenses/.

Image Formatting from Add an Image Window

The Add an Image window provides formatting options that allow you to present images with text wrapped around them, in various sizes, and with additional information attached for yourself or your readers.

These options appear when you upload images or view them in the Media Library. More formatting options are available after your images are in your blog post.

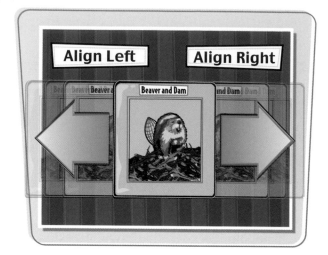

Edit Image

Expands an editing panel that allows you to crop, rotate, or resize your image.

Title

Text that appears when a viewer positions the mouse over an image in a published blog post.

Alternate Text

Lets you enter a short description of the image to be read aloud by a screen reader or other assistive device, or when a browser has images turned off. It is always a good idea to provide alternate text.

Caption

Typically provides information for readers about the photo, which may appear in the post with the photo depending on your theme's style sheet.

Description

Lets you record information of interest but does not display it.

Link URL

Associates the image with a URL you enter to the image's file by clicking **File URL**; or to the blog post's permalink by clicking **Post URL**.

Alignment

Provides the options of *no alignment*, meaning the image aligns according to surrounding formatting tags; or *left*, *right*, or *center* alignment, which provide text wrapping around the image in addition to aligning the image to the specified location. Note that the alignment setting defaults to whatever alignment you used last.

Size

Lets you display the image in one of the default sizes — thumbnail, medium, or large as determined on your Media Settings page — or *Full Size*, the size you uploaded. Note that the size setting defaults to whatever size you used last. The exact dimensions associated with each size appear beneath the size name. If no dimension appears, as is the case below Large in the figure, that is because the uploaded image is smaller than the default size.

Insert Into Post

Places image into post at the point where your cursor last was.

Delete

Starts process to delete an image from your Media Library. A confirmation message appears when you click **Delete**.

Save All Changes

Saves changes and stores the image in the Media Library but does not insert the image in post if it is not already there.

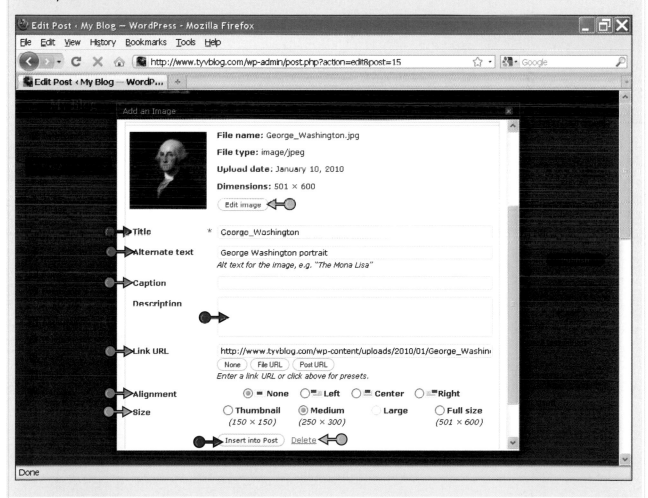

Image Formatting from Edit Image Window

Once an image is inserted into a post, you can move it around, adjust its size, alter or add its borders, and more. In other words, you can make it exactly the way you want it. It all starts by clicking the image in the Edit Post window.

Image Handles

Resizes image proportionally when you click and drag corner handle or stretches image when you click and drag a side handle. You also can click and hold anywhere within the image, and drag the image to a new location.

Edit Image

Opens Edit Image window, to edit size, link, caption, and alignment settings and Advanced Settings.

Delete

Deletes image from location in post, but not from Media Library.

Size Scale

Resizes image display to a percentage of the inserted size.

Edit Options

Lets you enter or change the information you provided when you uploaded your image.

Update/Cancel

Saves or cancels changes you made in Edit Image window and returns to Edit Post window.

Advanced Settings Tab

Opens Advanced Settings window.

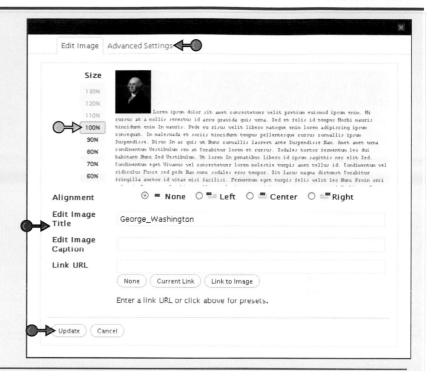

Image Properties

Add or alter borders and spacing around the image.

Advanced Link Settings

Edit characteristics of links associated with the image. These are useful if you are familiar with HTML and CSS.

Update/Cancel

Saves or cancels changes you made in Advanced Image Settings window and returns to Edit Post window.

Insert Images into Media Library

Depending on how you work, you may find it more convenient to upload your images without worrying about where they go in your blog posts. The Media Library lets you do just that, and it also provides a searchable repository for your images and other media.

Media embedded into your blog via other Web sites' URLs are not saved to your Media Library.

Insert Images into Media Library

① Click **Media** in the left menu bar.

The Media menu expands, and the Media Library window opens.

② Click **Add New**.

The Upload New Media window opens.

③ Click **Select Files**.

A browser window opens.

④ Select the file or files you want to upload.

⑤ Click **Open**.

WordPress uploads the files to your server and stores them in your Media Library.

⑥ Click **Show** if you want to edit information about the images.

The image's display expands and allows you to add and update information.

⑦ When finished, click **Save all changes**.

WordPress returns to the Media Library, which shows the new additions.

 TIPS

Can I just upload images with my FTP client?

Yes, if you have a self-hosted blog. Simply upload the images from your computer to the correct folder, or directory, or your server. See your Miscellaneous Settings if you are unsure where to upload your files.

How do I insert images from the Media Library?

When writing a post, click the **Insert Image** button (🖻), and then click the **Media Library** tab in the Add an Image Window. Click **Show** to the right of the image you want to use, which reveals its settings, and click **Insert into Post** to close the dialog box and add the image to the post or page.

Insert an Image Gallery

The WordPress Image Gallery gives you a quick and easy way to display a set of photos or other images on your Web site. The gallery displays thumbnails of the images, and then you can click the individual images to view larger versions.

To get started, upload images to your post while you are in the Edit Post window. After you have uploaded the images, click Save All Changes, rather than Insert into Post. Images are attached to your post this way, but not visible — yet!

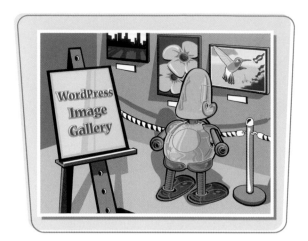

Insert an Image Gallery

① From the Add an Image window, accessible via the Insert Image button (▦), click **Gallery**.

The Gallery tab opens, listing all the photos that you have uploaded from the New Post or Edit Post window.

② Expand the Order Images By drop-down menu, and select the order in which you want your images to appear. For now, choose the **Menu order** option.

③ Type a number in each box to specify the order in which you want the images to appear.

④ Click **Save all changes**.

The images reappear in numerical order according to the number you assigned them.

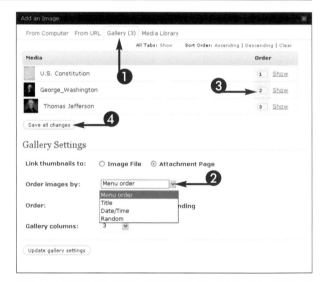

⑤ Click the **Image File** radio button (○ changes to ⊙).

⑥ Click **Insert Gallery**.

The Add an Image window closes.

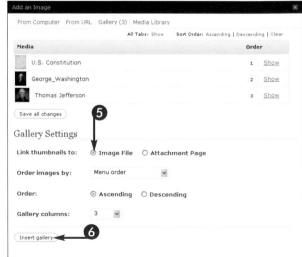

- The Gallery placeholder image appears in the Edit Post window.

7 Click **Update Post**.

8 Click **View Post** or **Preview Changes** to see your gallery.

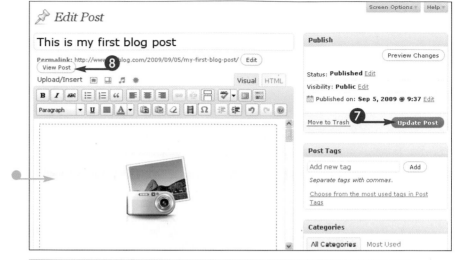

Your blog post opens and shows your gallery.

9 Click an image.

The image opens to its uploaded size in an otherwise blank browser window.

TIPS

Can I do a gallery that includes only three of the five images I uploaded to my post?

Although using various add-ons is a better alternative, you should be able to exclude images through the WordPress [gallery] shortcode. You can find more information at http://en.support.wordpress.com/ images/gallery/ for WordPress.com blogs and at http://codex.wordpress.org/Gallery_Shortcode for self-hosted blogs. Chapter 8 shows one option.

Why not use the Attachment Page option for viewing?

You are welcome to use it, of course. With that option, clicking an image thumbnail displays it full size on a separate page using your theme's image attachment template.

Add a Slide Show to Your Posts

Why limit yourself to an image or two, or even a gallery, if you can have a slide show simply and easily? If you use Picasa or Flickr to host or store your photos, you can make a Flash slide show for free with PictoBrowser, and you do not even have to sign up for anything new.

WordPress.com does not support PictoBrowser slide shows, but it has other options as described in the tips at the end of this task.

Add a Slide Show to Your Posts

① In your Web browser, go to www. pictobrowser.com and click **PictoBuilder**.

② In the screen that appears, click to indicate whether you are using photos from Flickr or Picasa (☐ changes to ☑).

③ Type the username for your Flickr or Picasa account.

④ Click **Continue**.

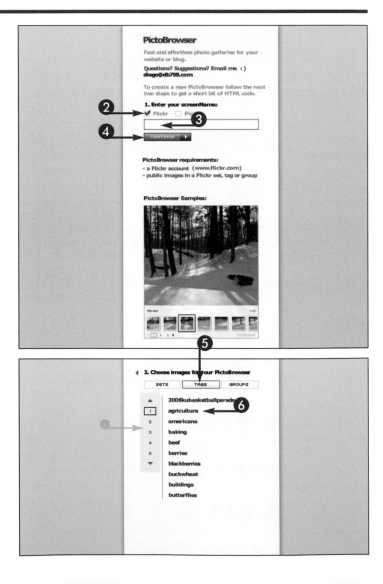

The Step 2 window opens.

⑤ Click to choose whether to view images according to sets, tags, or groups.

● A list lets you scroll through pages of sets, tags, or groups. In this case, the list displays tags.

⑥ Click your choice from the list.

7 In the PictoBrowser settings page, change any Image Settings for the size or alignment of your slide show.

8 Change Player settings for the size or title settings for the slide show window.

9 Change Background Color settings for the background color and transparency of the player.

● Adjustments appear in the preview.

10 When finished, click the **Get HTML Code** tab.

The left pane changes to reveal HTML code, which you need to select and copy.

11 On the New Post or Edit Post page, click the **HTML** editor tab.

The post box opens in the HTML editor.

12 Paste the copied HTML in the post box.

13 Click **Save Draft**.

The slide show now is embedded in your post.

Note: The slide show is not visible in the Visual version of the post box. You must look at the preview or your published blog post to see the slide show.

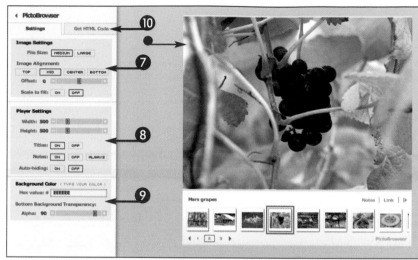

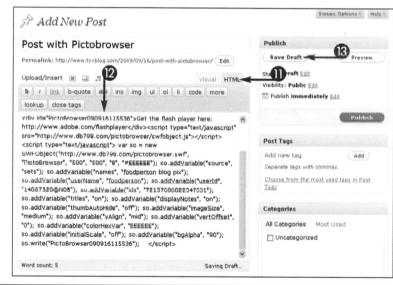

What slide show options are available for WordPress.com blogs?

Slide shows compatible with WordPress.com are available at Slide.com, RockYou.com, and SlideShare.com. Of those, only Slide.com lets you create slide shows from existing Flickr and Picasa accounts. Just go to the sites and follow the steps. They let you click WordPress.com as your host to make posting easier.

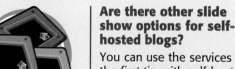

Are there other slide show options for self-hosted blogs?

You can use the services in the first tip with self-hosted blogs, but, as with PictoBrowser, you have to post the HTML in your post box on the New Post or Edit Post page. Self-hosted blogs also can use plugins, such as NextGEN Gallery and Smooth Slider.

Link to YouTube (and Other) Videos

Videos are a little more trouble to deal with than images, but they add a lot of visual energy to your blog posts. Using embedded videos through links may be the easiest way to get them up and running, and you do not have to use your own host space to store the videos.

You can link to most videos hosted at YouTube.com, and you can upload your own videos there, too.

Link to YouTube (and Other) Videos

1 After you find the video you want to post on YouTube.com, click the **Customize** button (⚙).

● The customizing options box opens, where you can change the display.

2 When you have finished customizing the display, click in the Embed box, and copy the code there.

3 In your blog's Dashboard in the New Post or Edit Post window, click the **HTML** tab of the post box.

4 Go to the spot in your post where you want the video to appear, and paste the code you copied from YouTube.com.

5 Click **Save Draft**.

6 Click the **Visual** tab.

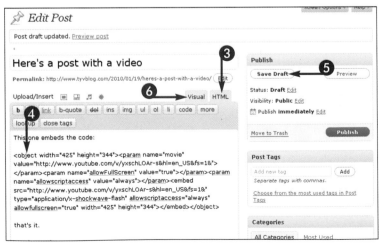

● The post box switches to the Visual editor, where a placeholder box for the video appears.

You can click and drag the box elsewhere in the post, if you want. (On WordPress.com blogs, you see a short link instead.)

7 Click **Save Draft**.

The post is published to your blog.

8 Click **Preview**.

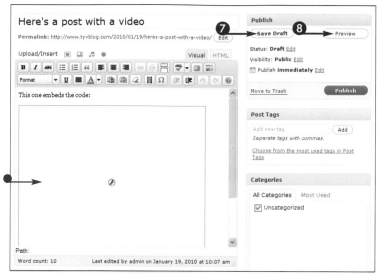

A preview of your post appears in a new window.

9 Click one of the **Play** arrows (▶) to view the video.

TIPS

Do I have to pay for the video add-in to post YouTube videos with WordPress.com?

No, because you are posting a *hotlink* to the video rather than hosting the video on your WordPress. com account.

Is there any other way to link to videos?

Starting with WordPress version 2.9, you can simply put the video's URL in a separate line in the HTML editor and save it. Another way is to click the **Add Video** button (▣) above the post box, click the **From URL** tab, and paste the URL in the Video URL box. Also, you can link to videos at other popular video hosts such as Vimeo.com, DailyMotion.com, and Metacafe.com. You can read about various video hosting services on Wikipedia.org.

Upload Video Files to Your Host

You have more control over the look and performance of your videos when you host them yourself. Doing so takes a few more steps than when you link to videos posted elsewhere.

If your blog is hosted on WordPress.com, your first step is to buy the VideoPress upgrade.

Upload Video Files to Your Host

Basic Installation on Self-Hosted Blog

① On the New Post or Edit Post page, click the **Add Video** button (▣).

The Add Video window opens.

② Click **Select Files**.

A browse for files window opens, from which you select the video you want to upload and then click **Open**. When you do, the Add Video window returns and shows the progress of the upload.

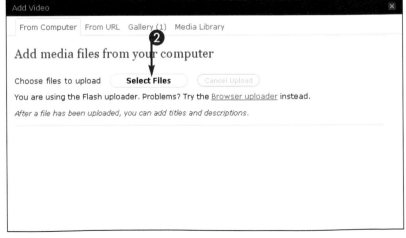

When the upload is complete, the Add Video window shows details about the video.

③ Click **File URL**, which pastes a link to the video location in the Link URL box.

④ If desired, change the video title, which by default is based on the video file's name.

⑤ Click **Insert Into Post**.

A *link* to the video file — but no image — appears in your post box.

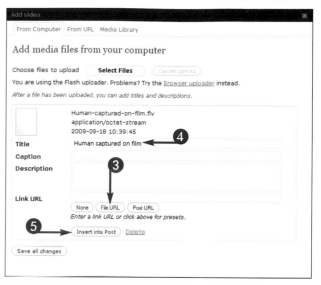

Full-Featured Installation on WordPress.com

① After clicking **Upgrades** in the left menu panel and then buying the VideoPress upgrade, go to a New Post or Edit Post page, and upload as described in steps **1** and **2** on the preceding page.

A message appears informing you that your video is being processed and will be ready in a few minutes.

② While you wait for the video to be processed, go to http://support.wordpress.com/videopress/ to read detailed instructions on setting up your video.

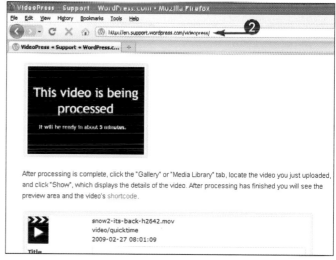

 TIPS

Is a link the best I can do for video on my self-hosted blog?

You can do much better, actually, but it requires use of a plugin. See Chapter 8 for information about plugins.

I get a message saying that my upload is too big on most videos. On others, they take forever to upload. What can I do?

With your self-hosted blog, you can speed things up and avoid that upload limit by uploading files directly to your uploads folder on your Web host. Unless you have customized your upload folder in your Miscellaneous settings panel, the default uploads folder is wp-content/uploads.

Link to a Podcast or Sound File from Your Blog

With audio files, you can give your readers the sound of your voice, of bird calls, of music. Linking to such files is much like linking to videos, but to have the files play in the background requires some additional steps.

First, you need to find the audio file that you want to link to.

Link to a Podcast or Sound File from Your Blog

1 From the New Post or Edit Post window, click the **Add Audio** button (🎵).

2 The Add Audio window opens, where you click **From URL**.

3 Type or paste the URL of your chosen audio file into the Audio File URL box.

4 Type a title for the audio file into the Title box.

5 Click **Insert into Post**.

The Add Audio box closes, and a link to the audio file appears in the post box of the New Post or Edit Post box.

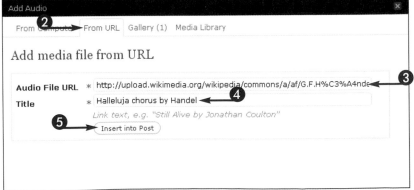

6 Click **Save Draft**.

7 Click **Publish**.

WordPress publishes the post to your blog.

Note: If you prefer, you can click Preview to view the link in the post.

8 Click **View post**.

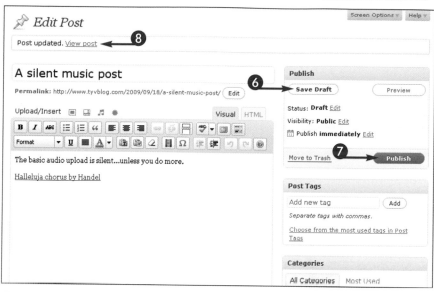

The post opens in your browser, where you can click the link to hear the sound file.

The sound file opens at its URL and begins playing.

● You can click the **Pause** button (⏸) if you want to pause the file.

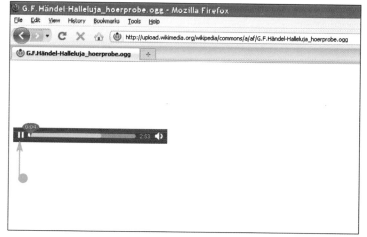

TIPS

Can I host files on my blog so that people do not get transferred to another location?

If your blog is self-hosted, the steps are the same as for uploading a video file described in "Upload Video Files to Your Host" earlier in this chapter. Just use the Add Audio link instead of Add Video. On a WordPress.com blog, you need to buy an upgrade if you want to upload an audio file.

Can I make music automatically play in the background?

It is not a good idea; many people object to that audio intrusion. Much better to make the file available and let people choose to listen or not.

Create and Install a Favicon for a Self-Hosted Blog

A favicon is the tiny icon that appears next to a Web address in many browsers. It also may appear in a browser's Favorites or Bookmarks list. You can stick with the favicon provided by your Web host.

Do not worry about pronouncing favicon correctly. There is no definitive pronunciation. Options include FAVE-icon, from the word's root as *favorite icon*, and FAVV-uh-con, with a short *a*, as in hat.

Create and Install a Favicon for a Self-Hosted Blog

① Go to DeGraeve.com/favicon, and click **Browse**.

A file upload window opens, where you browse your hard drive for an image that you want to convert to a favicon and click **Open**.

② When the path to your image appears in the Upload this Image box, click **upload image**.

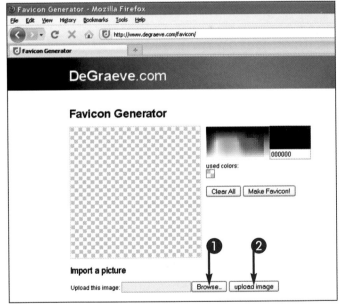

The image appears in a new window.

③ Click and drag, even stretch, the selection box until it surrounds the part of your image that you want to make into your icon.

④ Click **Crop picture**.

Note: The DeGraeve icon generator lets you crop from a larger image. Other icon generators, such as the one at Dynamicdrive.com, reduce an entire image to create a favicon.

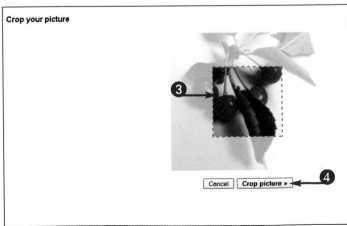

The browser returns to the Favicon Generator window and shows your pixilated favicon.

⑤ Click **Make Favicon!**.

The favicon appears on the screen. Follow the directions for saving the favicon to your hard drive. It is named favicon.ico.

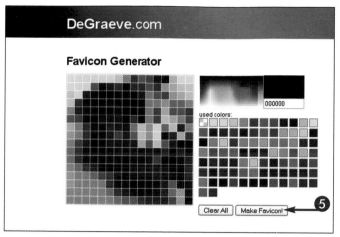

⑥ Using your FTP client, such as FileZilla, upload favicon.ico to the root of your blog site, as in /public_html. For good measure, you might also save it to /public_html/wp-content/themes/*yourtheme*, where *yourtheme* is the theme you are using.

● The file appears in the directory listing.

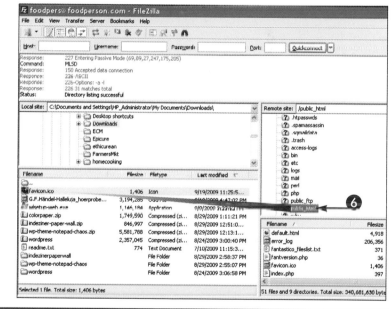

Is there some other way to make a favicon?

You can make your own custom favicon with a paint or image-editing program. Just make sure it is 16 x 16 pixels (although some browsers support 32 x 32 pixels) and is named favicon.ico.

I followed the directions, but the favicon is not appearing. Why not?

Most likely, it will not appear until your browser's cache has been cleared or until you wait a couple of weeks. If you have waited two weeks or so and it still does not appear, there is a chance that your theme needs to be modified to support favicons. Search the WordPress.org forums for help.

Create and Install a Favicon at WordPress.com

Blogs at WordPress.com can upload an image that works as a favicon to give your blog a unique identity. WordPress also makes it available in other sizes for display around the WordPress.com community.

Create and Install a Favicon at WordPress.com

① Click **Settings** in the left menu bar to get to the General Settings in your WordPress.com Dashboard.

② Click **Browse** to find the image on your computer that you want to use for your favicon.

③ An upload window opens, where you select the desired image and click **Open**.

④ When the path to the image appears in the box, click **Upload Image**.

The Crop Uploaded Image screen appears, with a box for cropping.

⑤ Click and drag, even stretch, the selection box until it surrounds the part of your image that you want to make into your icon.

⑥ When you are satisfied, click **Crop Image**.

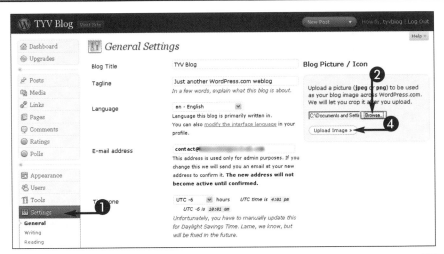

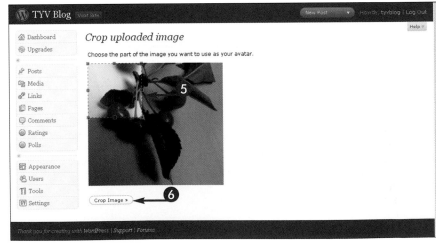

- After a moment, the All Done! screen appears, showing the favicon size (the smallest) and avatar (the medium). The largest size may appear in various other spots around WordPress.com occasionally.

7 Click **Back to blog options**.

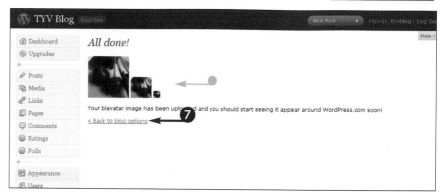

The General Settings window reappears and displays your new blog image.

- Your new blog image appears on the General Settings page, where you also have the option to remove it.

8 Click **Discussion** under Settings in the left menu bar.

9 When the Discussion Settings window opens, make sure you have selected **Show Avatars** in the Avatars section so that your avatar will appear on your blog pages.

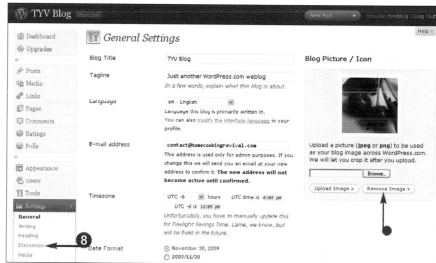

TIPS

The image is appearing on my General Settings page, but not on my blog. Why not?

It can take a little while before it shows up. Check back in half an hour or so.

I uploaded a blog image but I still do not have an avatar appearing when I leave comments. What can I do?

The blog image is different from the avatar associated with you as an individual. You can upload an avatar image by clicking **Users** in the left menu bar and then clicking your name to go to your profile. See "Create Your WordPress.com Profile" in Chapter 2.

Extend Your Options with Widgets and Plugins

Although WordPress software gets your blog up and running, WordPress widgets and plugins make your blog do cartwheels. These miniprograms add functions, ease effort, and do just about anything else you may want your blogging software to do. As usual with WordPress, these helpers generally do not cost a dime.

Introducing Widgets and Plugins..................138

Choose and Insert Widgets.........................140

Rearrange and Remove Widgets..................142

**Add Sidebar Items Using HTML in a
  Text Widget**.......................................144

Get a Key and Activate Akismet..................146

Find Plugins..148

Consider These Popular Plugins..................150

Install and Activate a Plugin.........................152

Introducing Widgets and Plugins

Widgets and *plugins* may sound like games, but they are seriously useful bits of code that extend your WordPress blog beyond the basics of writing and posting information on a regular basis.

Widgets for Sidebars

Widget is the term that WordPress uses for items that appear in the sidebars of your blog. Both hosted and self-hosted blogs come with a few standard widgets. If your theme supports widgets, your Dashboard prompts you to configure the widgets when you activate the theme.

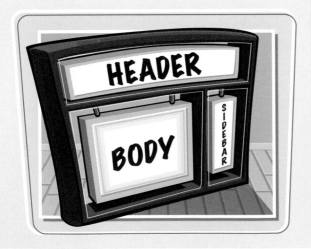

Plugins for Everything

Plugins are like miniprograms that do lots of things, from adding buttons to your post box interface to installing a media player so that you can play your own photo gallery, podcasts, and videos on your blog. Plugins can serve ads, increase your search-engine visibility, point out frequent commenters, and do lots, lots more.

Standard Widgets at Self-Hosted Blogs

At this writing, self-hosted blogs generally have widgets to display a monthly archive of posts, a calendar, blog categories, your blogroll, a *meta* section for logging in and other tasks, a list of static pages, a display of recent comments, a list of recent posts, the RSS feed of your choice, a search box, a tag cloud, and text widgets, which have lots of options, including for images and HTML.

Standard Widgets for WordPress.com Blogs

WordPress.com does not allow users to upload and install plugins, but the host makes up for it in large part by having numerous widgets in addition to most of those included on self-hosted blogs. You can add any of the widgets to your sidebar just by following some simple directions.

WordPress.com Widgets and What They Do

The following WordPress.com widgets are in addition to those that are standard on self-hosted blog installations.

Widget	What It Does
Akismet	Displays the number of spam comments caught by Akismet spam catcher.
Authors	Shows capsule information about all authors on your blog.
Blog Stats	Displays number of hits to your blog.
Box.net file sharing	Provides way to share files by way of the Box.net service.
del.icio.us	Displays your del.icio.us bookmarks according to your settings.
Flickr	Displays photos based at Flickr.com.
Gravatar	Shows your Gravatar image.
Meebo	Connects to the Meebo service to allow instant messaging on your blog.
Platial MapKit	Makes it easy for you to use an interactive map.
RSS Links	Provides links for readers to sign up for your RSS feed or feeds.
SocialVibe	Lets you connect with a commercial sponsor to earn donations to your choice of several charities.
Top Clicks	Lists blog links that get the most clicks.
Twitter	Displays your tweets.
Vodpod Videos	Inserts a Vodpod video player in your sidebar where readers can view videos you have selected through your Vodpod account.

Choose and Insert Widgets

You can add or remove widgets any time you want after you have your blog running. Widgets make it easy to add sidebar features on your blog. Take advantage of them!

Most themes these days support widgets. If yours does not and you want to use widgets, you might consider changing themes.

Choose and Insert Widgets

① In the left menu bar, click **Appearance** to expand the Appearance menu.

② Click **Widgets** to open the Widget panel, which lists available widgets in alphabetical order.

● Active widgets appear in the sidebar list. If your theme has more than one sidebar, a sidebar list appears for each available sidebar.

③ Use the scroll bar or page down until you see the Search widget.

④ Click and hold on the Search widget until ⬚ changes to ✛.

⑤ Drag the Search widget to the sidebar list.

When the widget reaches the list, a dotted line appears under the sidebar label indicating that you can release the mouse button.

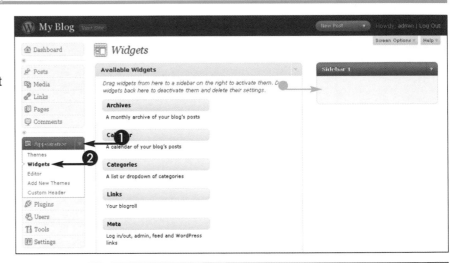

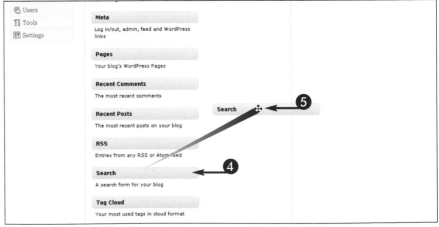

6 Type a title for your Search widget in the title box.

Note: Widget titles are usually optional.

7 Click **Save**.

Note: Options for each widget may vary from one theme to the next. If your theme's widget has no options, simply dragging it to the sidebar is all you need to do.

8 Click **Visit Site** to see your widget in action.

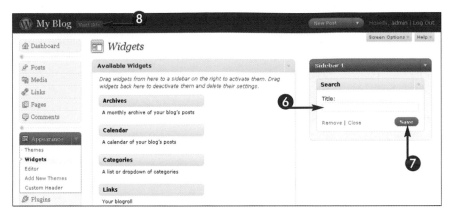

● The Search widget appears in sidebar in the default theme.

9 Click the **Back** button to return to the Widgets panel, where you can add more widgets to your sidebars.

TIPS

After I installed my first widget and looked at it on the site, all the other widgets that appeared with my theme are gone. Also, when I clicked the browser's Back button, even the widget I added does not appear in the sidebar on the Widgets panel. What did I do wrong?

Not a thing. Themes include numerous widgets as part of their installation. Once you configure your first widget, the default widgets go away. Back on the Widgets panel, after you click your browser's **Refresh** button, or click **Widgets** in the left menu bar, your newly activated widget reappears. Then, click and drag any other widgets you want to the sidebar or sidebars.

I have a self-hosted WordPress blog, but I have more widgets than the standard ones previously mentioned. How come?

Virtually every self-hosted WordPress blog has the standard widgets mentioned in "Introducing Widgets and Plugins." Some themes do have additional widgets. It just means your theme's developer automated more functions for you.

Rearrange and Remove Widgets

Another great thing about widgets is that they are as easy to remove as they are to add, which makes experimenting with different arrangements a simple task. You can rearrange and remove widgets — and even retain your settings if you want.

If you scroll down the Widgets panel, you can see an Inactive Widgets box below the Available Widgets.

To Rearrange Widgets

❶ Click and hold on the widget that you want to move in your sidebar (⬚ changes to ✛), and then drag the widget to the position you want it to have in your sidebar.

❷ When a rectangle with a dotted line appears at the desired location, release the mouse button.

The widget appears in its new position in the sidebar, and a rotating circle appears at the top of the sidebar for a moment to indicate that WordPress is storing your new arrangement.

To Remove a Widget and Retain Its Settings

❶ Click the expansion arrow on the widget you want to remove.

❷ Click **Remove**.

The widget disappears from the sidebar and reappears in the Inactive Widgets box on the lower portion of the Widgets panel. It keeps the title you assigned to it.

Note: *The Close link collapses the widget's full display.*

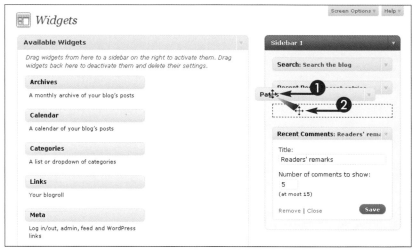

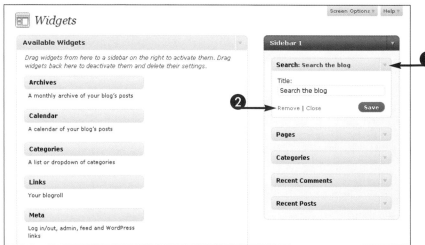

To Remove a Widget without Retaining Its Settings

1 Click and hold the mouse button on the widget you want to remove (⬚ changes to ✛). Drag the widget to the Available Widgets box of the Widgets panel and release the mouse button.

● A deactivate message appears at the top of the Available Widgets box, and the widget disappears from the Sidebar box.

To Reactivate a Saved Widget

1 Click and hold the mouse button on the widget you want to reactivate (⬚ changes to ✛). Drag the widget to the Sidebar box, and then release the mouse button when a dotted-line rectangle appears in the location where you want the widget.

The widget reappears in the Sidebar widget list.

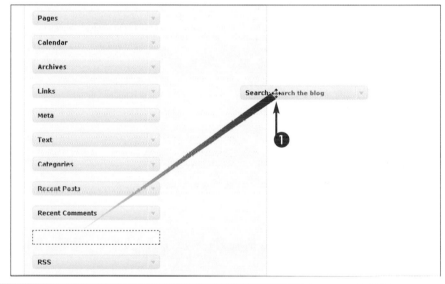

TIPS

I tried to remove and save a configured widget, but I cannot find the settings. Why not?
At this writing, the settings-retention function of the widgets does not seem to work for all widgets. This function is likely to improve in future WordPress updates.

Why do my widgets appear only on my front page?
Different themes vary in their widget displays. Some limit them to the front page or static pages. Others have some, but not all, appear on individual post pages. If you want them to appear on every screen of your blog, you may need to search for a theme that uses widgets in that way.

Add Sidebar Items Using HTML in a Text Widget

Among the many widgets WordPress themes offer is one innocuously titled Text. And, yes, you can use it to show, say, a favorite quote or a bio about yourself in a sidebar. But you also can use it to insert more complex additions that use HTML.

Like most other widgets, the text widget can be used multiple times simultaneously in your sidebars.

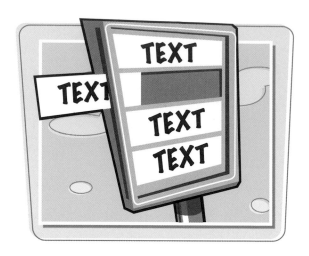

Add Sidebar Items Using HTML in a Text Widget

Add a Basic Text Widget

● After you click and drag a Text widget to a sidebar, a large configuration box appears.

① Type a title, if desired, in the Title box.

② Type your desired text in the text box.

③ Click **Save**.

The text appears in the sidebar location you selected using the formatting specified in your theme's style sheet.

④ Click **Close** to collapse the text widget box.

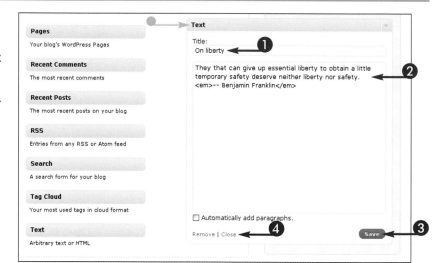

To Change Text Widget Format

① Type simple HTML tags around text you want to format, in this case `<em>` and `</em>` around the text to put it in italics.

② Scroll down and click **Save**.

Your formatting is saved and appears on the blog's sidebar.

Note: *If you navigate elsewhere and return to the Widgets panel, your formatting tags do not appear, but the formatting remains, as you can see by looking at your blog. Also, your theme's style sheet may override some HTML styling.*

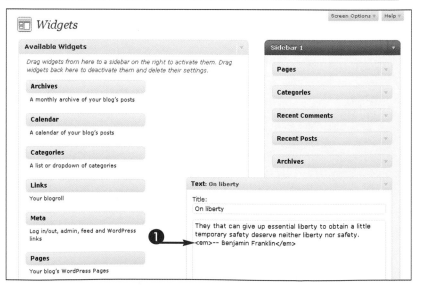

Adding Functional Content via Text Widgets

1 Go to www.clustrmaps.com in your Web browser.

2 Type your blog's complete URL in the URL box.

3 Type an e-mail address where you can receive a password.

Note: *Although you are required to enter an e-mail address, you do not need a password unless you want to customize your map.*

4 If you accept the terms and conditions, click **Make my map**.

ClustrMaps opens another page.

5 Scroll down to the Recommended Code box, and then select and copy all the code that appears there.

6 Paste that code into your Text widget and save. The ClustrMap for your blog appears in your sidebar.

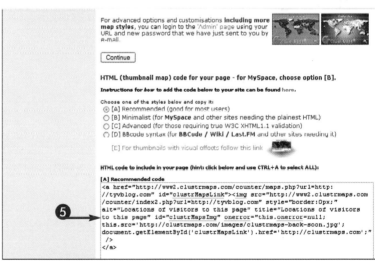

How can I put an image in a sidebar?

WordPress.com has an Image widget just for that purpose. If your blog is self-hosted, you use a Text widget, odd as that sounds. Simply drag a Text widget to the sidebar, and in the large box, type the HTML to call the image, such as `<img src="http://www.tyvblog.com/wp-content/uploads/2009/10/baked.jpg">`.

That map thing is cool! What else can I do in a text widget?

You can find a list of other content you can add via a Text widget at http://codex.wordpress.org/Plugins/WordPress_Widgets#Using_Text_Widgets. Note that WordPress.com does not allow many JavaScripts.

Sadly, junk producers have created junk comments just like junk e-mail. Happily, WordPress comes with the Akismet spam-capturing and spam-identification feature built in. WordPress.com bloggers have the service running by default. Users of self-hosted WordPress blogs have to take a couple of extra steps for Akismet to work for them.

First, self-hosted bloggers must register at WordPress.com — yes, the place that hosts WordPress.com blogs — to get a key to activate Akismet.

Get a Key and Activate Akismet

1 After you have registered at WordPress.com following the instructions in "Sign Up with WordPress.com" in Chapter 2 — you probably want to select the Just a Username option — log on to your self-hosted blog's Dashboard, and click **Profile** in the left menu bar.

The Profile panel opens.

2 Copy the API key that appears at the top of the screen.

3 Log out from WordPress.com.

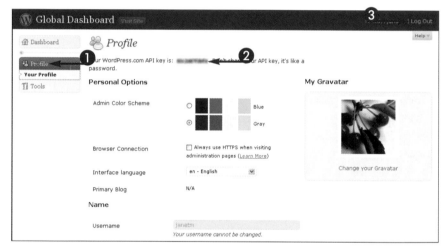

4 Log on to your blog's Dashboard, and click **Plugins**.

The Plugins menu expands, and the Manage Plugins panel opens to reveal installed plugins.

5 Click **Activate** in the Akismet section.

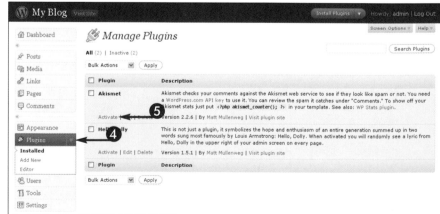

The Manage Plugins panel alerts you that the plugin is activated and prompts you to enter your API key.

⑥ Click **enter your WordPress. com API key**.

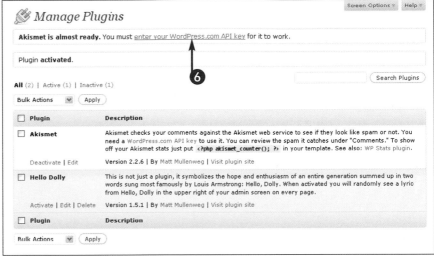

The Akismet Configuration panel opens.

● The Akismet Configuration panel includes instructions on how Akismet works.

⑦ Paste or type your API key in the API key box.

⑧ If desired, click the check box to discard spam comments after a month (☐ changes to ☑).

⑨ Click **Update options**.

WordPress confirms that your options are saved.

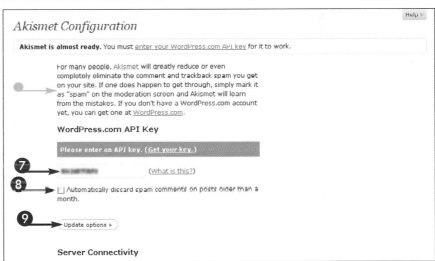

TIPS

How will I know if Akismet has caught any spam comments?

A count of comments in the spam comment queue appears at the top of the Edit Comments panel, which you reach by clicking **Comments** in the left menu bar of the Dashboard (or My Dashboard at WordPress.com blogs). You can see the comments by clicking the **Spam** link there.

Does Akismet ever catch comments that are not spam?

Rarely, but it does happen. That is why it is a good practice to check the junk comments listing periodically.

Find Plugins

Plugins provide all sorts of functions for your self-hosted WordPress blog besides those that are built in, from media players you can embed in your blog to post and comment rating systems and lots more. Finding plugins is easy; choosing less so!

You can investigate plugins from your admin panel or at WordPress.org.

Find Plugins

Find Plugins via the Admin Panel

① Click **Plugins** in the left menu bar.

The Plugins menu expands, and the Manage Plugins panel opens.

② Click **Add New**.

Install Plugins reveals several ways to search or browse for plugins:

● Search plugin lists based on those featured, popular, new, or recently updated at WordPress.org.

● Search by keyword, author, or tag.

● A tag cloud reveals popular plugin tags.

③ Click a link or do a search.

A list of the plugins that fit your selection appears.

● The plugin name links to the plugin's information page.

● The rating from plugin users appears here.

● A brief description of the plugin is shown here.

● A link to the plugin developer's home page finishes the description.

④ Click **Install**.

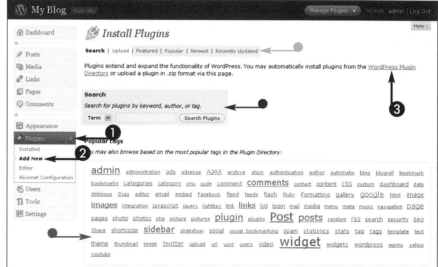

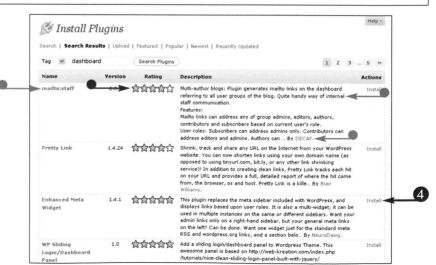

An information and installation window opens.

5 Read the information about the plugin by clicking each tab.

6 Click **WordPress.org Plugin Page**.

The WordPress.org Plugin Directory opens to the plugin page you selected, where you can click **what others are saying** to see what problems and praise others have made about the plugin.

7 Click to close the box and return to the Install Plugins panel.

Find Plugins via the WordPress.org Directory

1 In your browser, go to http://wordpress.org/ extend/plugins.

The Plugin Directory has all the search and browse options available on the Install Plugins panel. Use them to research plugins.

● The plugin tag cloud is accessible by clicking **More** next to Popular Tags in the Plugin Directory.

Why do I need to read plugin details before I install a plugin?
Doing so will help you avoid problems. As helpful as plugins are, they also can cause problems. Some plugins may conflict with other plugins, for example, or a plugin may not work on the version of WordPress that you are running. By doing a little research first, you can avoid headaches.

Consider These Popular Plugins

Even with thousands of plugins available, a few are consistently popular due to their success in helping blogs address certain ongoing needs, such as attracting search engine traffic and helping your blog to work efficiently. Some of them are sure to address your needs.

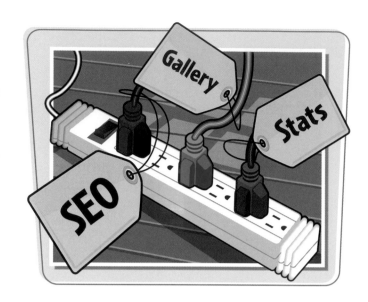

Spread the Word

Blogging is all about communicating, and some plugins aim to add to the buzz. Among them are the ShareThis and Sociable plugins. With one of these plugins active, your blog posts automatically include a button bar that lets your readers easily add the post to their favorite social networking site or send a link to friends via e-mail.

Save the Data

Keeping your WordPress data backed up saves you from disaster should your Web host lose or corrupt your blog. It *can* happen! The WP-DB-Backup plugin makes it easy for you to regularly back up your WordPress database, which stores all your posts, pictures, and other media.

Speed Blog Performance

The bigger your blog and the more photos and other content it has, the slower it can run. The WP Super-cache plugin speeds things up by automatically converting your dynamic blog pages to static pages for most blog visitors.

Pretty Galleries

The standard WordPress image gallery is fairly limited, and the plugins NextGEN Gallery and PageFlip are two plugins that give you more control over how images are shown on your blog, from determining their visual styling in NextGEN to a cool page-turning effect in PageFlip.

Search Engine Optimization

Search engine optimization, or SEO, aims to make your site its most attractive to search engines. All-in-One SEO is an SEO workhorse, allowing you to add keywords and to create a special keyword-rich post title and post summary from boxes right on the Edit Post panel.

Statistics Trackers

Two plugins specialize in giving you the details about your blog's traffic. The Google Analyticator takes advantage of the Google Analytics' data to show what is happening on your blog. The WordPress.com Stats plugin gives the same data for your self-hosted blog that WordPress.com gives its users.

Install and Activate a Plugin

Once you have identified the plugins that you need — or simply want — installing them is easy. Most plugins can be installed with a few clicks from the Add Plugins panel, but even manual installations are easy.

Once installed and activated, each plugin may have other settings and operations that you configure according to the instructions on the plugin's information screens.

Install and Activate a Plugin

From the Add Plugins Panel

① After you have found your chosen plugin in the Add Plugins panel and clicked **Install** to get that plugin's details, click **Install Now**.

A progress indicator appears on the screen, and then the Installing Plugin panel, which gives further progress information.

② After *Successfully installed* appears in the Installing Plugin panel, click **Activate Plugin**.

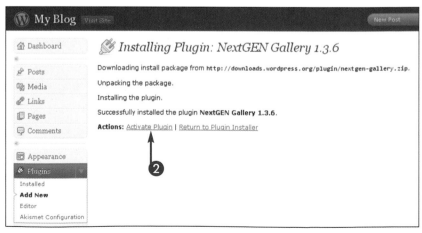

The Manage Plugins panel appears, which confirms the activation and lists the new plugin. You now can use or configure the plugin according to the instructions provided on the plugin information pages.

Manual Plugin Installation

① After you find the plugin's page in the WordPress Plugin Directory, click **Download**.

A browser download window opens, from which you choose to save the ZIP file.

② After extracting the ZIP file, connect to your site using your FTP client or Web host FTP panel, and click the extracted plugin folder on your computer.

③ Drag or copy that folder to the Plugins directory in your blog's wp-content directory.

The plugin is installed and can be activated on the Manage Plugins panel.

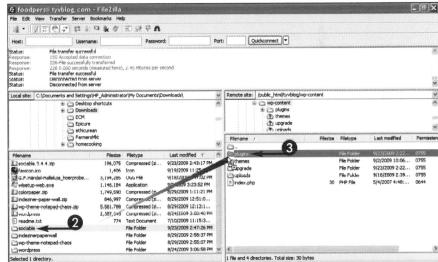

TIPS

I installed my plugin, but it does not seem to be working. What do I do?
Click **Visit plugin site** in the plugin's listing on the Manage Plugins panel for more information.

The plugin I installed has a notice and link about donating money for the plugin. What is that about?
Individuals develop plugins and make them available for free to WordPress users, and many developers ask for donations. Giving money is optional, but it is a good way to assure that developers maintain their plugins and develop new ones as the need arises.

9

Make Your Blog Content Appealing

A good-looking blog is all well and good, but in the end the content is king. You can improve your content's appeal with careful editing and attention to typography and organization.

Edit What You Write.................................156

Use Typography to Enhance Posts..............158

Use Images to Enhance Posts.....................160

Use the More Option to Break Your
    Posts in Two.......................................162

Understanding Categories and Tags............164

Create Categories....................................166

Create Tags..168

Apply Categories and Tags to Posts............170

Convert Categories and Tags.....................172

Getting your message online is good, but getting it out there in an appealing and readable way is even better. By editing your posts you give your blog greater credibility and make reading it easier for your readers. Yes, spelling does matter!

① Click **Posts** in the left menu bar, or in the Right Now module of the Dashboard.

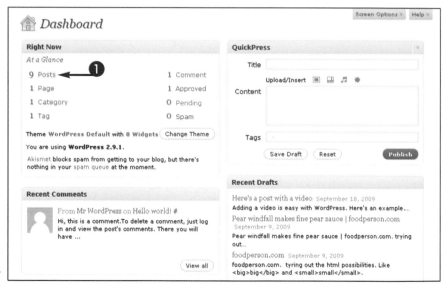

The Edit Posts panel opens, listing all posts you have written, whether published or not.

② Click the name of the post you want to edit.

The Edit Post panel opens, where you can edit and save changes.

Note: *You also can click **Edit** under the post name, which appears when you position your mouse in that post's row in the list.*

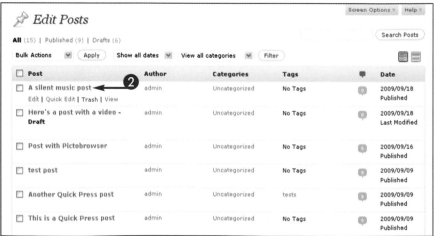

Proofreading at WordPress.com

1 Click the **Proofreading** button (⌘).

The built-in spelling and grammar checker underlines misspelled words in red, grammar errors in green, and questionable style use in blue.

2 Right-click an underlined word.

A list of possible corrections appears, and you can click a word to replace the questioned word or select an *Ignore* option.

3 When you are finished editing, click **Update Post**.

Spell-Checking on Self-Hosted Blogs

1 Click the down arrow next to the Spell-Checker button to choose the language to check.

2 Click the **Spell-Checker** button (⌘).

Red dotted lines appear under misspellings.

3 Right-click a misspelled word.

A list of options appears from which you select a suggested spelling or ignore the spelling.

4 Click **Save Draft**.

Note: If you have already published the post, click Update Post instead.

Can I get the proofreading tools for my self-hosted blog?

Yes. They are available as the After the Deadline plugin via the WordPress.org plugin directory. Note that it also allows you to choose among several style-checking options, such as whether to check for clichés, on the Profile panel of your blog.

Can I spell-check more than one language at a time?

No, but you can check your English spelling and then choose a different language and check the spelling in that language. Doing so can be useful if you have a phrase in a different language; naturally, most of your English will appear to be misspelled in the other language.

Use Typography to Enhance Posts

You can make your blog posts easier to read by using headings, subheadings, bulleted lists, numbered lists, and other typographical tools. Knowing when and when not to use these tools makes the most of them.

Chapter 6 covered how to format type. Now you can find out the best way to use your formats.

Choose Your Visual Style

Try to make decisions early in your blogging experience as to when you will use headings, lists, and other style options, because presenting a consistent look is a key part of your blog's identity. You can experiment with draft posts to see how various features look in your theme.

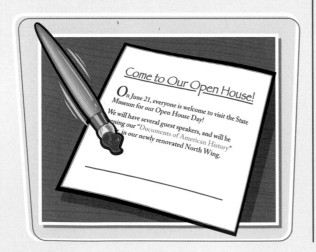

Headings for Hierarchy

Headings do more than change the size, and perhaps other characteristics, of type. Headings also create a hierarchy for your Web posts, and search engines use headings to index your pages and their content. Use heading formats accordingly, with Heading 1 formats for the most important headings, Heading 2 for the next most important, and so on, with Heading 6 the least important heading.

Use Bullets for Unordered Lists

An *unordered* list is one in which the order of the items does not matter, such as a list of groceries to buy or a list of WordPress features. When you use bullets for such a list, a reader does not assume, for example, that the first grocery item must be purchased first.

Use Numbers for Ordered Lists

Reserve numbered lists for when you want to communicate that the order of the listed items matters, such as a sequence of steps or items listed in order of importance.

Use Blockquote for Quotes

The *blockquote* format was created particularly for when you insert text quoted from another source. You can use it for another purpose if you want, but be consistent in how you apply it so as not to confuse readers.

Formats for Computer Code

Special formats for computer or Web developers' blogs are the Address and Preformatted paragraph formats and the Code format in the HTML editor. If you are not a developer, you still may be interested in Preformatted because it is the only standard format that retains extra spaces that you insert.

Use Images to Enhance Posts

If one picture is worth a thousand words, one picture *plus* a thousand words must be worth five thousand words, as long as the words and pictures complement each other. A consistent pattern again improves your blog's visual identity.

Chapter 7 identified your image formatting options, and now you can see how and when to use them.

Art for Interest

You can use images like headings to break up a large block of uninterrupted text. If you do not have a suitable image, you can consider microstock images in addition to the public domain images mentioned in Chapter 7. Two popular microstock sites are iStockPhoto.com and Shutterstock.com.

Take Advantage of Images' Words

Besides providing information for visitors using screen readers or other assistive devices, the alternate text in your images also can lead search engines to your photos. Even the image name can lead searchers your way. So, rather than name your photo img0235.jpg, give it a descriptive name, such as autumnleaves.jpg.

Captions Not Required

Just because your WordPress image-inserting window allows you to type a caption does not mean you must use that option. The caption feature generally puts a border around the image with the caption included. You may not like that look. If not, consider putting captions on a separate line under photos, or providing caption information at the end of the post. And some images require no captions at all.

Consider Wrapping Text

You may want a powerful image to stand alone on a line using the *none* or *center* formats. An image that mainly illustrates your words, however, might work better with text wrapping around it using the left or right alignment. Make sure the photo is small enough to allow at least three or so words to fit on every line beside it.

Offer Two Display Options

You can upload a large photo, say one that is 800 by 1200 pixels, but insert it in your post using the Thumbnail option or a percentage display. That represents the size that the image appears in the post, but readers can click the small image and see its larger version in another window.

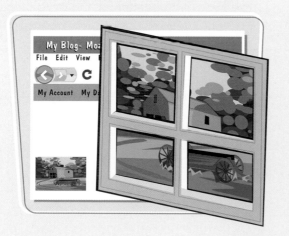

Give Credit

It is useful to readers — as well as to artists and photographers, perhaps including you — if you credit the source of your images. You can do it in alternate text, but doing it on screen is nicer. Some people recommend doing it both places. Also, if you do not want others to use your photos, declare your copyrights with each image.

Use the More Option to Break Your Posts in Two

If you would rather your readers see more headlines and less text on your blog's front page, the More option is just the thing for you. When you increase the number of posts that appear on your front page, you get an entirely different look.

Use the More Option to Break Your Posts in Two

Insert the More Tag

① On the New Post or Edit Post panel, click the location in your post where you want to split the post.

② Click the **Insert More Tag** button (⊞).

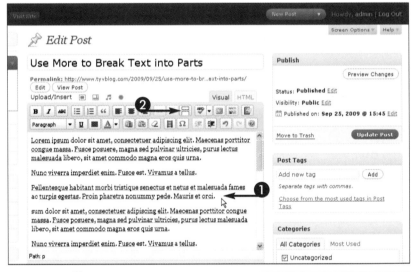

● The More marker appears in the post.

③ Click **Save Draft**.

④ Click **Publish**.

The post is published to your blog.

Note: *Clicking **Preview** does not reveal anything about the More tag.*

⑤ Click **Visit Site**.

The home page of the blog opens, with only part of the divided post showing.

6 Click **Read the rest of this entry**, which appears at the location where you inserted the More tag.

The post page opens, revealing the full text of the post.

Note: *The wording that refers readers to the full post varies from theme to theme.*

Remove the More Tag

1 In the Visual text editor of the Edit Post panel, click the line or tag where More appears.

A box with handlebars appears around the More tag.

2 Press Delete or Backspace, and the More tag disappears.

Note: *You also can click the More tag and drag the box that appears to another location in the post.*

I added More tags but still show only four posts on my front page. How can I change that?

Click the **Settings** menu in the left menu bar, and then click **Reading**. On the Reading Settings panel, change the number next to **Blog pages show at most** to the number of posts that you want on the front page.

Can I just use the More tag on some of my posts, rather than all?

Certainly! Many bloggers like to use it only on very long posts, which is a great use for the More tag.

Understanding Categories and Tags

Well-thought-out categories and tags make a convenient way for readers to navigate through your blog. Although you can add them as you go along in your blog, they are likely to be more useful if you do a little planning.

Categories versus Tags

If you think of your blog as a book, think of categories as chapters and tags as index items. In other words, categories work best for bigger concepts, and tags work best for details. Also, every blog post must be assigned to at least one category, but tags are optional.

Default Category

If you do not specify a category when you create a post, WordPress assigns it to the default category, which initially is *Uncategorized*. You can name and choose your default category, and probably come up with something more pertinent to your topic than *Uncategorized*.

Category Display

Most blog themes include an option for displaying a category list in a sidebar, and the category of a post also may appear at the end or beginning of each post. Sidebar display options include a simple list and a drop-down list. These links take readers to an archive-type page that shows post headlines and, often, excerpts in the selected category.

Categories and Subcategories

You have the option of creating subcategories, or *child* categories, as well as categories. For example, if you have a gardening blog, you might have *Flowers* as a category with *Annuals*, *Perennials*, and *Biennials* as subcategories. You might also want a *Vegetables* category and *From the Garden* as your default category's name. Tags have no hierarchy.

Why Use Tags

Although tags are optional, tags are useful because they provide another means to help and encourage readers to view more of your blog, and because they provide another means for search engines to find your blog posts.

Best Practices

Your blog will look more professional and be easier to understand if you decide on and apply some rules to provide consistency for category and tag names. For example, you may want to make your categories nouns and capitalize them and your tags verbs and lowercase. Doing so also reduces odds that you will accidentally create both *Seeds* and *seeds* tags.

Create Categories

The Categories panel lets you create multiple categories, but you also can create categories on the fly, if you will, on the posting panel. Either way, you end up with categories to help organize your blog posts.

Create a Category in the Categories Panel

1 After clicking **Posts** in the left menu bar and the Posts menu expands, click **Categories**.

The Categories panel opens.

2 Type a category name.

3 Type a category slug.

Note: The Category Slug box does not appear in WordPress.com blogs.

4 Type a description.

5 Click **Add Category**.

The category appears in the list at right on the Categories panel.

Create a Subcategory

1 Type a subcategory name.

2 Type a category slug.

3 Click the Category Parent drop-down arrow.

4 Click the category that you want as the parent of your subcategory.

5 Type a description.

6 Click **Add Category**.

The subcategory appears in the list at right on the Categories panel.

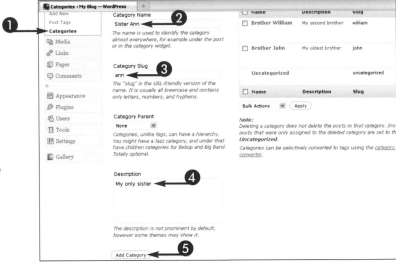

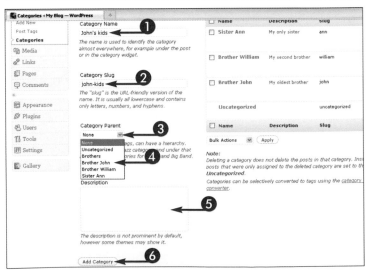

Create a Category in the Post Panel

① On the New Post or Edit Post panel, click **Add New Category** at the bottom of the Categories module.

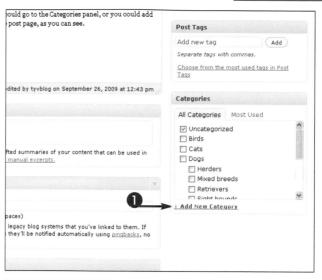

Two boxes appear under Add New Category.

② Type the new category in the first box.

③ If the new category is a subcategory, click the Parent category drop-down list, and click a category on the list

④ Click **Add**.

The new category appears in the Categories box.

How do I change the default category?

You can click **Uncategorized** in the list on the Categories panel to open the Edit Category panel. Then, change *Uncategorized* to the name you prefer. Another option is to click **Writing** under Settings in the left menu bar and then choose the default category from the Default Post Category drop-down menu on the Writing Settings panel.

What is a category slug?

It is what appears in the URL for a page that lists your posts by category. If you do not enter a slug, WordPress converts your category name to a slug by making it all lowercase, stripping it of punctuation, and inserting hyphens where you had spaces.

Create Tags

Tags are like keywords attached to individual blog posts. Tags provide a convenient way for readers to search for information. Unlike categories, they are not hierarchical, so you cannot have child and parent tags.

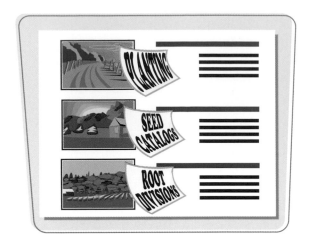

Create a Tag in the Tags Panel

1. After clicking **Posts** in the left menu bar and the Posts menu expands, click **Post Tags**.

   The Tags panel opens.

2. Type a tag name in the Tag Name box.

3. Type a category slug in the Tag Slug box.

   Note: The Tag Slug box does not appear in WordPress.com blogs.

4. Type a description in the Description box, if desired.

5. Click **Add Tag**.

   The tag appears in the list on the right side of the Tags panel.

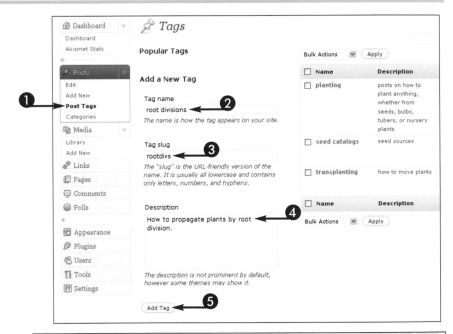

Create a Tag in the Post Panel

1. On the New Post or Edit Post panel, click in the **Add new tag** box in the Post Tags module.

168

② Type the desired tag or tags in the Add New Tag box, using a comma between tags.

③ Click **Add**.

The new tags appear below the Add New Tags box. The tags also are added to your blog's Tags panel and attached to the post you are editing.

Note: *If you want your tag to include a description, you must go to the Tags panel.*

④ Click **Save Draft** (or **Update Post** if editing a published post).

Remove Tags in Edit Post Panel

① Click the **Cut Tag** button (🔲) next to the tag you want to remove.

The tag disappears from the Edit Post panel.

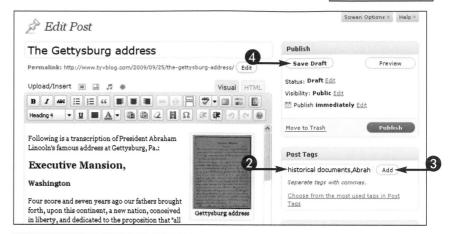

TIP

What are global tags?

Global tags are a feature of WordPress.com. WordPress.com collects tags from all the blogs it hosts to create a way that readers can easily view a large number of blogs posts across WordPress.com that used a particular tag.

Apply Categories and Tags to Posts

You can apply categories and tags as you create or edit your posts, or you can add them after the fact, including in bulk, from the Categories and Tags panels. You can use whichever technique fits best into your workflow.

You can use these techniques after you already have created some categories and tags.

From the Post Panel

1 In the Post panel of a new or existing post, click **Choose from the most used tags in Post Tags** in the Post Tags module.

A tag cloud opens.

2 Click the tag you want to add to your post.

The tag appears above the tag cloud.

3 In the Categories module, click the check box next to the category you want to assign the post to (☐ changes to ☑).

4 Click **Update Post**.

The post is now assigned to the categories and tags you specified.

Bulk Edit from the Edit Posts Panel

1 Click **Posts** in the left menu bar.

The Edit Posts list opens.

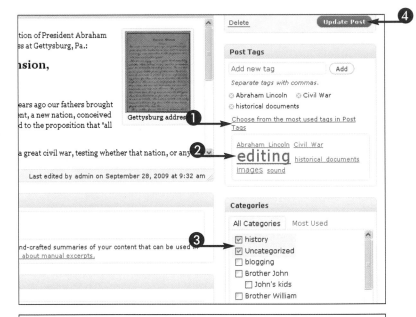

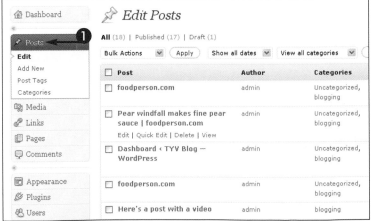

② Click the check box next to posts you want to edit (☐ changes to ☑).

③ Click the arrow next to Bulk Actions to expand it.

④ Click **Edit**.

⑤ Click **Apply**.

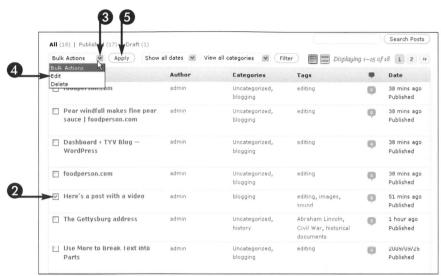

The Bulk Edit Posts pane opens.

⑥ Click the check box next to categories you want to assign to the posts (☐ changes to ☑).

⑦ Type tag names you want to apply to selected posts, separated by commas.

⑧ Click **Update Posts**.

The categories and tags you selected are added to the posts.

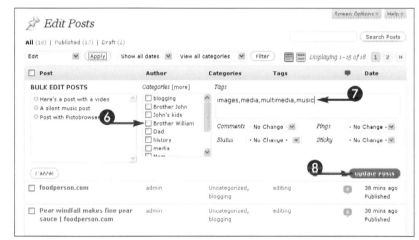

TIPS

Is there a limit to the number of tags or categories I can have?

No, but it is good practice not to attach too many to a single post. A large number may confuse readers and search engines. Go for three or four of each at most.

Can I use the Bulk Edit box to remove a category from a group of posts?

No. You must either individually edit each post to remove a category or delete the entire category. If the posts are already assigned to other categories, those category assignments remain. If the posts do not have another category assignment, they are assigned to the default category.

Convert Categories and Tags

If you imported your blog to WordPress from another blogging platform, you may find that all your old tags are now categories. Or maybe you just changed your mind on how you want to classify your posts. Fortunately, WordPress has a tool that lets you convert categories to tags and vice versa.

① On the Categories panel, which you can reach from the Posts section of the left menu bar, scroll to the bottom of the page and click **category to tag converter**.

	Mom		mom	0
	Sister Ann	My only sister	ann	0
	— Ann's kids	Ann's children	ann-kids	0
	Uncategorized		uncategorized	17
	Name	**Description**	**Slug**	**Posts**

Bulk Actions ☑ (Apply)

Note:
Deleting a category does not delete the posts in that category. Instead, posts that were only assigned to the deleted category are set to the category Uncategorized.

① → *Categories can be selectively converted to tags using the category to tag converter.*

The Convert Categories to Tags panel opens.

② Click the check box next to each category that you want to convert to a tag (☐ changes to ☑).

③ Click **Convert Categories to Tags**.

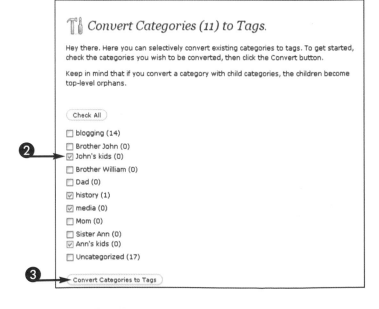

🔧 *Convert Categories (11) to Tags.*

Hey there. Here you can selectively convert existing categories to tags. To get started, check the categories you wish to be converted, then click the Convert button.

Keep in mind that if you convert a category with child categories, the children become top-level orphans.

(Check All)

☐ blogging (14)
☐ Brother John (0)
② → ☑ John's kids (0)
☐ Brother William (0)
☐ Dad (0)
☑ history (1)
☑ media (0)
☐ Mom (0)
☐ Sister Ann (0)
☑ Ann's kids (0)
☐ Uncategorized (17)

③ → (Convert Categories to Tags)

WordPress displays the conversion progress.

④ Click **Tags to Categories**.

The Convert Tags to Categories panel opens.

⑤ Click the check box next to any tag you want to convert to a category (☐ changes to ☑).

⑥ Click **Convert Tags to Categories**.

WordPress displays the conversion progress and converts the selected tags to categories.

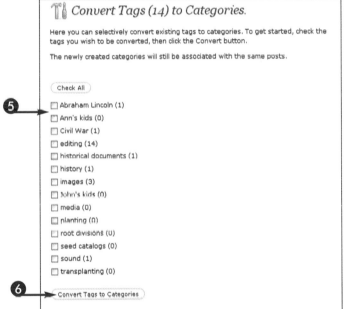

What happens to the posts when I convert categories and tags?

The names are still attached to the posts they previously were assigned to, but as categories instead of tags, or vice versa. Because categories are required, though, if you changed all categories assigned to a particular post, the post automatically is now assigned to the default category.

What happens if I convert a top-level category to a tag but do not convert its subcategory?

The subcategory becomes a top-level category.

10

Build Traffic to Your Blog

Unless you are among the minority of blog publishers who wants to keep your blog private, you probably are publishing a blog because you want people to see it and read it. They are much more likely to do so if they know you are there! That is where building traffic comes in.

Create a Comment Policy 176

Comment on Someone Else's Blog 178

What to Say on Someone Else's Blog..........179

Moderate Comments 180

Edit a Comment...182

Respond to Comments on Your Blog 184

Deal with Comment Spam...............................186

Allow Threaded Comments............................188

Understanding Trackbacks
    and Pingbacks 190

Understanding and Joining RSS Feeds........192

Add a Feed to Your Sidebar............................194

Use FeedBurner to Track Feed Traffic 196

Offer FeedBurner E-mail Subscriptions 198

Connect with Twitter..200

Promote Your Blog via Social Media 202

Optimize Your Blog for Search Engines.....204

Use Surveys and Polls......................................206

WordPress gives you the power to decide who can and cannot comment on your blog and under what conditions. You can even choose on a post-by-post basis whether people can comment on your blog. In other words, you can be the lone voice or the leader of a free-for-all. It is your choice.

How Thick Is Your Skin?

Sharing opinions with readers sounds like a good idea until you get your first *flame*, a searingly critical comment, or *troll*, a commenter whose remarks are aimed at provoking argument, often by being nasty. If you love the kind of debate that those provoke, you may not need a comment policy. Otherwise, give it some thought.

Time Considerations

Moderating comments can be a time-consuming task, especially if you manage to attract a lot of comments. Do you have time to manage that? Discussion Settings that give a pass to previous commenters, that ban words you specify, or that hold comments with numerous hyperlinks can reduce the load while making your blog somewhat less vulnerable to trolls.

Consider Your Audience

It is best if your policy takes into consideration not only your preferences but also those of your readers. If you are aiming at members of your church, you may want to block profanity. If you are aiming at American teens, you probably need to allow abbreviations commonly used in instant messaging and texting.

Aim for a Balance

Keep in mind that a major appeal of blogs for readers and publishers alike is the ability to interact by way of comments. Commenting that is too restricted or delayed, as when waiting for the moderator, can be frustrating for readers, but frequent malicious comments are a turn-off for lots of people. Try to strike a balance with your policy.

State Your Policy

Having a written comment policy is good for two reasons. One, creating it causes you to think into what is and is not acceptable to you. Two, it gives you something to point to when people complain about comments being deleted, edited, or excluded. Let your readers know where you stand.

Put It Where People Will Find It

Your About page is a good place for a comment policy, because the About page is the most frequently viewed page on most blogs. If you are comfortable making a few adjustments with your theme, you could put your policy next to your comment form on your blog pages.

Comment on Someone Else's Blog

Commenting on others' blogs is a recognized means of attracting people to your blog. How? When others read your insightful remarks, they cannot wait to read what else you have to say. They therefore click the link in your comment that leads to your blog.

Comment on Someone Else's Blog

① On the post that you want to comment about, click the link to the comments form.

Note: Comment link location and text will vary from one blog to another.

② Type your name in the Name box.

③ Type your e-mail in the Email box if required.

④ Type your blog's URL in the Website box.

⑤ Type your comment in the space provided.

⑥ Type the words or letters of the *captcha* (or in this case ReCaptcha) box, if present.

Note: Captcha is a spam-avoidance tool, which you can add to self-hosted blogs with a plugin. See Chapter 8 to find and install plugins.

⑦ Click **Submit Comment**.

Your comment is published or submitted for moderation.

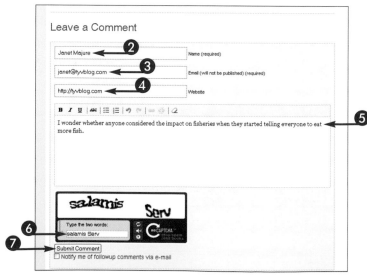

What to Say on Someone Else's Blog

Well-placed and considered comments prompt readers of other people's blogs to click through to read what else you have to say. Reading and commenting contributes to the blogging community and adds to your standing.

What to Say

Add something *useful* to the conversation. Useful might be anything from adding a bit of helpful advice based on your experience with the subject to sharing the good resources you know about. Useful also may mean to pose a question related to the blog post; pertinent questions expand the conversation.

What Not to Say

New bloggers, eager to attract readers, often are tempted to visit numerous blogs and comment, "Great post!" or "Thanks for writing this!" Although there is little harm in such comments, they rarely have the desired effect. Self-promotional comments are rarely welcome, unless you really do have *the* solution to the problem being discussed.

Moderate Comments

Chances are you will need to moderate, or review, comments occasionally, even if you have a fairly wide-open comment policy. Doing so reduces comment spam and keeps the commentary within your comments policy.

Moderate an Individual Comment

① Click **Comments** in the left menu bar of the administrative interface.

The Edit Comments panel opens.

● The number of comments awaiting moderation appears here.

● Comments awaiting moderation appear in the Recent Comments module with a note, *[Pending]*, and a pale yellow background.

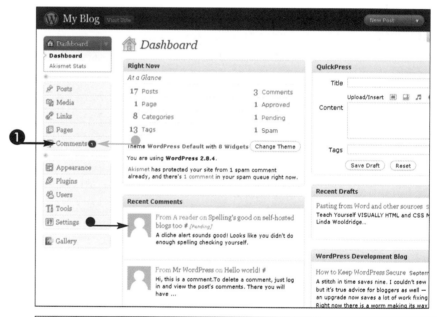

② Position your mouse over the area of the comment awaiting moderation, which has a pale yellow background.

A set of options appears.

③ Click **Approve** to approve the comment.

The comment is published to your blog, and the background turns white.

Note: *The other options are discussed later in this chapter.*

Moderate Multiple Comments

1 Click the check box next to the comments you want to moderate (☐ changes to ☑).

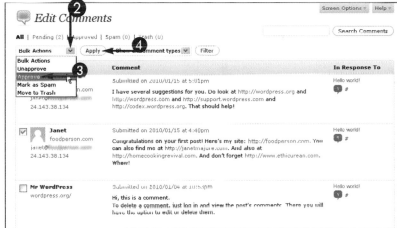

2 Click the arrow next to Bulk Actions.

The Bulk Actions menu expands.

3 Click **Approve**.

4 Click **Apply**.

All checked comments are approved and published.

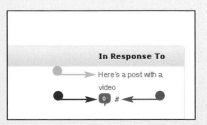

TIPS

What do I do about the e-mail I got asking me to moderate a comment?

Just click the appropriate link to approve the comment, delete it, or "Spam it." Or, you can click the fourth link, which takes you to the moderation panel, otherwise known as the Edit Comments panel.

What is that information under the In Response To heading?

● Link to Edit Post panel for the post associated with the comment

● Link to Edit Comments panel filtered to show only comments on the post associated with the comment

● Link to published post

In Response To

Here's a post with a video

Edit a Comment

Editing comments lets you correct typos, tone down rhetoric, or make comments conform to your comment policy. Editing often is a nicer alternative to approving or deleting troublesome comments.

From the Edit Comment Panel

1 Click **Edit** next to the comment you want to change.

The Edit Comment panel opens.

Note: *When you are logged into your blog, some but not all themes provide links from the comment display to the Edit Comment panel. You can always click **Edit** in the Edit Comments panel.*

2 Make any changes you want, including formatting, in the HTML editing box.

Note: *A WYSIWYG comment editor is not available at this time.*

3 Edit the publication time if desired.

4 Click **Update Comment**.

WordPress saves the changes and returns you to where you clicked Edit on the blog post panel or Edit Comments panel.

From the Quick Edit Pane

1. Position your mouse over the comment you want to edit, and click the **Quick Edit** link that appears.

The Quick Edit pane expands.

2. Make any changes you want, including formatting, in the HTML editing box.

Note: *Editing options in this pane are limited to the comment text, author, e-mail, and URL.*

3. Click **Update Comment** when you are done.

The changes are saved, and the Quick Edit pane closes.

 TIPS

Why would I want to edit the published time?

You may have occasions in which you want to change the order in which comments appear. Editing the times can change the order.

Is there a way that commenters can edit their own comments?

If you have a self-hosted blog, you can make that happen with the WP Ajax Edit Comments plugin. See Chapter 8 for information about plugins.

Respond to Comments on Your Blog

If you think blogs are all about conversation, then you will want to respond to your readers' comments. When you do, you also build readers' sense of involvement in your blog, which can increase loyalty and readership.

Respond to Comments on Your Blog

From the Blog Page

1 If you are logged in, simply type your response in the comment.

2 When you are finished, click **Submit Comment**.

Your comment is published to the site.

Note: *If you are not logged in as administrator, you have to enter a name and e-mail address just as any other commenter would.*

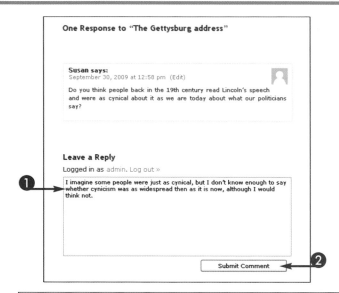

From the Dashboard

1 After going to the Edit Comments panel by clicking **Comments** in the left menu bar, position the mouse over the comment you want to respond to and click **Reply**.

The Reply to Comment pane opens.

② Type your response in the space provided.

③ Click **Submit Reply**.

The Reply to Comment pane closes.

The Edit Comments panel lists the reply, which also is published to your blog site.

④ Click the date and time display

The link takes you to the published comment.

TIPS

Can I respond to several comments at once?

If you are looking for a bulk response option, none exists. What most bloggers do is to write one comment but refer to previous comments by the writers' names as shown on their comments. For example, you might write, "Susan, I agree with you. Bill, you make a good point, but I think ..."

How do I link to a particular comment?

The date and time display with each comment on the Edit Comments panel has a permalink to the comment embedded in it. You can right-click the link and choose **Copy Link Location** to copy the comment's permalink. Then, use that permalink as needed.

Deal with Comment Spam

Even by setting hurdles for commenters to clear, comment spam still gets through. Your blog will look better and be more appealing if you make sure that spam comments get zapped as soon as possible.

The Akismet tool covered in Chapter 8 is the primary means by which WordPress bloggers handle spam comments.

Spam that Got Published

❶ After clicking **Comments** in the left menu bar to open the Edit Comments panel, find the offending comment in the list, position your mouse over the comment to reveal the options, and click **Spam**.

The comment disappears from the list and moves to the Spam queue.

Note: *Spam comments do not appear in the ordinary Edit Comments list, even when you click the **All** option under Edit Comments.*

From an E-mail Notice

❶ After getting an e-mail notice to moderate a comment and clicking the link to "spam it," click **Spam Comment** to confirm the item is spam.

The item goes to the Spam comment list, and information goes to the Akismet database to contribute to its spam-catching ability.

● Naturally, you need to click **No** if you realize the comment is not spam.

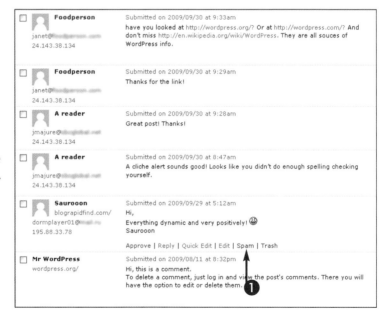

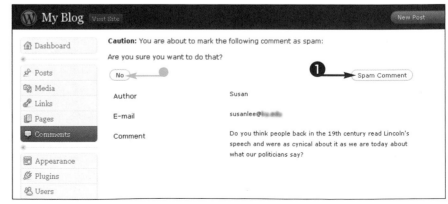

Review Spam Comments

1 Click **Comments** in the left menu bar to open the Edit Comments panel.

2 Click **Spam**.

The comments list reveals comments marked as Spam. Review to make sure no valid comments are incorrectly identified as spam. You can position the mouse over any valid comments and click the **Approve** link that appears.

3 After approving any valid comments incorrectly labeled as spam, click **Empty Spam**.

The spam comments disappear.

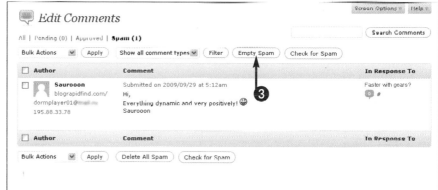

 TIPS

How often do I need to review the Spam list?

It depends on how active your blog is. You need to check it periodically, though, to make sure that your spam queue is not eating up your disk space and to make sure valid comments are not getting caught.

Why not just click Trash when a spam comment shows up in the regular comments list?

When you simply click **Trash** rather than **Spam**, you are not letting Akismet learn which senders and IP addresses are sending you spam comments. So, click **Spam** when you get a spam comment. You can delete it later.

Allow Threaded Comments

You can reply — and let readers reply — directly to specific comments others make on your blog. The result is stair-stepped, *threaded*, comments, and you can make them several levels deep.

Enable Threaded Comments

1 Click **Settings**.

The General Settings panel opens and the Settings menu expands.

2 Click **Discussion**.

The Discussion panel opens.

3 Click **Enable threaded (nested) comments** (☐ changes to ☑).

4 Click the arrow next to 5, the default level setting.

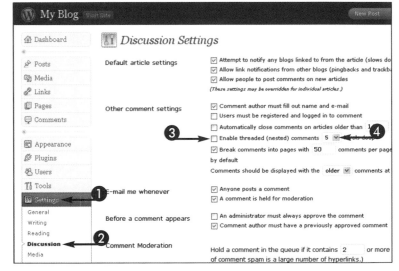

The level number drop-down menu opens.

5 Click the number of levels of threaded commentary you want.

6 Scroll to the bottom of the page and click **Save Changes**. A confirmation message appears.

7 After saving changes, click **Visit Site**.

Your blog opens for you to check the comments.

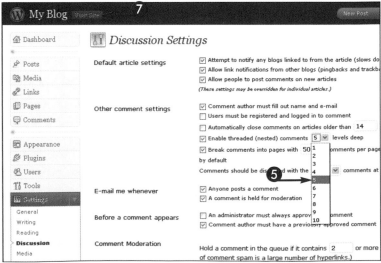

Work with Threaded Comments

1 After going to the comments on a post, click **Reply** in the comment box that you want to reply to.

The regular Reply box disappears, and a Reply box that combines with the comment appears.

2 Type your reply in the Leave a Reply box.

3 Click **Submit Comment** when done.

● The comment appears as a *subcomment* of the selected comment.

TIPS

I cannot get the threaded comments to work. What do I do?

Threaded comments are a relatively new feature of WordPress, and many themes may not fully implement them. Contact the theme developer or the WordPress or WordPress.com support sites for suggestions.

Can I create a threaded comment by clicking Reply on a comment in the Edit Comments panel?

Yes. Just click **Reply** under the appropriate comment. Note that if you want to add a comment that is *not* threaded, you need to go to the blog post and create a new comment there.

Understanding Trackbacks and Pingbacks

Trackbacks and pingbacks automatically alert blogs when other bloggers have linked to them. When you publish trackbacks and pingbacks as miniature "comments" you also let readers see that your blog has credibility elsewhere.

Why Send Trackbacks and Pingbacks

Sending trackbacks and pingbacks to blogs that you have referred to builds community among bloggers and promotes your blog to the sites to which you link. It is a nice way to give credit and to let others know you exist.

Why Publish Trackbacks and Pingbacks

Publishing the trackbacks and pingbacks that other blogs have sent to your site similarly encourages community. It lets you and your readers discover other sites, and it is a way of saying thank you to the blogs that have linked to your site.

Trackbacks versus Pingbacks

Trackbacks are manual, and pingbacks are automatic if you have enabled them. With pingbacks, that means that if you link to another site, WordPress automatically sends a sort of mini-comment to the other site showing that you have linked to the site.

How to and Why Send a Trackback

You may want to send a trackback when you mention or give credit to a blog but do not specifically link to it. To do so, enter the URL of the blog or blog post in the Trackback module of the Edit Post/New Post panel.

How to Enable Trackbacks and Pingbacks

Whether to routinely allow trackbacks and pingbacks is part of the default article settings mentioned in Chapter 5. The *Attempt to notify* setting is for sending pingbacks, and the *Allow link notifications* is for publishing them. You can change settings for individual posts in the Discussion module of the Edit Post or New Post panel.

Stopping Unwanted Self-Pingbacks

To prevent a pingback from appearing on an old post that you link to in a newer post, type only the part of the previous post's URL that comes after the domain as your link. In other words, instead of using *http://www.myblog.com/2010/03/12/oldpost/* as the link, use */2010/03/12/oldpost/*. If that fails, use the HTML editor to enter the link.

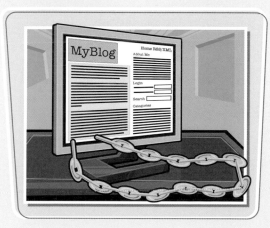

Understanding and Joining RSS Feeds

By providing an RSS feed from your blog, you are giving people who use feed readers ready access to your new content. Feed readers let someone read the updates of all his or her favorite Web sites by going to a single location. When you read feeds, you too can keep up with your favorites.

What Is RSS?

RSS stands for *Really Simple Syndication*, and it really is simple to use. All it takes is a feed reader and feeds from your favorite sites. Blogs and news sites typically provide feeds. When you open your feed reader, you see content from each site that has been added since you last read that site's feed.

Feed Readers

Feed readers, also called aggregators, may be Web-based, such as Google Reader and Bloglines. Some, such as FeedDemon for Windows, are *client* programs based on your local computer that download your feeds. Others are browser extensions. You can find a comparison list at http://en.wikipedia.org/wiki/Comparison_of_feed_aggregators.

Identify Feeds

Internet Explorer and Firefox make it easy for you to identify pages that have feeds. IE shows the standard orange RSS logo in its toolbar. Firefox shows the logo in the address bar. In either case, clicking the logo opens a feed sign-up window. Also, many Web pages display text or logo or both, inviting you to subscribe.

Subscribe to Feeds

Choose a feed reader for yourself, and then start subscribing to feeds. It is a good idea to subscribe to at least a few blogs in your topic area to see what others are saying. Sign up for your feed, too, so that you can make sure that your feed is functioning properly.

Decide Feed Settings

Your blog's Reading Settings under Settings in the left menu bar specifies whether your feed includes an entire post or a summary. If you choose summary, the feed will send an Excerpt if you wrote one on the Posts panel. If you did not, it will send a *teaser* — the words before a More tag — and if there is no More tag, the feed sends the first 55 words of your post. WordPress.com blogs have added options.

Invite Your Readers to Subscribe

You can do more to promote your blog's feed than rely on the RSS logos in browsers and perhaps within your theme. Consider writing a post from time to time specifically about your feeds — WordPress comes with one for your new posts and one for comments — or adding a line at the end of each post encouraging subscriptions.

Add a Feed to Your Sidebar

You can continue to build community or keep your readers up-to-date on your blog entries by posting an RSS feed or two on your blog's sidebar. A WordPress widget simplifies this task once you choose what feeds to feature.

Add a Feed to Your Sidebar

① After you identify a feed you want to subscribe to, click its subscribe link to open a subscriptions page, and copy the URL in the address box.

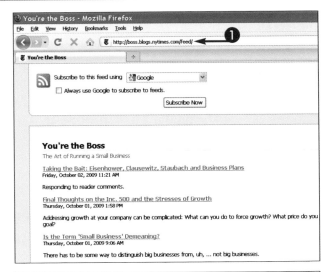

② After going to **Widgets** under Appearance in the left menu of your Dashboard, scroll to the RSS widget, and click and drag the widget to the sidebar panel where you want the feed to appear.

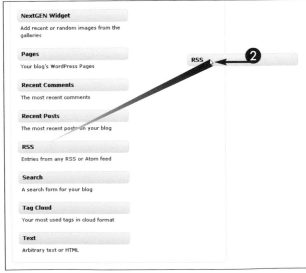

The widget opens.

③ Paste the URL of the feed in the first box.

④ Type a name for the feed.

⑤ Click the check box next to any display option you want (☐ changes to ☑).

⑥ Click the arrow next to **How many items** and click to choose the number of feed items you want to display.

⑦ Click **Save**.

⑧ Click **Close**.

● The feed is published to your sidebar.

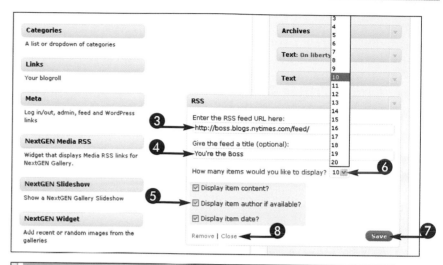

Can I publish my own feed this way on my blog?

No, you need to use the Recent Posts widget instead. You can read about widgets in Chapter 8.

What is the difference between the RSS widget and the RSS Links widget?

The RSS Links widget, available as a default only on WordPress.com, lets you promote your own feeds in your sidebar. You can choose whether the links are text only, image only, or text plus image, and if you use image only, you can choose the color of the RSS logo. Similar plugins are available for self-hosted WordPress blogs.

Use FeedBurner to Track Feed Traffic

If you wonder how many people are subscribed to your feed, you can get a pretty good idea by opening an account with FeedBurner, a service that Google acquired in 2007. You can get other helpful services through FeedBurner, too.

You need to have or create a Google logon to use FeedBurner.

Use FeedBurner to Track Feed Traffic

① Type **feedburner.com** into your Web browser, and when the FeedBurner home page opens, enter your Google account e-mail name if it is not present.

② Type your password in the Password box.

③ Click **Sign in**.

The FeedBurner MyFeeds page opens.

● If you do not have a Google Account, you can start by clicking **Create an account**.

④ Type your blog's URL into the Burn a feed box.

⑤ Click **Next**.

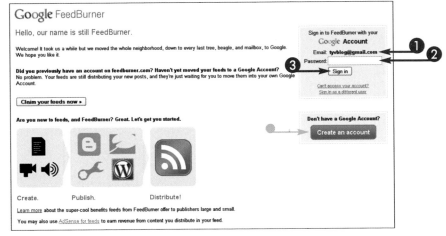

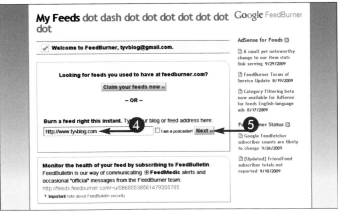

The Identify Feed Source page opens. It lists all feeds available at your home page URL.

⑥ Click the radio button next to the feed you want to track (○ changes to ⊙).

⑦ Click **Next**.

⑧ FeedBurner confirms the feed, and you click **Next**, which opens a page saying that your feed is ready.

⑨ Scroll down on the page until you see WordPress logos.

⑩ Click **Use this plugin** (or **Publish a chicklet** if your blog is at WordPress.com).

A page opens that gives further instructions.

Note: *Additional FeedBurner plugins are available through the Plugins panel on self-hosted blogs.*

Next time you go to FeedBurner, it displays your feeds and subscribers.

⑪ Click a feed to get more details about your feed traffic.

TIPS

What if I want both my posts and my comments feeds tracked?

Click the **My Feeds** tab at the top of FeedBurner page when you are logged in. You can type another feed URL or put in your blog URL, click **Next**, and then select another feed to track.

How can I tell if the feed is working correctly?

Click a feed link on your blog. The subscribe page that appears mentions FeedBurner if your feed is redirecting via FeedBurner. Wait a day or two to make sure everything is up and running.

Offer FeedBurner E-mail Subscriptions

Not everyone wants go to the Internet to get blog updates. Fortunately, FeedBurner lets you offer e-mail subscriptions to your feed. It is simple to do, so there is no reason not to offer this service.

If you have not already set up an account with FeedBurner, see "Use FeedBurner to Track Feed Traffic" on the preceding pages. WordPress.com has a widget for e-mail subscriptions.

Offer FeedBurner E-mail Subscriptions

① After logging into your FeedBurner account, click the feed on which you want to offer e-mail subscriptions.

My Feeds エンジョイライフ！

Google FeedBurner

✔ **Welcome back, tyvblog@gmail.com.**

FEED TITLE	SUBSCRIBERS
▣ My TYVBlog	**1**
▣ TYV Blog	**1**

Burn a feed right this instant. Type your blog or feed address here:

☐ I am a podcaster! **Next »**

Export Feeds: Get a list of your burned feeds as an OPML file
Export Feed Stats: from this month ▾ for all feeds. **Export as CSV »**

AdSense for Feeds ▣

📄 "Afternoon, Frank." "Hey howdy, George." 11/13/2009

📄 AdSense policy clarification on using AdSense for feeds and AdSense for content 11/9/2009

📄 AdSense for feeds now available directly in Blogger 10/30/2009

FeedBurner Status ▣

📄 AWeber stats will be temporarily under-reported 10/7/2009

② The Feed Stats page opens, where you click the **Publicize** tab. When the Publicize Your Feed page opens, click **Email Subscriptions** in the left sidebar. The Email Subscriptions page opens.

③ On the Email Subscriptions page, click **Activate**.

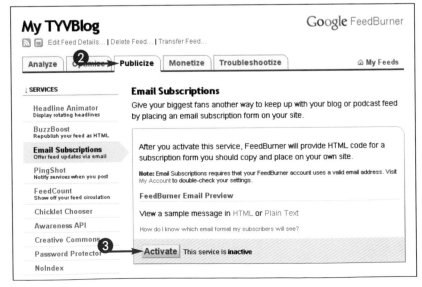

My TYVBlog

Google FeedBurner

▣ ▣ Edit Feed Details... | Delete Feed... | Transfer Feed...

| Analyze | Optimize | **Publicize** | Monetize | Troubleshootize | ⌂ My Feeds |

↓ SERVICES

Headline Animator
Display rotating headlines

BuzzBoost
Republish your feed as HTML

Email Subscriptions
Offer feed updates via email

PingShot
Notify services when you post

FeedCount
Show off your feed circulation

Chicklet Chooser

Awareness API

Creative Commons

Password Protector

NoIndex

Email Subscriptions

Give your biggest fans another way to keep up with your blog or podcast feed by placing an email subscription form on your site.

After you activate this service, FeedBurner will provide HTML code for a subscription form you should copy and place on your own site.

Note: Email Subscriptions requires that your FeedBurner account uses a valid email address. Visit My Account to double-check your settings.

FeedBurner Email Preview

View a sample message in HTML or Plain Text

How do I know which email format my subscribers will see?

Activate | This service is **inactive**

④ The Email Management panel opens, where you scroll down to the second box of code.

⑤ Copy all the code under Preview Subscription Link.

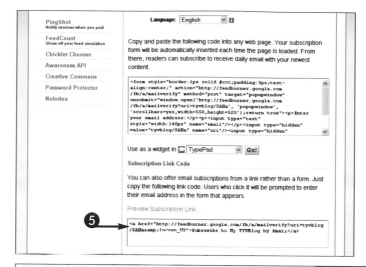

⑥ Go to your blog's Widgets panel, available under the Appearance menu in the left sidebar.

⑦ Drag a Text widget to the sidebar, and when the widget pops open, paste the code in the lower box.

⑧ Give the sidebar link a title.

⑨ Click **Save**.

The link is published to the designated sidebar.

 TIPS

Can I use the FeedBurner e-mail subscription form code instead?

Yes, if you have a self-hosted blog. WordPress.com blogs, however, do not support forms codes as used for the subscription form.

After I set up the link and subscribed to my own feed, I put up a new post, but I have not gotten it in my e-mail. How do I find out what I did wrong?

FeedBurner sends a daily digest of all your postings. You can set a two-hour time window by clicking **Delivery Options** under Email Subscriptions in the Publicize panel at FeedBurner. Check out the other options there, too.

Connect with Twitter

WordPress and Twitter let you communicate more than ever. Your blog readers can keep up with your Twitter feed right on your blog, and self-hosted WordPress blog users also can automatically update Twitter followers about new blog postings.

You need a Twitter account, available at www.twitter.com, to get started.

Via RSS Feed

1 On your Twitter profile page or home page, copy the link contents for your RSS feed.

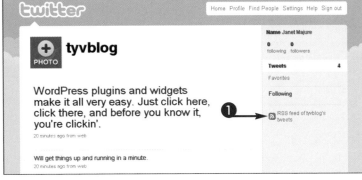

2 From your blog's Dashboard, expand Appearance and click **Widgets**.

The Widgets panel opens.

3 Drag an RSS widget to the sidebar where you want your feed to appear.

The RSS widget opens, where you paste the Twitter feed you copied in step **1**. After you save, the Twitter feed appears in your sidebar.

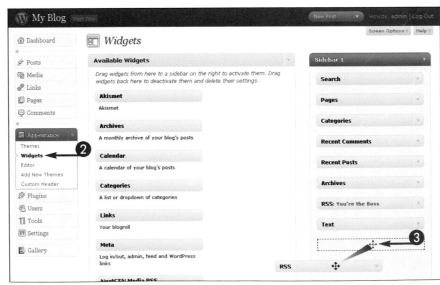

Using Twitter Widgets on WordPress.com

1 Instead of using an RSS widget, drag a Twitter widget to a sidebar on the Widgets panel.

2 Type your Twitter username in the box.

3 Add a title.

4 Click **Save**.

The Twitter feed is published to your blog sidebar.

Using Twitter Widgets on Self-Hosted Blogs

1 Go to https://twitter.com/goodies/widgets.

2 Click **My Website**.

A list of website widgets appears.

3 Click **Profile Widget**.

4 The Customize Your Profile Widget page opens, where you supply the information requested. When finished, click **Finish and Grab Code**, paste the code in a text widget on your blog's Widgets panel, and save the widget. The custom Twitter feed appears on your sidebar.

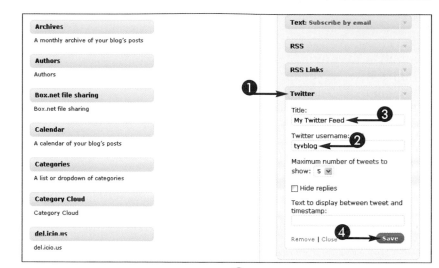

TIPS

How do I get my blog posts, or at least the headlines, to publish on Twitter?

If you are on WordPress. com, go to My Blogs under the Dashboard menu, and click the check box next to Twitter in the Publicize column (☐ changes to ☑). With a self-hosted blog, use a plugin such as WP to Twitter to add tweets when you post.

Can I post other people's Twitter feeds?

Sure can. Just follow the same steps as for your own feed. One exception: If a Twitter user has chosen *Protect my tweets* on their Twitter settings page, you will not be able to post their feed.

Promote Your Blog via Social Media

Even if you are not a member of Facebook, LinkedIn, MySpace, Digg, or other online communities, you can be sure some of your readers are. If you take advantage of that situation, you not only can promote your blog, but your readers can promote it, too. And do not forget bookmarks!

Blog to Network Widgets

Both hosted and self-hosted WordPress blogs let you display *badges*, or graphic emblems, from the social networks such as Facebook that you belong to. Just put HTML that you get from the networks in a text widget on your blog. Those badges link your blog readers to your social network site and may show your social network updates on WordPress.

Understanding Social Bookmarks

Del.icio.us, Digg, StumbleUpon, Reddit, and numerous other social bookmarking sites let you store favorite links, sort of like your browser's Bookmarks or Favorites lists but on steroids. You can comment about stored links and recommend them to other people. These sites can help boost traffic to your blog, so it is nice to make it easy for readers to add you to their lists.

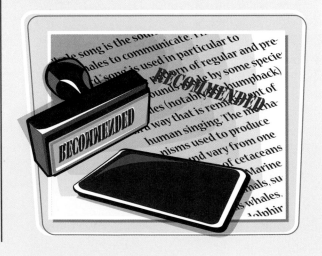

Blog to Network Promotion Plugins

Self-hosted blogs can get readers to promote blog posts by providing links from their blogs to readers' social networking sites. Such plugins include simple ones like Add to Facebook or farther-reaching ones like Socialize and ShareThis, which provide links to numerous bookmarking sites, too.

WordPress.com to Network Promotion Code

A blogger developed a little application, GetSocial for WordPress.com users, that produces a set of social networking buttons without a plugin or scripts, which WordPress.com does not allow. It works for Windows machines, and is available at http://hillelstoler. com/2008/05/18/ getsocial-social-bookmarking-for-wordpresscom.

Share Your Social Bookmarks

Some networking sites, such as Del.icio.us, Digg, and StumbleUpon focus more on sharing blog post or Web site *bookmarks*, or recommendations, than on personal information. You can publish your bookmarks on your WordPress.com blog with the Del. icio.us widget, and the Postalicious plugin for self-hosted blogs covers several bookmarking options.

Network to Blog Application

WordPress has developed an application that publishes your blog posts to your profile page on LinkedIn. To set that up, go to http://www.linkedin. com/static?key=application_directory. Click the WordPress icon, then click **Add Application**, and follow the instructions provided.

Optimize Your Blog for Search Engines

You will draw more readers to your blog when they are able to find it through search engines, such as Google and Yahoo. *Search engine optimization*, or SEO, means taking steps to help search engines do just that.

How SEO Works

Search engine companies do not reveal exactly the process they use to rank Web pages found in their searches. Whatever their specific algorithm, you can be sure it is based on words. WordPress gives multiple opportunities for you to feature words that highlight your blog and specific blog posts.

Use Keywords

Keywords are key to SEO. Think of keywords as words or phrases that people might use when searching for information that you have in your blog post. Therefore, if you have a post with great information about health problems in golden retrievers, use the term *golden retrievers* frequently, and not just your dog's name, *Bruno*.

Use Meaningful Blog Post Titles

Keywords need to appear in your blog post titles, or headlines, too. They are more search-engine friendly if they are specific rather than general. For example, a title reading *8 Easy-to-Care-for Tropical House Plants* is likely to get more search engine traffic than a title reading *My Favorite Plants.*

Choose Custom Permalinks

If you have a self-hosted blog, choose a post permalink structure that includes the post title or headline. You can do that on the Permalinks panel available under Settings in the left menu bar. (WordPress.com blogs automatically include the post title.) You can shorten the permalink when you create a post if you think it is too long.

Select Meaningful Category Names

Category names also provide words that search engines scan, or *crawl*. Again, specific names are better than general ones. Naming a category *Pet Care Books* is better than naming it simply *Books*, even if your blog topic clearly is pet care.

Other SEO Opportunities

You can and should use keywords in the alternate text of your images (see Chapter 7). If you have a self-hosted blog, you also might consider a plugin such as the All-in-One SEO plugin described in Chapter 8.

Use Surveys and Polls

Surveys and polls get readers involved in your blog, and when readers feel involved, they want to come back for more. WordPress.com has a PollDaddy poll tool built in, and self-hosted blogs can get similar functions with a PollDaddy plugin. Other poll plugins also are available.

If your blog is self-hosted, first go to PollDaddy.com and register. Then install the PollDaddy Poll plugin. You can read about plugin installation in Chapter 8.

① Click the **Add Poll** button (⊚) in the media tools list.

② The Polls (Add New) window opens, where you click the **Add New** link or **Create One** link.

Note: *The first time you use this feature from a WordPress.com blog, a window titled Polls in WordPress appears. Click **Do it: I want some polls!** to automatically register with PollDaddy. com.*

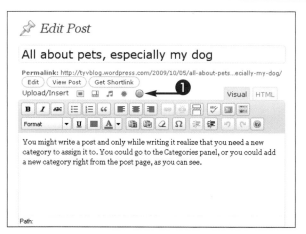

③ Type a question in the first box.

④ Type your proposed answers in the Answers boxes, clicking **Add another** if you need more answer blanks.

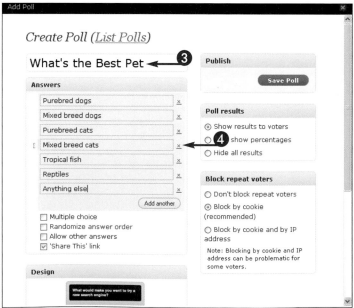

⑤ After scrolling down to reveal the Design module, click the double arrows on either side of the sample poll until you find a design you like.

⑥ After you are satisfied with your poll selections, click **Save Poll**.

The window name changes to Edit Poll and confirms a poll has been created.

⑦ Click **Send to Editor** (either link).

A *shortcode* appears in your Edit Post box, looking something like this: *[polldaddy poll=1234567]*. When you save and publish your post, the poll appears, too.

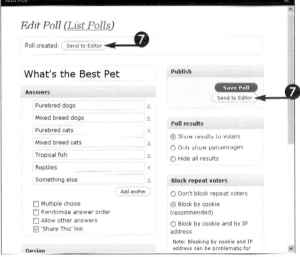

TIPS

Does the Polls menu that gets added to the menu bar in self-hosted blogs (and appears by default in WordPress.com blogs) do anything different from the Add Poll button in the media tools line?

If you click **Polls** (●) in the menu bar, a Polls list panel, rather than a separate window, opens. It allows you to create and edit polls without going through a post.

How do I put a poll in a sidebar?

Instead of sending the shortcode to the editor, find the poll in your polls list, get the HTML, and paste it in a text widget.

Tweak Your Theme

If you are like lots of people, you like your blog's theme but just a few little changes would make you like it *so* much better! Fortunately, you can make many adjustments to your WordPress theme, and most adjustments are quite simple.

Customize Your Header Art with a Built-in Tool................................210

Understanding the Theme Editor.................212

Add Copyright Information to the Footer..214

Change the Title on Your Blogroll...............216

Create and Use a Page Template................218

Introducing CSS...220

Try CSS with the Web Developer Toolbar...222

Add a Category RSS Feed Link......................224

Customize Your Header Art with a Built-in Tool

Using your own header art distinguishes your blog visually from others that use the same theme. The header art can be a photo, drawing, or other graphic. You can find themes with a built-in tool by using the Custom Header option when searching for a theme.

This example uses the Connections theme for WordPress.com or Connections Reloaded for self-hosted blogs.

Customize Your Header Art with a Built-in Tool

Change Header Art

① With your theme activated, click **Custom Header** under Appearance in the left menu bar.

The Your Header Image page opens.

② Click **Browse** to find the image on your computer that you want in your header.

③ Click **Upload**.

The image is uploaded to your Web host.

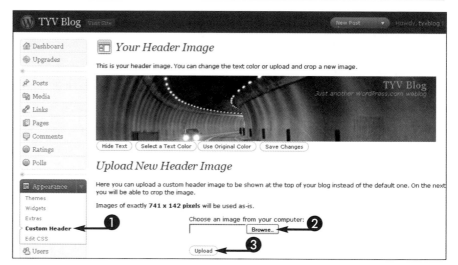

④ Stretch, shrink, or move the crop box to crop the image.

⑤ Click **Crop Header** when you are satisfied.

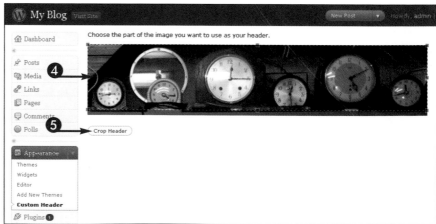

Header complete! appears, and the new header image is published to your blog.

Adjust Header Text

① Click **Custom Header** under Appearance in the left menu bar.

The Your Header Image page opens.

② Click **Select a Text Color**.

A color selection tool opens.

③ Click in the circle to select the hue of the header text.

The text color changes in the preview box on the page.

④ Click in the box to select the hue's tint, tone, or shade — that is, the amount of white, black, or gray to add to it.

The text color changes in the preview box on the page.

⑤ Click **Save Changes** when you are satisfied.

The text color is saved to your site.

⑥ Click **Visit Site** to see how your new header looks on your front page.

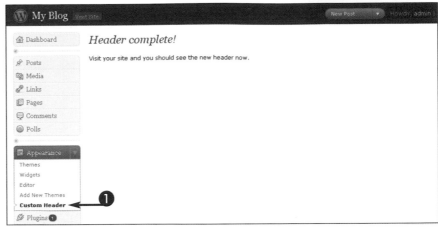

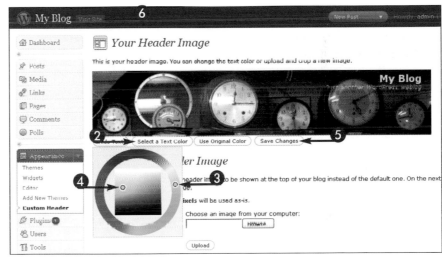

TIPS

I do not like the way my image looks after it was resized for the header. Any suggestions?

To get the results you want, use a paint program or image editor to create your header image, and make it the size specified on the custom header page. You have more control that way.

I do not see a Custom Header option under Appearance.

Different themes use different terminology, but the process is essentially the same. Yours might say Theme Options or Header Options, for example, and it might not provide for changing text color.

Understanding the Theme Editor

If you do not mind getting your fingers a little dirty digging in the code (not for WordPress.com blogs), you can personalize your theme even more by making adjustments to your theme in the theme editor, listed as Editor under Appearance in the left sidebar. You do not have to be a programmer to make it happen.

Theme Editor Components

Edited File Title

Shows which theme file is being edited.

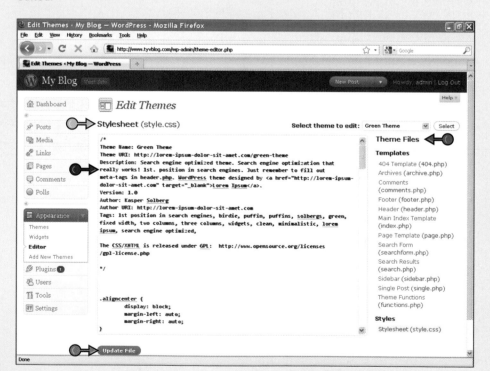

Edit Theme File Box

Portion of theme editor where you make changes.

Theme Files

Lists files available for the theme being edited.

Update File Button

Saves changes to theme files.

Theme Files

WordPress themes consist of several *PHP* templates, that is, files written in the PHP scripting language, plus at least one cascading style sheet, or *CSS* file. All themes have a file called index.php and most have such files as header.php, sidebar.php, footer.php, comments.php, and more. You can make changes — carefully — to any of them.

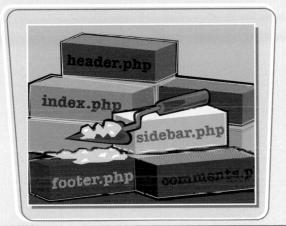

Theme Editor Alternatives

If you are not comfortable using the theme editor, you may edit theme files in a text editor on your computer and upload them to your theme's folder. If you save an unedited version of the files, you can reload them if your changes mess anything up. Free source code editors such as Notepad++ or Komodo Edit make editing the files easier.

Common Changes

If you do not know PHP or HTML, it is best to keep changes simple. You may want to edit files to change text in templates or to insert code, such as from an affiliate advertiser, in a location, such as a footer, that does not have a widget to do it for you. CSS files also are commonly changed.

What to Change

It can be scary editing theme files. To be safe, *do not* change anything between a pair of angle brackets that start with <?php; *do not* change items beginning <div class= unless you know CSS; but *do* change text between common HTML tags such as <h3> and </h3>.

Add Copyright Information to the Footer

Adding a copyright statement to your blog's footer lets readers see at a glance what rights you retain. Deciding what copyright notice to use requires some thought or even legal advice. Publishing the notice, though, is a good way to dip your toe into theme editing.

The example on these pages uses the default, or Kubrick, theme.

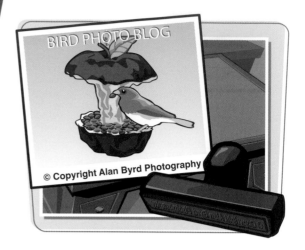

© Copyright Alan Byrd Photography

① On your blog front page, scroll to the bottom to take note of how your footer looks and what it says, and decide where in that area you want your copyright notice to appear.

② After going to the Dashboard and clicking **Appearance** and then **Editor**, click **Footer (footer.php)** under Theme Files.

Footer.php opens in the edit theme file box.

● The blog name's *call* in PHP.

● Text that will appear on blog is shown here.

● Links in HTML appear here.

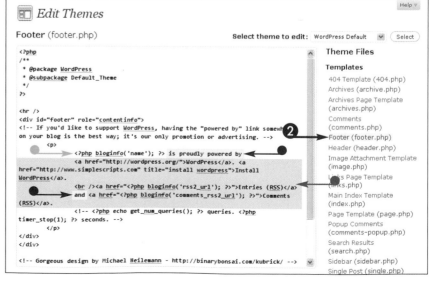

3 Click the mouse just before "is" in the first bit of text to place the cursor there, and then type what you want your statement to say, such as "**is licensed under the Creative Commons Attribution-Share Alike license and . . .**".

4 Click **Update File**.

The changes are saved.

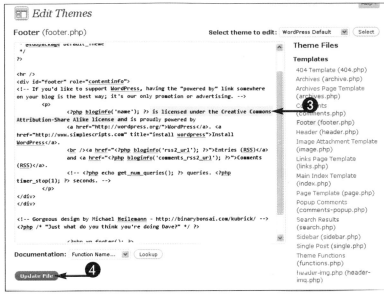

5 On your blog's front page, scroll to the bottom to review your changes.

TIPS

Can I make a link in the copyright statement?

Certainly. Just use the HTML to do so. It is `<a href="http://www.placetolink.com">`*the link name*`</a href>`, where *www. placetolink.com* is the place you want to link to and *the link name* is the text you want to appear as a hyperlink.

Where can I find out more about copyrights?

You can get more information at www. copyright.gov. You also may be interested in the Creative Commons licenses, which you can read about at http://creativecommons.org.

Change the Title on Your Blogroll

Hate the term *blogroll* that appears above your links list? Or maybe your theme has a blogroll title that duplicates the name of a link category. You do not have to live with it; you need to edit a theme file. Knowing which file is not always obvious.

Check first to see whether changing the name in your Links panel does the trick. The example on this page uses the theme Green Theme.

Change the Title on Your Blogroll

① Determine the blogroll title on your blog's front page.

② After going to the Dashboard and clicking **Appearance** and then **Editor**, click **Sidebar (sidebar. php)** under Theme Files.

Sidebar.php opens in the edit theme box.

Note: *The sidebar file is the first place to look.*

③ Search the edit theme box for "Links" in this case, or whatever title, such as "Blogroll," that your theme uses.

④ If you find the term to change, then edit as desired. But if you do not find the title to change in the sidebar file, click **Theme Functions (functions.php)**.

Note: *You may have to inspect other theme files to find the right location.*

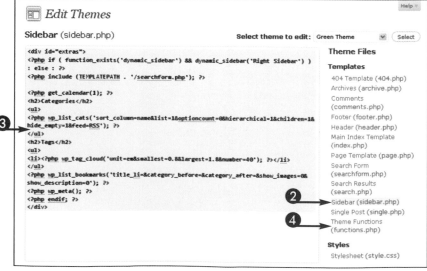

Functions.php opens in the edit theme box.

5 Find the text to edit.

6 Type **Check Out These** in front of the word Links.

7 Click **Update File**.

The changes are saved.

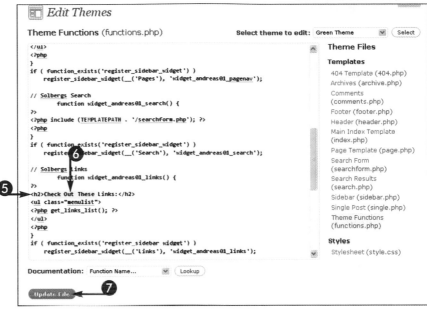

8 After clicking **Visit Site**, scroll to the spot on the page and review the change.

 TIPS

Can I change or add HTML tags to text in the theme files?

Yes. It should work just fine as long as you use proper opening and closing tags.

Is there an easy way to find the text I am looking for in the edit theme box?

You can use your browser's find function, accessible by pressing Ctrl + F (or ⌘ + F for Mac). Internet Explorer gives you a search window to use. If you use Firefox the search bar at the bottom of the screen also has a handy Highlight All option (●), which highlights every instance of the term you seek.

Create and Use a Page Template

By creating your own page templates, you can add pages to your theme that fit your needs. Perhaps you want a page that does not include a sidebar. You can have it by creating your own page template.

This option is not available for users at WordPress.com. In this example, you create a template for a page without a sidebar.

① Using your FTP program, save a copy of the file page.php from your theme directory to your computer.

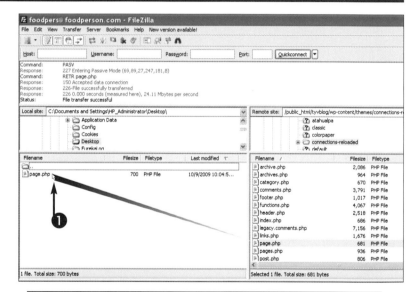

② Open page.php with a text editor or a source code editor and save the file as nosidebarpage.php, or a name of your choice, but it must have the .php ending.

③ Type `<?php /* Template Name: NoSidebarPage*/ ?>` at the top of the file.

④ Find and delete the lines reading `<div id ="sidebar"><?php get_ sidebar(); ?></div>`.

Save the file, and upload it to the directory where you found page. php.

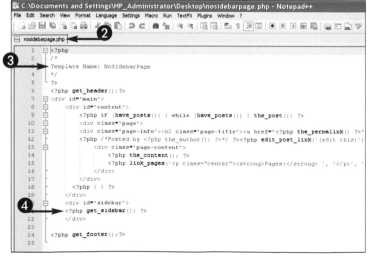

5 In your WordPress Dashboard, expand the Pages menu and click **Add New**.

The Add New Page panel opens.

6 Click the arrow next to Default Template to expand the templates list.

7 Click **NoSidebarPage** to select the new template.

Note: *The list of templates varies from theme to theme.*

8 After typing a title in the title box and entering text or other content in the page box, click **Save Draft**.

9 When your page is ready, click **Publish**.

Your page is published using the new template.

10 After going to your site, click the page name.

Your page from the new template opens, and it has no sidebar!

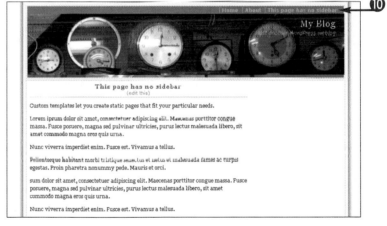

Where do I find the page. php file?

You find it on your Web host in your blog directory at wp-content\themes*your_ theme*\page.php, where *your_ theme* is the name of the theme for which you want to create a page template.

What else can I do with page templates?

Just about anything you want, but it is helpful to know more about HTML, cascading style sheets (CSS), and PHP.

Introducing CSS

Cascading style sheets, or CSS, allow you to create standard styles for your blog's appearance. Your theme comes with a style sheet file, usually called style.css, which stores those standards. By using your style sheet, you can change most aspects of your blog's look without changing the way it works.

You can use custom CSS on WordPress.com blogs only if you pay for the CSS upgrade.

What CSS Affects

Your style sheet determines what font you use, the colors of headlines and links, whether images have borders around them, how text is aligned on the page, how lists are shown, and just about anything else visual on your page — even the page layout.

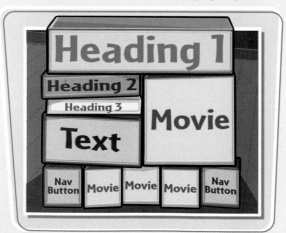

How CSS Works

Your WordPress theme is composed of a set of templates, and each template tells the Web browser that displays your blog to get presentation information from your style sheet, which is exactly what happens.

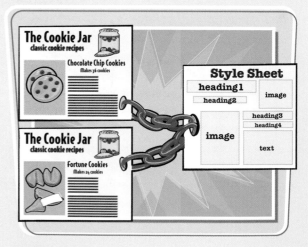

Style Sheet Comments

You can open your style.css file in a text or source code editor. The file may have comments in it to help you understand its parts. Comments do not affect presentation. Comments appear between the characters /* and */.

Style Sheet Rules

Each CSS rule consists of a *selector*, or the HTML element you are defining, and a *declaration*, which is the rule you are applying to that HTML element. In the CSS rule `body {background-color:beige}`, *body* is the selector and *{background-color:beige}* is the declaration.

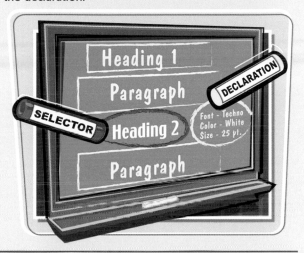

CSS Declarations

CSS declarations consist of a *property:value* pair, where *property* is the aspect of the element you want to define, and *value* is the definition. In the previous example, *background-color* is the property, and *beige* is the value.

More CSS Information

If you want to learn CSS, which *can* get complicated, the authority is W3C, the World Wide Web Consortium. It has information on learning CSS at www.w3.org/Style/CSS/learning — in 40 languages! See also the excellent and free tutorials at www.yourhtmlsource.com and www.w3schools.com.

Try CSS with the Web Developer Toolbar

Fortunately, you can test CSS changes without being a CSS whiz. When you use the Firefox Web Developer Toolbar, you can see how changes to your blog's CSS will affect your blog's presentation.

If you do not have the Firefox browser, you can download it from www.mozilla.org.

Try CSS with the Web Developer Toolbar

1 With Firefox running as your browser, go to http://addons.mozilla.org, and type **Web Developer** into the search box.

2 Click the search arrow (▶).

A list of Web developer add-ons appears, including the one you need, Web Developer by Chris Pederick.

3 Click **Add to Firefox**.

4 A download window opens. Agree to the download, the installation, and the restart of Firefox. The Developer Toolbar appears. If it does not appear, click the **View** menu and select **Developer Toolbar**.

5 With your blog page open in Firefox, click **CSS** in the new toolbar.

6 Click **Edit CSS**.

Your style.css file opens in the Edit CSS pane of your browser.

⑦ As an example, change the font size in the body section near the top of the style sheet.

● The type size changes instantly in the main part of your browser window.

Note: *The browser displays what would happen if you changed the style sheet, but it does not actually change the style sheet.*

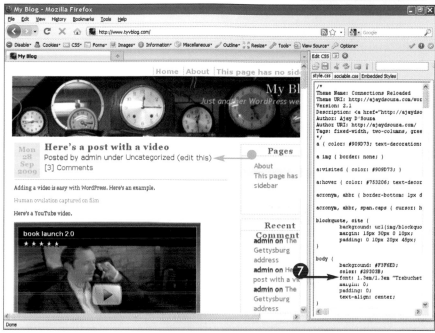

TIPS

All I want to do is change the color of the headlines. How do I do that?

You need to specify the color in hexadecimal notation, such as #000000, which is black, or with one of 16 Web standard names: aqua, black, blue, fuchsia, gray, green, lime, maroon, navy, olive, purple, red, silver, teal, white, and yellow. You can find hexadecimal notations and additional widely accepted color names at www.w3schools.com/css/css_colornames.asp. Finding the right selector can be the trick.

So how do I find the selector?

The Web Developer toolbar can help: Click the **Information** button (●) on toolbar and select **Display Element Information**. Now, click a headline whose color you want to change. The toolbar displays information about the headline's styling here (●) and in a pane at the far right of your browser.

Add a Category RSS Feed Link

If your blog has categories that may appeal to different audiences, you can set up separate feeds for those audiences. For example, you may have a needlework blog. You can create separate feeds for your knitting, needlepoint, crewel, and crochet categories. WordPress has the code built in; you just need to point your readers to it.

① From your blog's administration pages, click **Posts**.

The Posts menu expands.

② Click **Categories**.

The Categories page opens.

③ Select and copy the slug of the category to which you want to provide a feed link.

④ Click **Appearance**.

The Appearance menu expands.

⑤ Click **Widgets**.

The Widgets page opens.

⑥ Drag a Text widget to a sidebar.

The widget pops open.

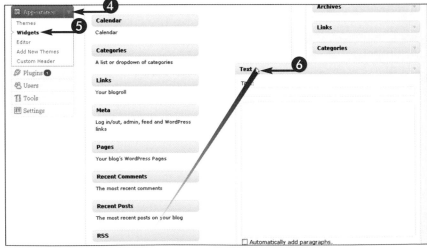

7 Give your widget a title, if you want.

8 Type an HTML link to the category feed like so: `<a href="http://www.yourblog.com/category/category_slug/feed">link name</a>`, where *www.yourblog.com* (yourblog.wordpress.com) is your blog's URL; *category_slug* is the slug for the desired category; and *link name* is what you want your link to say.

9 Click **Save**.

The widget is published to your Web site.

10 On your blog's front page, find the new sidebar widget, and click the new subscription link.

A feed subscription window opens.

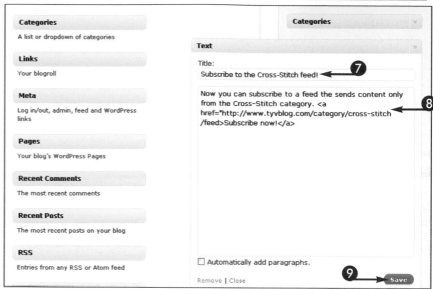

TIPS

WordPress.com does not show feed slugs, so do I just put the category name?

Basically, yes. Convert your category name to a slug by making it all lowercase, deleting punctuation, and inserting hyphens where spaces are.

I entered the URL right, but when I click my new link to subscribe, it just shows my regular feed. What did I do wrong?

You may be using a plugin to manage feeds through FeedBurner, and the plugin is fouling things up. Try deactivating the plugin; if the link works then, go to the plugin's Web site, which you can find on your blog's Plugins panel, and look for FAQs. If that does not help, contact the plugin author for help.

Use WordPress for Content Management

Content management systems, or CMS, get much attention in Web computing these days for the way they let multiple users work together or separately to create, edit, publish, and manage Web content without having to fiddle with computer code. WordPress lets you manage authors, members, and content, and you can do even more if you are willing to touch code.

Understanding User Capabilities 228

Add Authors and Contributors 230

Create a Member Community 232

Add a Forum to Your Blog 234

Manage Documents 236

Use a Static Page as Your Home Page 238

Add a Blog to an Existing Static Web Site 240

Create a Portfolio of Your Photos or Art ...242

Considerations for Your Portfolio 243

Place Ads on Your Blog 244

Add Google Ads to Your Site 246

Add Amazon Affiliate Ads to Your Site 248

Use Sticky Posts to Control Page Content 250

Understanding User Capabilities

As the blog owner, you can decide who gets to write, edit, and publish content to your site. A critical aspect of using WordPress to manage content generated by multiple users is the permissions that you can assign to each user.

User Roles and Capabilities

WordPress provides a standard set of user *roles*, which specify what *capabilities*, or tasks, a user can perform. The standard roles are Administrator, Author, Editor, Contributor, and Subscriber. The subscriber role does not exist at WordPress.com.

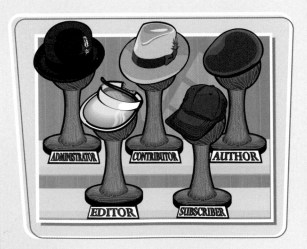

Administrator Capabilities

If you set up the blog, you have Administrator capabilities. An Administrator can do anything, from writing posts to changing themes and adding users. In most cases, the blog owner runs the site as the Administrator, but more than one person can have the Administrator role. If you add an Administrator, make sure it is someone you absolutely trust!

Editor Capabilities

As implied by the role's title, the Editor role can write, edit, publish, and delete posts and pages by herself or by others. The Editor role also can moderate comments and manage categories, tags, and blogroll. An Editor can do a lot but cannot change themes, plugins, users, and the like.

Author and Contributor Capabilities

Authors can write, edit, publish, and delete posts that they wrote, but they cannot alter anyone else's posts. They also can upload images for their posts. Contributors can write and edit posts, but an Editor or Administrator must review and publish them. Authors and Contributors cannot create pages.

Subscriber Capabilities

If you have open registration available, Subscriber is the default role. Some blogs require registration to comment on blog posts, and when a reader registers, he or she gets the Subscriber role. A Subscriber can read blog posts, comment, and have a subscriber profile that defines his or her name, password, and so on. A WordPress.com registration fulfills that role for WordPress.com blogs.

Determining Roles

If you own a blog and want to have several contributors, a good practice is to give any new users the fewest capabilities that they need to complete their jobs. Limiting broader capabilities to only the very few who need them deters both miscues and malicious changes.

Add Authors and Contributors

You can turn your blog into a group blog by adding editors, authors, and contributors. At the same time, you can control — or not — when and how content is published by setting permissions to fit your blog's needs.

Add Authors and Contributors

In Self-Hosted Blogs

① In the administrative pages, click **Users**.

The Users menu expands.

② Click **Add New**.

The Add New User panel opens.

③ Type a username in the Username box.

④ Type the person's e-mail in the E-mail box.

⑤ Give the user a password and confirm it.

⑥ Confirm that the Send Password check box is selected (the default).

⑦ Click to expand the Role drop-down menu, and click a role.

⑧ Click **Add User**.

WordPress adds the user, sends the person an e-mail, and opens the Users list with the new user.

⑨ Click the username.

The user's profile opens. You or the new user can add or change settings.

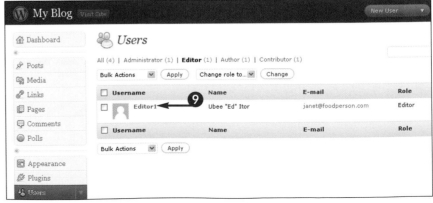

At WordPress.com for WordPress.com Users

1 Click **Users**.

The Users panel opens.

2 Type the e-mail address of a WordPress.com member.

3 Click the Role drop-down menu, and click the role you want for that user.

4 Click **Add User**.

WordPress adds the user, sends the person an e-mail, and opens the Users list with the new user.

At WordPress.com for People Not at WordPress.com

1 Click **Invites** under the Users menu.

The Invites panel opens.

2 Type the e-mail address of the person you want to add.

3 Personalize the default message.

4 Click **Send Invite**.

WordPress sends the person an e-mail inviting him to register.

How do new users add content?
New members of your site can access your administrative pages the same way you do, with their username and password, by going to www.*yourblog*.com/wp.admin. There, they can do whatever tasks their role allows.

Create a Member Community

You can avoid the formality of creating authors with certain WordPress options and plugins such as Alkivia Open Community. Be forewarned, though, that opening your blog to the world may invite *unwanted* contributions. At self-hosted blogs, using a plugin is a safer way to go.

Use a Theme, Self-Hosted Blogs

1 After installing and activating the theme P2, which allows posting from the front page, click **Settings**.

The Settings menu expands, and the General Settings panel opens.

2 Click the **Anyone can register** check box (☐ changes to ☑).

3 Expand the drop-down menu next to New User Default Role, and click **Author**.

4 At the bottom of the page, click **Save Settings**. Any visitor now can register as an author, allowing him or her to write and publish posts.

Use a Theme at WordPress.com

1 After activating the theme P2, which allows posting from the front page, expand the Appearance menu and click **P2 Options**.

The P2 Options panel opens.

2 Click the **Allow any WordPress.com member to post** check box (☐ changes to ☑).

3 Click **Update Options**.

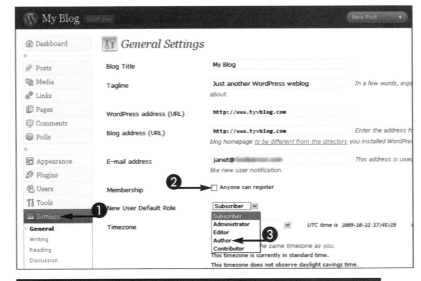

Use a Plug-In

1 After installing and activating Alkivia Open Community, click the **Alkivia** menu in the left sidebar.

The Alkivia General Settings panel opens.

2 Select a page from the drop-down menu where you want community information to appear.

*Note: If you do not want to use an existing page, such as About, you must first choose **Pages** and then **Add New** and create a community page.*

3 After reviewing other options on the page, click **Save Changes** at the bottom of the page.

Your selection and other settings are saved, and the User Profiles link appears on the Alkivia menu.

4 Select the privacy options you prefer.

5 At the bottom of the page, click **Save Changes**. Registered members' profiles are available to visitors.

TIPS

Where can I get more information about Alkivia Open Community?

Go to the plugin's home page or support forum, both of which are accessible from the Alkivia General Settings panel.

Is there any other theme that allows front-page posting?

At this writing, there is another such theme, called Prologue. It is available for self-hosted or WordPress.com blogs. It is an earlier version of P2, lacks the P2 options, and may require the administrator to add new users.

Add a Forum to Your Blog

If a blog does not provide enough commentary to satisfy you, you can add a forum to your blog. Doing so allows visitors to start topics and respond to other people's topics, even if the visitors are not regular contributors to your site. The solution at self-hosted blogs is called Simple:Press Forums, a plugin.

This plugin is not available through the Install Plugins panel.

① Go to http://simplepressforum. com/download in your browser.

② Click the download icon under Default Skin and Icons Only.

A ZIP file downloads.

③ Click the download icon under For WP Standard and MU.

An RTF file downloads. Open and read the file for WP Standard installations.

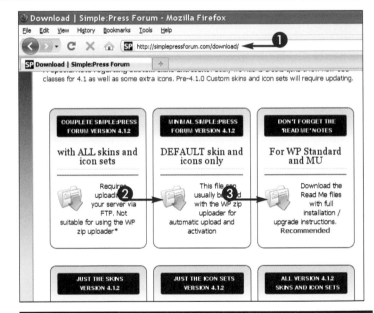

④ Expand the Plugins menu in your WordPress Dashboard and click **Add New**.

The Install Plugins panel opens.

⑤ Click **Upload**.

An upload box opens.

⑥ Click **Browse**, locate the Simple:Press Forum ZIP file on your computer, and then click **Open** in the Upload File window.

⑦ Click **Install Now**.

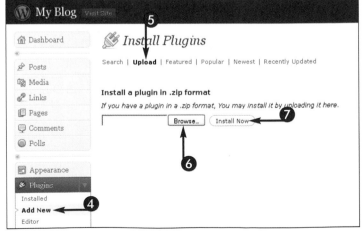

WordPress uploads the files from the ZIP file.

8 Click **Go to Forum Admin**.

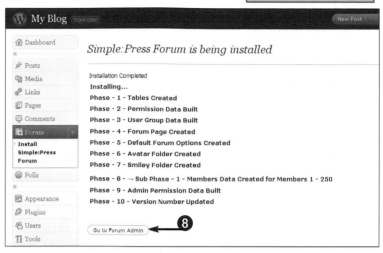

The SPF Administration panel opens.

9 Go to the Simple:Press:wiki's Getting Started pages at http://wiki.simplepressforum.com/doku.php?id=getting_started.

10 Use the instructions there to set up your forum.

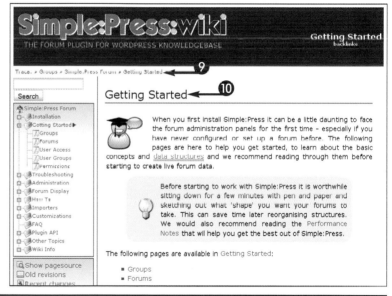

 TIPS

Can I add a forum for my WordPress.com blog?

Not directly, but there are indirect ways to do so. First, do a Google search on free forum hosting and set up a forum at the site of your choice. Then, create a link to your forum in a Text widget.

Could I do that with my self-hosted blog?

Sure! It will not be integrated with your blog the way the Simple:Press Forum is, but it should work fine. Simple:Press Forum is not as complicated as it looks if you use the wiki and go step by step.

You can use your WordPress site as a portal to assorted documents that you want to store online and make accessible to others. Using the same technique as uploading images, you can upload word processing documents, spreadsheets, and PDFs for sharing.

For this example, you make a page just for documents.

Manage Documents

1 Create a new page by clicking **Pages** then **Add New**.

2 On your page, type the categories of the documents you want to upload.

3 Click where you want a link to your first document to be listed.

4 Click the **Add Media** icon (⊡).

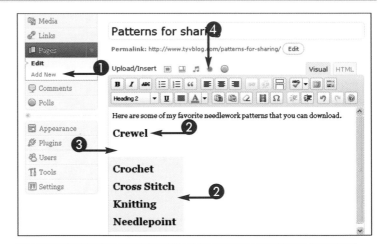

The Add Media window opens.

5 Click **Select Files**.

6 A file selection window opens. When you locate the file you want to upload, click **Open**, and WordPress uploads the file and displays information about it in the Add Media window.

7 Change the title, which by default is the file name, to what you want the link to the document to say.

8 Click **Insert into Post**.

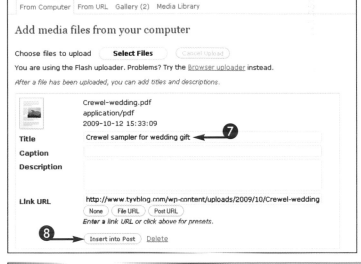

● A link to the file is inserted into the page where you left your cursor.

9 Click **Save Draft**.

The page draft is saved, and you can add as many more links to documents as you like.

TIP

Is there a way I can upload a bunch of documents at once?

Yes. After you click **Select Files** and the file selection window opens, you can click multiple files as long as they are in the same folder on your computer. Press and hold Ctrl (⌘ on Mac) as you make your selections. After all the files are uploaded, click **Show** next to each one to change the title and insert into your file.

Use a Static Page as Your Home Page

You can give your site an entirely different feel by making your front page a static page, rather than the usual reverse-chronological presentation of blog posts. When people go to your domain, they see photos, text, or whatever else you want to display.

① Click **Pages** in the left menu bar.

② Click **Add New**.

The Add/Edit Page panel opens.

③ Type **Home** in the title box.

④ Click the Template drop-down menu, and select a template.

Note: If your theme has only one page template, you will not see Template menu.

⑤ Click **Save Draft**.

⑥ Click **Publish**.

The new page is published.

⑦ Click **Add New**.

A new Add/Edit Page panel opens.

⑧ Type **Blog** in the title box.

⑨ Click the Template drop-down menu, and select a template.

⑩ Click **Save Draft**.

⑪ Click **Publish**.

The new page is published.

⑫ Click **Settings**.

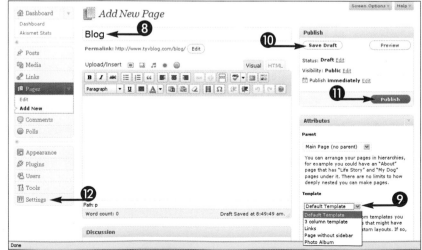

The Settings menu expands.

⑬ Click **Reading**.

The Reading Settings panel opens.

⑭ Click the **A static page** radio button (⊙ changes to ⊚).

⑮ Click the Front page drop-down menu.

⑯ Click **Home**.

⑰ Click the Posts page drop-down menu.

⑱ Click **Blog**.

⑲ Click **Save Changes**.

Visitors to your domain name now land on the page called Home and must click Blog to read blog posts.

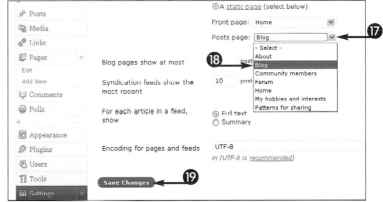

TIPS

Why is my home page blank except for the sidebar?
You must create the content that you want for your home page. Do it as you would create content for any other static page.

Do I have to name the blog page Blog?
No. You can name it whatever you like. If Blog does not fit the tone of your site, you can always call it News or Announcements or something else altogether.

Add a Blog to an Existing Static Web Site

You can add a WordPress blog to your existing Web site with very little effort. That way, you get to keep the Web site you are known for while adding the dynamic content you can easily create with WordPress.

You can add a self-hosted blog via a subdirectory or subdomain, but if your blog is hosted at WordPress.com, you must use a subdomain.

Add a Blog to an Existing Static Web Site

Use a Subdirectory for Self-Hosted Blogs

① Create a subdirectory, or folder, called *blog* or some other name, in the root directory of your existing site.

② Install WordPress into the blog directory.

Note: *See Chapter 3 for installation information.*

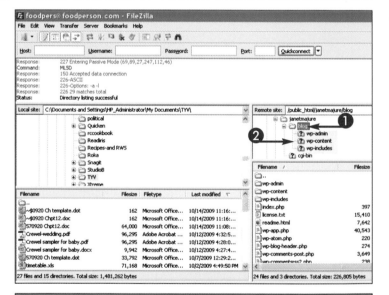

③ In your browser, type the subdirectory name in the address bar using the format **http://www.yourdomain.com/blogdirectory**, where *yourdomain.com* is the domain of your Web site and *blogdirectory* is the name of the new subdirectory.

Note: *Do not forget to link to your blog from your site's home page.*

Your blog page appears in your browser.

Use a Subdomain

① Type **blog** as the subdomain in your Web host's subdomains tool.

Note: *This example uses the cPanel Subdomains tool. Check your Web host for more information.*

● This field shows the directory where your blog content is stored.

② Click **Create**.

A subdomain called blog. yourdomain.com is created.

For a self-hosted blog, install WordPress into the subdomain's directory and you are ready to blog.

Map a Subdomain to WordPress.com Blog

① After you have created a subdomain, create a new CNAME record at your domain registrar. It will look something like this:
```
blog.yourdomain.com.
IN CNAME myblog.word
press.com.
```
— where *myblog* is your WordPress.com username.

② Go to the WordPress.com Dashboard and click **Upgrades**.

③ Click **Mapping** and follow the steps to add the subdomain and buy the mapping upgrade.

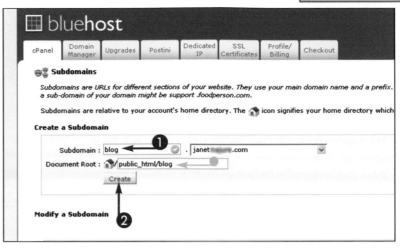

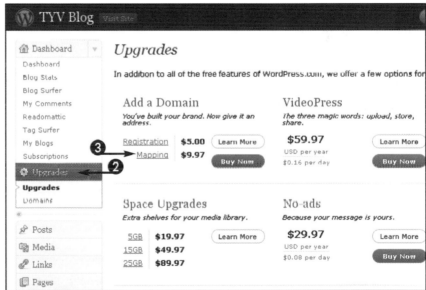

I am trying to direct my subdomain to my WordPress.com blog, and it is not working for me. Help!

You may find the instructions at http://en.support.wordpress. com/domain-mapping/map-subdomain/ helpful. If not, contact your Web host or post a question on the WordPress.com support forums at http://support.wordpress.com.

I added WordPress to a subdirectory at my site, but I cannot seem to log on to the administration panels. What do I do?

Your WordPress blog works just as if it were a stand-alone self-hosted blog, using http://www.*yourdomain.com/ blogdirectory*/wp-admin to get to the administration pages. Be sure to use the logon information you received from WordPress for your administration pages, not your Web host logon information.

Create a Portfolio of Your Photos or Art

The easiest and probably best way to create a portfolio blog of your photos or art is through your choice of theme. Your portfolio or photoblog site is more than a blog with pictures; it is a blog where the images are the focus, rather than illustrations of the words.

Create a Portfolio of Your Photos or Art

① After expanding the Appearance menu, click **Add New Themes**.

The Install Themes panel opens.

② Click the **Photoblogging** check box (☐ changes to ☑).

***Note:** This option is not available at WordPress. com.*

③ Click **Find Themes**.

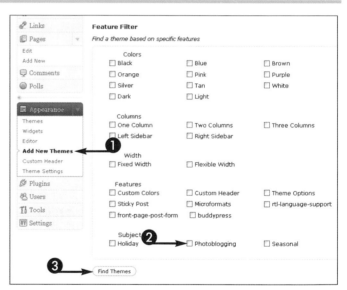

A selection of themes tagged photoblogging appears, which you can preview.

④ Click **Install** to install the theme of your choice.

The Install window opens, where you confirm that you want to install the theme. After the theme is installed, activate it.

Considerations for Your Portfolio

When you are choosing a theme or a plugin to operate your photoblog, consider ease of use, whether it resizes photos for you, and whether it displays your photos to best advantage. After all, that is why you have a photoblog! On the other hand, you *can* put other themes to work for photos.

WordPress.com Themes to Consider

WordPress.com offers two themes, Monotone and Duotone, made specifically for images. If you do not care for them, here is an option that may work well for you: Choose a plain theme such as The Journalist, set the Reading settings to display just one post per page, and insert your images. They will be the focus.

WordPress.org Themes to Consider

Your self-hosted blog offers numerous photoblogging themes. Among them is AutoFocus, which has a slick front page display; Phantom, which automatically creates and displays thumbnail images of recently posted photos, and HoPE, which has an easy, built-in image link to your Picasa or Flickr photostream.

Place Ads on Your Blog

If making money is part of your blog plan, you have plenty of company, and there is a lot to learn. Entire books have been written about making money on your blog, but here is an introduction to ways your blog can use advertising to earn income.

Advertising Possibilities

Advertising essentially is a means by which someone pays you for displaying their ad on your blog. You can contract directly with advertisers, sign up for an ad service or network, or use affiliate programs. Payments may be made for clicks on ads; for *impressions*, or the number of times the ad was viewed; or as sales commissions.

WordPress.com Limits

You can place any ads you want on your self-hosted blog. WordPress.com, however, significantly restricts advertising. Read the WordPress.com Terms of Service or contact support at WordPress.com if you have questions. Generally, Amazon Associate links are acceptable, but only if they are part of an original commentary about the item you are linking to.

Advertising Networks or Services

The most popular system is Google's AdSense, which offers text and display ads. Other popular ad systems include Text Link Ads, Chitika, and BlogHer. Most often, these networks select ads to place on your site based on the content of your site.

Affiliate Programs

Numerous individual businesses offer affiliate programs, with Amazon being the best known. Many smaller businesses offer affiliate programs through affiliate networks, such as Commission Junction, LinkShare, or ShareASale. With affiliates, *you* choose the merchant or product to advertise, instead of the ad network choosing for you.

How They Work

Typically, ad networks provide a bit of code that you place on your site via a widget or by inserting it into your theme's files. The code keeps track of impressions, clicks, or both. Various plugins are available, such as AdServer, that you can use to manage ads, including ads that you sell directly to blog sponsors.

Ad Considerations

Some blogs make a lot of ad income, but most do not. Before you decide whether to include ads on your site, you may want to consider whether they are worth the effort to include and whether ads will detract from your blog content.

Add Google Ads to Your Site

Placing Google AdSense ads on your site lets you earn a few cents every time someone clicks on an ad. Google lets you choose among a variety of ad types, and you can customize the ads to make them fit in with your blog design.

As a first step, you need to have or create a Google account and log on. WordPress.com does not allow use of Google AdSense.

① Go to www.google.com and click **Advertising Programs**.

② The Advertising Programs page opens, where you click **Sign up now** under Google AdSense.

The Google AdSense page opens.

③ Type your site's complete URL.

④ Select a language from the drop-down list.

⑤ Click the check boxes to agree to Google's terms (☐ changes to ☑).

⑥ Provide the information requested in the Contact Information section.

⑦ Scroll down to complete all the information, then agree to the Policies and click **Submit Information**.

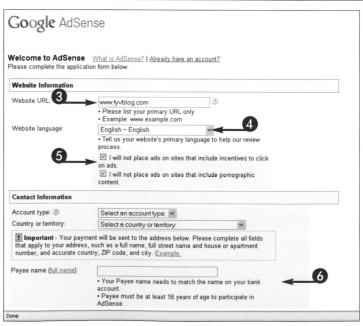

246

8 A confirmation page appears. Answer the questions on that page, and click **Continue**.

9 Google sends an e-mail asking you to confirm your email address. Click the link in it to complete your application.

10 After your application is approved, sign in at google.com/adsense.

11 Click the **AdSense Setup** tab.

12 Click **AdSense for Content**.

13 The Choose Ad Type page opens, where you leave the default settings and click **Continue** and then work your way through pages for creating your ad. When your ad selections are complete, click **Submit and Get Code**.

The AdSense code appears on a new page.

14 Copy the code in the code box.

15 On your blog administration panel, create a text widget, and paste the code into it. Ads start appearing in the widget space after a few minutes.

How long does it take to get approved as an AdSense publisher?

Google says two to three days is typical for application review. Check https://www.google.com/ adsense/support/ for a wealth of information about AdSense.

Is a widget the only way to implement AdSense?

No. You can incorporate it into your blog's theme templates by pasting the code in the location where you want the ads to appear.

Add Amazon Affiliate Ads to Your Site

If you find yourself recommending products on your blog, you can make a little money by providing a link to a place where someone can purchase them — and earn a commission for you through an affiliate program. Amazon.com Associates is the most popular such program, and you may be able to use it at WordPress.com. See "Place Ads on Your Blog" earlier in this chapter.

As a first step, go to https://affiliate-program.amazon.com/ and sign up.

Add Amazon Affiliate Ads to Your Site

① After signing in, click **Links & Banners**.

● The Get Started Now button provides an introduction for new associates.

② The Links & Banners page opens, where you click **Add Product Links now**.

③ The Product Links page opens, where you search for the item you want to link to. When you find the item in the search results, click **Get Link**.

The Customize and Get HTML page opens.

④ Click the **Text Only** radio button (○ turns to ◉).

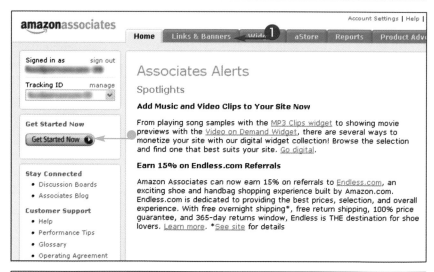

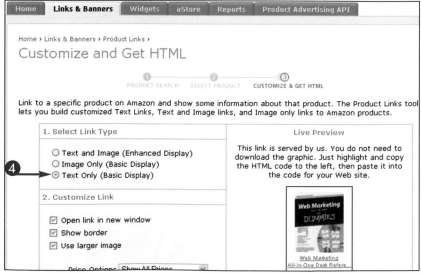

The page changes to display text link options.

⑤ Edit the link text, if desired.

● The text in the preview box changes as you type.

⑥ Click **Highlight HTML**.

⑦ Press Ctrl + C (⌘ + C for Mac) to copy the code.

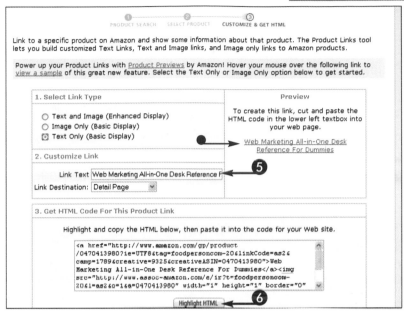

⑧ After logging into your blog's administration pages and going to the post where you want to add the text link, click **HTML** to go to the HTML post editor.

⑨ Paste the code in the place where you want the link to appear.

⑩ Click **Update Post**.

The post is updated with the coded text link to the product you recommend.

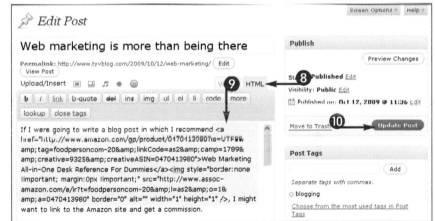

TIPS

Can I use the other kinds of ads and links that Amazon offers?

Yes, you can, and you also can put Amazon and other affiliate ads in your sidebar. Many bloggers like the text links because they are unobtrusive.

What are the Amazon widgets?

They are a form of dynamic ads. Find out more about them and other Amazon Associates products and issues at the Help page, https://affiliate-program.amazon.com/gp/associates/help/main.html.

Use Sticky Posts to Control Page Content

You can make your blog's home page partly static and partly *dynamic*, or changing, thanks to sticky posts. Just mark one or more posts as *sticky*, and it or they stay at the top of your front page, with your latest blog post right after them. Sticky posts are a great way to welcome readers or announce policies.

Use Sticky Posts to Control Page Content

From the Edit Posts List

1 Click **Posts** to expand the Edit Posts list.

2 After positioning the mouse over the desired post to reveal the Quick Edit link, click **Quick Edit** and then click the **Make this post sticky** check box (☐ changes to ☑).

3 Click **Update Post**.

The post is published to the top of your home page, and the Quick Edit pane collapses.

From the Edit Post Panel

1 With the Edit Post panel open for the post you want to change, click **Edit** next to the Visibility setting.

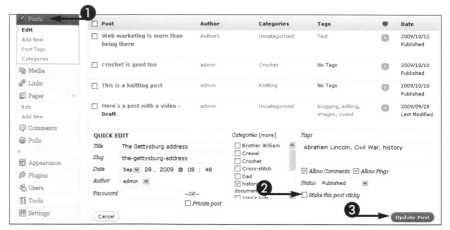

The Visibility pane opens.

2 Click the **Stick this post to the front page** check box (☐ changes to ✓).

3 Click **OK**.

4 Click **Update Post**.

The post appears at the top of the blog front page, and a note reading *Sticky* appears beside the post in the Edit Posts list.

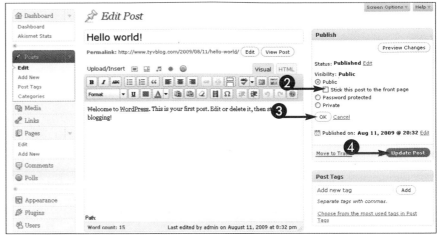

To Suppress Date on Sticky Posts

1 Under Appearance, click **Editor**.

2 Click **index.php**.

3 Find the code reading `<?php the_time( 'F jS, Y') ?>` and replace it with

```
<?php if (!is_
sticky() ) { ?>
<?php the_time('M jS,
Y'); ?> <?php }
?>
```

4 Click **Update File** at the bottom of the Edit Themes panel.

Your sticky posts do not show the original posting date.

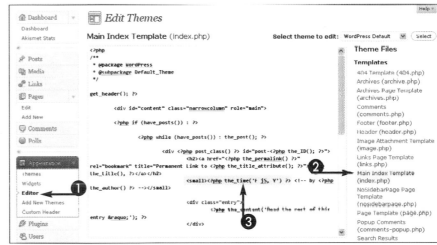

TIPS

Is there a limit to how many sticky posts you can have?

You can have multiple stickies, but if you wind up with a whole front page of static posts, consider using a page for the front and blog posts elsewhere as described earlier in this chapter.

I tried to suppress the dates on the sticky posts as you suggested, but it did not work. What to do?

It works with the default (or Kubrick) theme, but you may need to do things differently with your theme. Check with the theme developer or WordPress forums.

13

Maintain Your WordPress Blog

Now that your WordPress blog is up, running, and getting readers, you want to make sure that it continues to work smoothly. Although WordPress.com users have fewer maintenance tasks than do self-hosted bloggers, everybody can benefit from a little blog maintenance.

Understanding WordPress Backups............**254**

Get to Know WordPress Support Options....**256**

Upgrade WordPress Automatically..............**258**

Automatic Upgrade Troubleshooting..........**259**

Upgrade WordPress Manually......................**260**

Clean Out Outdated Drafts............................**264**

Check Your Site for Outdated Links............**266**

Sign Up for a Statistics Tracker....................**268**

Understanding Your Statistics......................**270**

Install Plugin Upgrades................................**272**

Read Blogs that Focus on WordPress..........**273**

**Use WordPress.com in Languages
   Besides English**..**274**

**Self-Hosted WordPress Blogs in
   Languages Besides English**........................**275**

Make a Suggestion..**276**

Steps To Take When Your Blog Breaks......**278**

Understanding WordPress Backups

If you have a self-hosted blog, you are responsible for backing up your Web site. Doing regular backups assures that you do not lose data — or at least not much — should your database become corrupted or your host crash for whatever reason.

What to Back Up

You need especially to back up the MySQL database that you created when you installed WordPress. That is because the database stores all your blog posts and comments. You also need to back up the *site*, however. It contains your plugins, themes, uploads, scripts, and a few other files as well as the core WordPress files.

When to Back Up

You are wise to back up your files on a regular schedule so that you do not forget. Some people do it daily, others monthly. Frequency depends on how active your site is — or how much you are willing to lose. In addition, you should always back up before updating to a new version of WordPress.

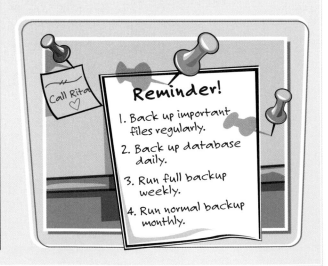

Backup Methods

There are several backup methods for you to consider. You can use a plugin, such as WordPress Backup; a backup tool provided by your Web host; or a manual backup method. You may want to try more than one method to see which works best for you.

Web Host Tools

Web hosts that use the cPanel control panel have two backup tools, one called Backup Wizard and the other simply Backups. Others provide phpMyAdmin, an interface you can use for backing up your site and database. Find more information by searching on *backups* at codex.wordpress.org.

How Long to Save Backups

Some people discard old backups when they create a new one. WordPress experts recommend keeping the latest three backups, just in case something has gone wrong along the way. Let your risk aversion be your guide.

Backup Instructions

Most Web host tools are fairly self-explanatory, but contact your Web host if you have questions. WordPress.org provides step-by-step instructions for backups using phpMyAdmin and MySQL tools. If you have trouble, also consult the WordPress.org forums.

Get to Know WordPress Support Options

The multiplicity of WordPress support options means you are almost certain to find the answer to your particular question. You can find it quicker if you go to the right places: WordPress.*org* sites for self-hosted bloggers, and WordPress.*com* if your blog is hosted there.

The WordPress.org Codex

A *codex* is a bound manuscript, and that is the name that WordPress.org chose for its set of support articles, which you can find at http://codex. wordpress.org. Note that numerous contributors write Codex articles, and some are definitely better and more up-to-date than others.

Official WordPress.com Support

As a host, WordPress.com is a bit more formal about its support pages, which you can find at http://support.wordpress.com. The main page has topics that you may find helpful. Occasionally, WordPress. com Support articles may be helpful even to self-hosted bloggers.

Search for Answers

Both the WordPress.org Codex and the WordPress.com Support pages have search options, and both allow you to search the documentation as well as the forums. If you do not identify what you need by browsing the documentation, search the documentation and the forums. You are likely to find an answer.

Do Not Miss WordPress.TV

WordPress has numerous instructional and informational videos you may find useful. You will find them at http://wordpress.tv. Although many of the videos focus on WordPress.com, you also can find videos from WordCamps, conferences for WordPress enthusiasts of all descriptions.

Pose a Question

If you fail in your attempts to find an answer, you are welcome to post a question to the thousands of WordPress users who read the forums. You need to be logged in to post a question — or an answer.

Posting Etiquette

Things that might be considered bad manners on the forums:

- Posting a question that has been answered many times before. Search first!

- Posting a .com question on the .org forum or vice versa.

Good manners include posting a link to your site, being specific, and using standard grammar and spelling.

Upgrade WordPress Automatically

If you have a self-hosted blog, you need to keep up with WordPress updates, a task that WordPress.com does for its users. Updating WordPress is a simple process, and it assures that you have the latest features and the latest security measures installed.

You will see an alert on your Dashboard when an upgrade is available. If you click it, which takes you to the upgrade panel, it provides a link to information about backing up your site.

Upgrade WordPress Automatically

① After you have backed up your site and database, click **Tools**.

The Tools menu expands.

② Click **Upgrade**.

The Upgrade WordPress panel opens.

③ Click **Upgrade Automatically**.

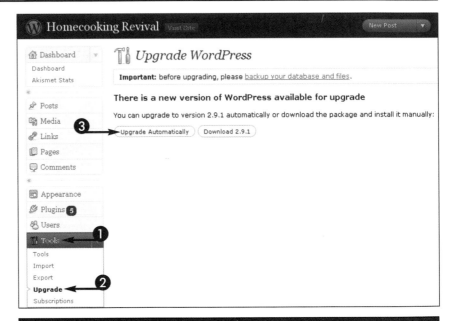

The update progress appears on the screen.

④ Click **Visit Site**.

Your site appears. You need to navigate through the site and check to make sure all is working correctly.

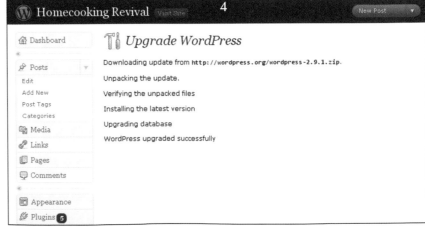

If your automatic upgrade failed for some reason, you are among the unlucky few. Worry not, however; you still should be able to upgrade successfully. If an automatic upgrade does not work for you, you can upgrade manually. Here are some troubleshooting tips.

You must upgrade manually if you are upgrading from a version earlier than WordPress 2.7.

Automatic Upgrade Troubleshooting	
Error	*Likely Solution*
Installation Failed message	Simply try again; you may have had some Internet connection interruption.
First message says *WordPress Upgraded Successfully*, but another message says *An automated WordPress update has failed to complete - please attempt the update again now.*	Using your FTP program, open the directory or folder where WordPress is installed — that is, the folder that contains the WP-Admin folder. Look for and delete a file named .maintenance. Then, try the automatic upgrade again.
Fatal Error message	Go to your plugins list and deactivate all plugins. Then, try the automatic upgrade again. When the upgrade is complete, reactivate the plugins.
Repeated failure	Ask at the WordPress.org forums for help, or do a manual upgrade, as described on the next page.

Maybe you are a hands-on kind of person, or maybe you have had trouble with the automatic upgrade. In any case, you can orchestrate a WordPress upgrade manually.

1 After you have backed up your site and database, click **Tools**.

The Tools menu expands.

2 Click **Upgrade**.

The Upgrade WordPress panel opens.

3 Click **Download X.X.X**, where *X.X.X* is the updated version number.

The file downloads to your computer, where you save it.

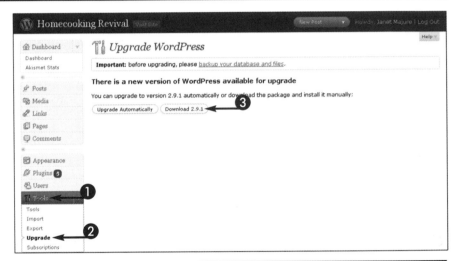

4 Click **Plugins**.

The Manage Plugins panel opens.

5 Select all plugins (☐ changes to ☑).

6 Click the Bulk Actions drop-down menu and select **Deactivate**.

7 Click **Apply**.

The plugins are deactivated.

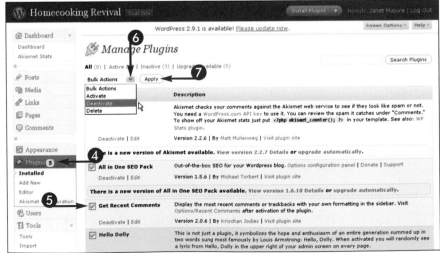

Important: Before proceeding with the next step, go back and verify that you can extract your downloaded backup files and that you can open the folders.

⑧ Using your FTP program, delete all files and folders in your root directory **except**:

● wp-config.php file

● wp-content folder

● .htaccess file, if you have added custom rules to it

● Custom content and/or plugins

 wp-images folder, if present

Note: Remember to **leave** the above files and **delete** everything else.

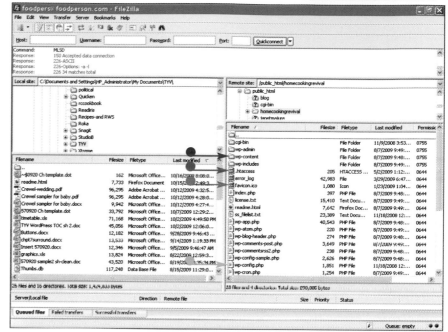

TIPS

What files do I delete exactly?

Delete wp-*everythingelse*, that is, all files starting *wp-*, except those listed above, plus readme.html, xmlrpc.php, license.txt, the wp-admin folder, the wp-includes folder, and index.php. If your installation has them, also delete wp.php, wp-content/cache folder, and the widgets folder found inside wp-content/plugins.

Do I have to do anything special if I use WordPress in German or another non-English language?

If you have a languages folder inside the wp-includes folder, that is, wp-includes/languages, move the languages folder to the wp-content folder before deleting wp-includes.

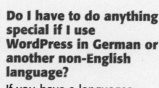

continued

Deleting files, rather than overwriting them, ensures a cleaner installation of your WordPress upgrade. Because you backed up your files, you can replace the deleted files if necessary.

Upgrade WordPress Manually *(continued)*

9 Upload all the extracted files in the downloaded WordPress folder **except** the wp-content folder.

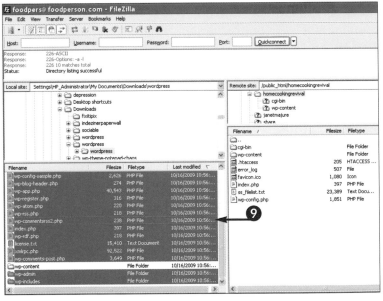

10 In your FTP program, open the wp-content folder on your local computer.

11 Open the wp-content folder on your Web host.

12 Do nothing with the plugins, themes, and uploads folders, but copy anything else in the local folder to the Web host.

In this case, copy index.php from the local computer to the Web host.

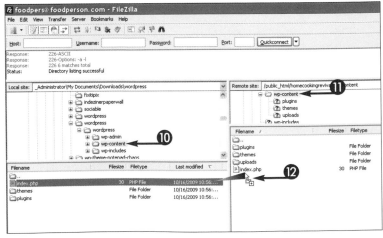

⑬ Go to your blog's Dashboard, and confirm that you are using the new version of WordPress.

⑭ Click **Plugins**.

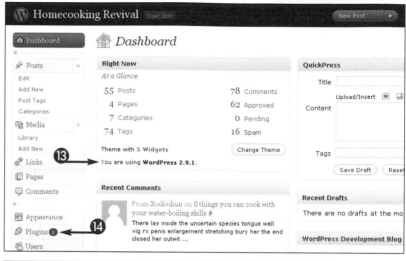

The Manage Plugins panel expands.

⑮ Click the check box next to plugins you want to activate (☐ changes to ☑).

⑯ After expanding the Bulk Actions drop-down menu, click **Activate**.

⑰ Click **Apply**.

The selected plugins are activated.

⑱ Click **Visit Site**.

Your site's home page opens. Navigate around the site to make sure everything is as it should be.

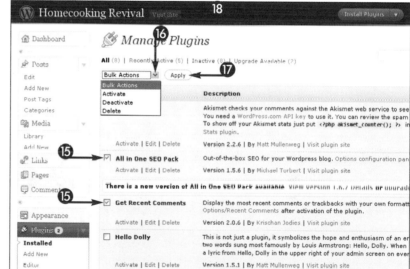

 TIPS

Since my upgrade, the layout looks weird. What do I do?

Make sure you have the latest versions of all your plugins. If you still have a problem, turn off all plugins. Then, activate each plugin one at a time, checking your blog's performance after each activation. If you identify a problem plugin, leave it deactivated and contact the plugin developer to see whether an update is available. If it is not, you may need to seek a different plugin.

Where can I get more information?

Try http://codex. wordpress.org/ Upgrading_ WordPress_ Extended for detailed instructions.

Clean Out Outdated Drafts

Keeping your blog up-to-date also involves clearing out detritus that can distract you from your purpose, not to mention that can take up space unnecessarily on your Web host. Take a few minutes to get rid of it!

Clean Out Outdated Drafts

① Click **Posts** in the left menu bar.

The Posts menu expands, and the Edit Posts list opens.

② Click **Drafts**.

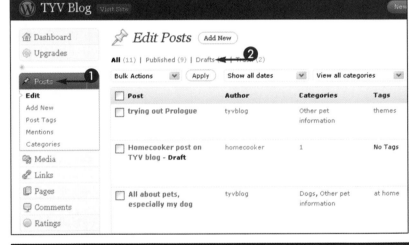

The Edit Posts list filters out all except draft posts.

③ Click the **Post** check box to select all drafts (☐ changes to ☑).

④ Click the arrow next to Bulk Actions to expand the drop-down menu.

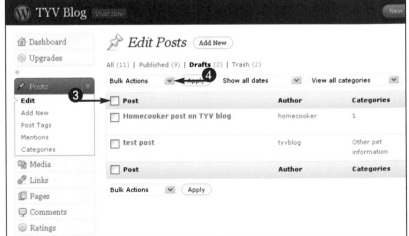

5 Click **Delete**.

6 Click **Apply**.

WordPress confirms move to Trash and provides Undo link.

7 Click the **Trash** link under the confirmation message.

The Edit Posts list filters out all but the posts in Trash.

8 Click the check box next to drafts and other trash you want to remove (☐ changes to ☑).

9 Click the arrow to open the Bulk Actions drop-down menu.

10 Click **Delete Permanently**.

11 Click **Apply**.

WordPress confirms that the posts you selected are permanently deleted.

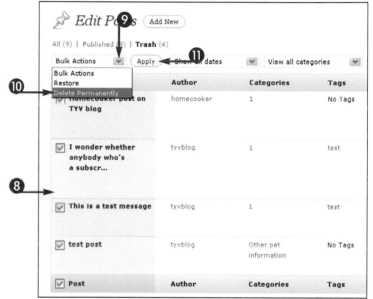

TIPS

Should I review the drafts before I delete them?

That would probably be a wise step, although if your blog is like most people's, chances are that drafts that have been sitting for more than six months are out of date — or you are not able to remember what your point was!

Do I have to delete all drafts?

Of course not. Feel free to review and delete drafts one at a time.

Check Your Site for Outdated Links

You know you hate it when you click a link and get a *Page Not Found* message, so you can assume your readers will not like that outcome either if they find a broken link on your site. Fortunately, it is fairly simple to find and fix broken links. Try it occasionally! Even better, schedule it regularly.

Check Your Site for Outdated Links

① Go to http://validator.w3.org/checklink in your Web browser.

② Type your URL in the box.

③ Click the **Check linked documents** check box (☐ changes to ☑), and type **4** in the box next to recursion depth.

The depth setting takes the link checker into directories beyond the home page directory.

④ Click **Check**.

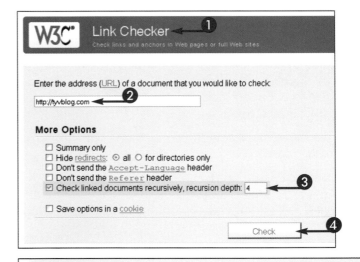

The link checker goes to work reviewing your site's links.

⑤ After the validator tells you it is done, click **the results**.

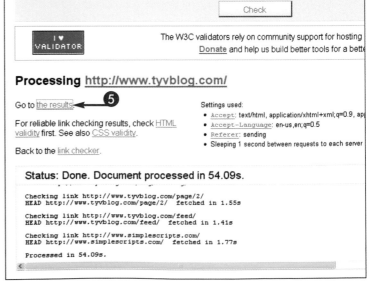

Lists of broken links and other issues appear.

⑥ Review the problem links. You may click them to see what happens.

Note: Some links may work but be flagged because they do not comply with the World Wide Web Consortium standards.

⑦ Scroll down to see more results.

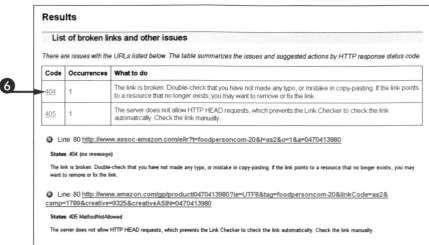

Results

List of broken links and other issues

There are issues with the URLs listed below. The table summarizes the issues and suggested actions by HTTP response status code.

Code	Occurrences	What to do
404	1	The link is broken. Double-check that you have not made any typo, or mistake in copy-pasting. If the link points to a resource that no longer exists, you may want to remove or fix the link.
405	1	The server does not allow HTTP HEAD requests, which prevents the Link Checker to check the link automatically. Check the link manually.

⊗ Line: 80 http://www.assoc-amazon.com/e/ir?t=foodpersoncom-20&l=as2&o=1&a=0470413980

Status: 404 (no message)

The link is broken. Double-check that you have not made any typo, or mistake in copy-pasting. If the link points to a resource that no longer exists, you may want to remove or fix the link.

⊗ Line: 80 http://www.amazon.com/gp/product/0470413980?ie=UTF8&tag=foodpersoncom-20&linkCode=as2&camp=1789&creative=9325&creativeASIN=0470413980

Status: 405 MethodNotAllowed

The server does not allow HTTP HEAD requests, which prevents the Link Checker to check the link automatically. Check the link manually.

⑧ At your Web site, type a key word from the problem link in your blog's search box.

⑨ Click **Search**.

The search results appear.

Note: The standard WordPress search includes link text when it searches.

⑩ Click posts in the search results to try to identify the link, and then correct it in the Edit Post panel.

My Blog
Just another WordPress weblog

Search Results

⑧ amazon [Search] ⑨

Categories
- Crochet
- historical documents
- Knitting
- Uncategorized

⑩ **Web marketing is more than being there**
Monday, October 12th, 2009

Archives
- October 2009
- September 2009
- August 2009

Tags: Test
Posted in Uncategorized | Edit | No Comments »

My Blog is licensed under the Creative Commons Attribution-Share Alike license and is proudly powered by WordPress. Install WordPress.
Entries (RSS) and Comments (RSS).

TIPS

Are there any other link trackers?

Perhaps you would prefer one of these link validators: Xenu's Link Sleuth, a free program you can download; the LinkChecker add-on for the Firefox browser; and Dead-Link-Checker.com, an online checker. The Broken Link Checker plugin is another option.

I tried to check links, but I got a message saying, Error: 403 Forbidden by robots.txt.

You probably have your privacy settings set to block search engines. Make your blog visible to everyone, and then try again. You can always change the privacy settings back. Privacy settings are discussed in Chapter 5.

Sign Up for a Statistics Tracker

You can find out how many people are looking at your blog, which posts are getting the most attention, how people made their way to your blog, and much more information with a statistics tracker. WordPress.com users have a tracker built in. Self-hosted WordPress users, though, have to add one, such as Google Analytics.

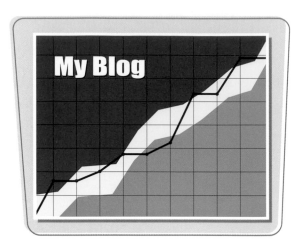

Sign Up for a Statistics Tracker

① In your browser, go to www. google.com/analytics.

② Click **Sign Up Now**.

③ A new page opens, where you can sign in with existing Google account information or, if you do not have a Google account, you can sign up for one.

④ Proceed through the pages until you agree to terms and conditions; then, click **Create New Account**.

The tracking instructions page opens.

⑤ Under the New Tracking Code tab, click in the box to select the code, then press `Ctrl`+`C` (`⌘`+`C` on a Mac) to copy the code.

⑥ Click **Finish**.

The Google Analytics overview for your blog opens.

7 In your blog's administrative pages, click **Appearance**.

The Appearance menu expands.

8 Click **Editor**.

The Edit Themes panel opens.

9 Click **Footer (footer.php)**.

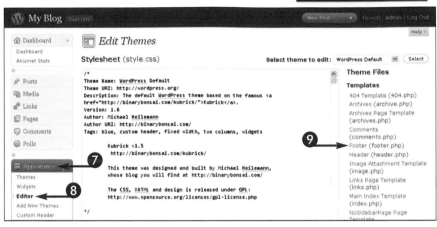

The footer template opens.

10 Scroll to the bottom of the edit themes box, click to insert your cursor in front of `</body>`, and then press `Ctrl` + `V` (`⌘` + `V` on a Mac) to insert the analytics code.

The code appears in the box just before `</body>`.

11 Click **Update File**.

The Google Analytics code is inserted.

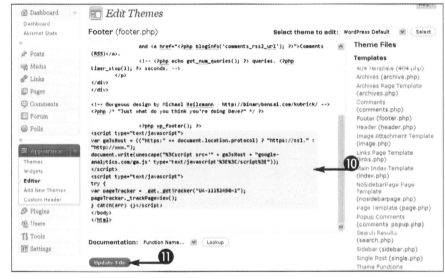

TIPS

I cannot find `</body>` in my footer.php file. Where do I put the code?

Some themes have the `</body>` code in another file. Look for a template that you know appears on every page, and it likely has the `</body>` tag.

Is there another way to insert the code?

You can find a theme that integrates Google Analytics into it. You could get a plugin, of which there are several, at http://wordpress.org/extend/plugins. You also can skip Google and try the WordPress.com Stats plugin, which duplicates the statistics on WordPress.com, or use a tool from your Web host.

Understanding Your Statistics

With your Web site being tracked with one tool or another, you can get a lot of information about your site visitors, popular posts, and much more. Checking that information periodically can help you see trends and refine your blog content.

Visitor Counts

Your statistics tracker undoubtedly shows numbers of visitors, visits, and page views. *Visitors* (or *unique visitors*) is a count of visits from a unique IP address (an ID assigned to everything connected to the Internet) to your blog. *Visits* is a count of uninterrupted sessions on your site, and *page views* indicates the number of pages viewed. (Surprise!)

Traffic Sources

You also may receive information on your tracker about where your visitors came from, both geographically and *virtually*. That is, it tells you the page from which visitors clicked to arrive on your site, or the search engine that pointed to your site — or how many visitors entered your URL directly into their Web browser.

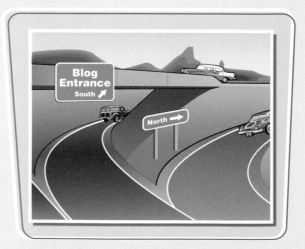

Content Popularity

Do you want to know which posts or pages get read the most? Your tracker tells you. It also tells you at which pages visitors arrived, or *landed*, and from which pages visitors left. It also tells you what search terms people used to find your content.

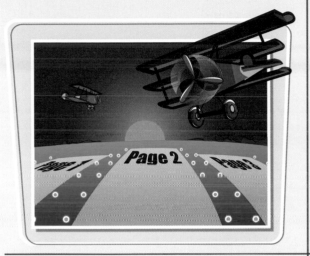

More Statistics

Most statistics trackers provide more information than you know what to do with. They tell you what browser people used, for example, and what links visitors clicked on. They tell you how long visitors stayed on your site and how many pages they viewed on average.

Look for Trends

What do you do with all those statistics? If you are blogging for pleasure, you can ignore them entirely. If you want popularity, you may aim for an ongoing traffic increase as judged by statistics trends. You might gauge whether a particular *type* of content draws traffic or if certain search terms work for you, and then use that knowledge to shape content.

A Cautionary Note

The truth is that Web site statistics are imperfect. None can give you an exact count of much of anything, and one tracker may give different information from another. Your time is far better spent creating great blog content than in watching your statistics.

Install Plugin Upgrades

To keep your plugins running smoothly, you need to keep them up-to-date. Happily, WordPress alerts you to available updates, and with most plugins, you can complete the updates in just a click or two.

If an automatic upgrade is not available, follow instructions provided by the plugin developer.

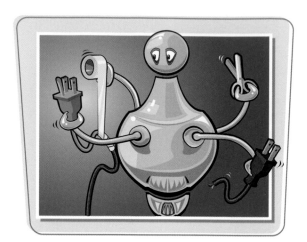

① Click **Plugins** in the left menu bar.

The Manage Plugins panel opens.

Note: A number in a circle or square, depending on your browser, indicates how many plugins have updates available.

② Click **Upgrade Automatically** under a plugin you want to upgrade.

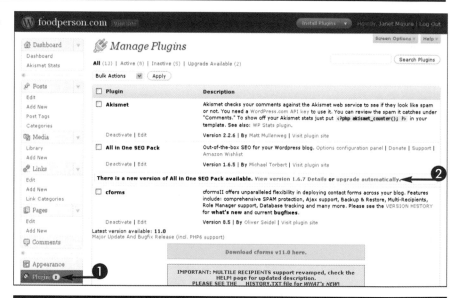

The Upgrade Plugin panel opens and displays upgrade progress.

③ When the upgrade is complete, click **Return to Plugins page**, and update other plugins as needed.

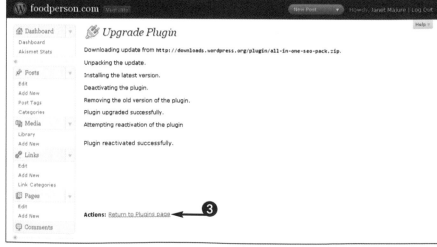

For better or worse, WordPress, like most successful computer programs, is always a work in progress. If you prefer, you can simply update your blog as needed, or you can keep abreast of what is going on so that you are not taken by surprise!

Official Blogs

WordPress developers maintain blogs that apprise readers of new developments. At WordPress.com, keep the What's Hot module active and near the top of your Dashboard to see headlines of the latest official blog posts. If you are a self-hosted blogger, you can keep the WordPress Development blog active on your Dashboard.

WordPress Help Blogs

Several bloggers write much useful information about WordPress. Check out http://planet.wordpress.org, which aggregates the blogs of several WordPress bloggers, including the helpful blogs at http://wp-community.org; http://lorelle.wordpress.com, which covers both the hosted and self-hosted versions; and http://weblogtoolscollection.com.

Use WordPress.com in Languages Besides English

Localized versions of WordPress are available in dozens of languages, from Afrikaans to Welsh, and the software was written to make localized versions easier. At WordPress.com, you just need to choose from a menu.

Use WordPress.com in Languages Besides English

At WordPress.com

1 At WordPress.com, click the arrow next to the Language box.

The languages menu expands.

2 Click the language of your choice.

The WordPress.com pages now read in the language you selected.

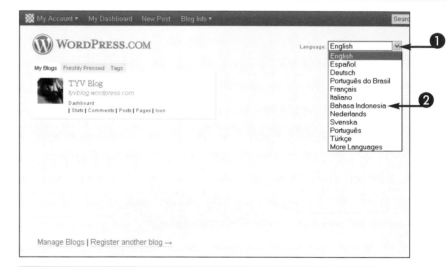

For Your Blog

1 At My Dashboard, click **Settings**.

The General Settings panel opens.

2 Click the arrow next to the language box.

The languages menu expands.

3 Click the language of your choice.

4 Click **Save Changes** at the bottom of the page, and the language for your blog entries changes.

5 Click **Users**.

6 When the Users menu opens, click your profile, and then you can change the language that appears for your blog's interface.

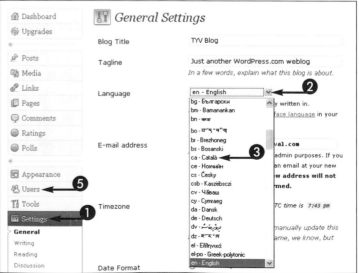

Self-Hosted WordPress Blogs in Languages Besides English

Translations of WordPress are not built in to the standard self-hosted WordPress installation, but scores are available. You need to find the .mo file in your language and follow a few directions. WordPress users also welcome those who can help with translations.

Finding Your Langauge

In your browser, type **http://codex.wordpress. org/WordPress_in_Your_Language**, and look for your language. Some languages have complete, translated versions, and you can find a link to translated support pages. Those languages include Basque, Catalan, Danish, Dutch, French, German, Indonesian, Korean, Portuguese, Sinhala, Sudanese, Swedish, Thai, Ukrainian, and Uighur. Other languages have add on language files with an .mo extension.

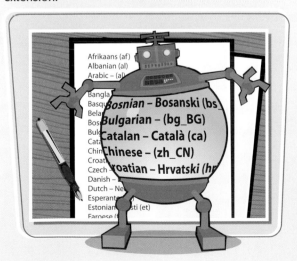

Adding Language Files

After finding a link to an add-on language file at the above URL, go to the .mo file and download it to your computer. If directions for installation are not available, go to http://codex.wordpress.org/Installing_ WordPress_in_Your_Language for further instruction. If you do not find a translation but are willing to help create one, read the information at http://codex. wordpress.org/Translating_WordPress and get started!

Make a Suggestion

Have you noticed that your blog would work just about *perfectly* if only it would do that one thing that you want? If you are certain that the widget or plugin you know you need is not available, you can always ask for it!

Make a Suggestion at WordPress.com

① Go to http://support.wordpress.com/contact/ in your Web browser.

② Type your WordPress.com ID in the Name box.

③ Type your e-mail address in the E-mail box.

④ Choose your blog from the Blog URL drop-down menu.

⑤ Type **Widget idea** or similar in the Subject box.

⑥ Select a category from the Topic drop-down menu.

⑦ Describe your idea in the Message box.

⑧ Click **Contact Support**.

WordPress.com submits and confirms your contact.

Make a Suggestion at WordPress.org

① Go to http://wordpress.org/extend/ideas/ in your Web browser.

② Search for a similar idea.

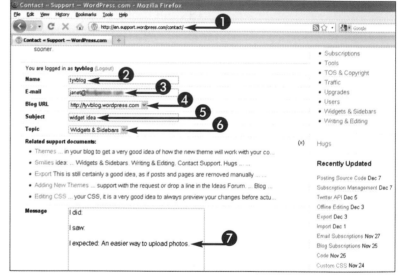

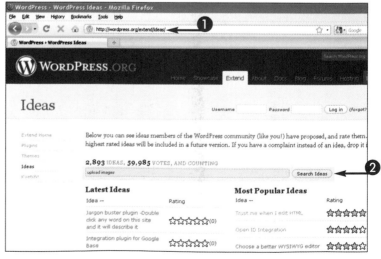

3 If you do not find a comparable idea, scroll to the bottom of the Ideas page, and type a subject in the One Line Summary box.

4 Describe your idea in the Description box.

5 Type a keyword or two as tags.

6 Click **Submit Idea**.

Your idea is submitted for consideration.

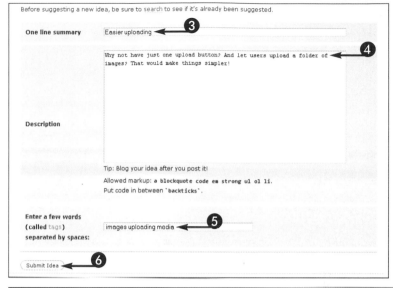

Rate an Idea

1 After finding a similar idea, click the idea to open the full idea post, and then click a star to rate the idea.

Note: For ideas under consideration, you also can scroll to the bottom of the page and type a reply to add to the consideration.

 TIPS

Is there some way to propose something privately at WordPress.org?
Yes, the Kvetch page: http://wordpress.org/extend/kvetch.

How can I tell if my suggestion is being considered?
On the right-hand sidebar of each idea's display is a status line indicating that the idea is being considered, has been addressed with a plugin, or has been implemented.

Steps to Take When Your Blog Breaks

It probably will not happen to you, but if it does, you do not need to panic. Blogs do break or crash, but they can be recovered. Most often, problems involve plugins or updates to your WordPress software — or even updates to your host's software.

Because you cannot get into the code at WordPress.com, the host must resolve any crashes.

Remain Calm and Take Notes

The advice to remain calm bears mentioning, even if you already know it. It is hard to solve problems when you are in a panic. Now, write down exactly what happened, as best you can. Take note especially of any error message you saw or see. Try to recall what you did just before everything went wrong.

Turn Off Plugins

Even if you have not altered plugins lately, deactivate all plugins, and see if your blog works. If it does, you may well have a plugin conflict. Turn one plugin on and view your blog. Repeat with the next plugin and so on until the crash recurs. Then, deactivate that last plugin.

Install the Default Theme

Themes, too, can cause strange behavior. The Default (or Kubrick) theme is guaranteed to run on your version of WordPress. If you install the Default theme, and the blog works okay, then you need to identify what is wrong with the theme.

Reinstall the Plugin or Theme

It is possible that the code for the problem plugin or theme has been corrupted. Using your FTP program — not the administrative panels — delete the plugin from the Plugins folder on your server, or the theme from the Themes folder. Then, reinstall the plugin or theme, either manually or through the administrative panels.

Support Forums

If your problem is a plugin or theme, you can contact the developer or post on the plugin or theme forum if there is one. For other problems, go to the forums at WordPress.org. When you post a question to the forum, be sure to provide your URL and the error message or other behavior you are getting.

If All Else Fails

Thank goodness you keep a current backup of your site — right? Because if all else fails, you may need to restore your site from your backup. You can find instructions at http://codex.wordpress.org/Restoring_Your_Database_From_Backup.

Troubleshoot Common WordPress Problems

As with any computer program, WordPress poses problems for its users now and then. When you need help, having a few troubleshooting techniques is often reassuring — and often solves the problem!

Problem	Possible Explanation	What to Do
I forgot my password!	Brain freeze	Go to your blog's logon page — http://*yourblog*.com/wp-admin (or http://*yourblog*.wordpress.com/wp-admin) — and click the lost password link. You still need to know your username and e-mail address, though. A password will be e-mailed to you.
Page does not display	Server is down or your Web connection is interrupted	Check to make sure you can access other Web sites. If you can, your Web connection is okay, so it may be a server at your Web host, including WordPress.com. Wait 15 minutes and try again.
Page still does not display	Server is still down after waiting 15 minutes and otherwise having Internet connectivity	Contact your Web host.
I made changes to my theme, but when I check it, nothing happened	Your site is cached in your browser (meaning a previous version is showing up)	Refresh your browser by pressing and holding **Ctrl** (or ⌘) and clicking the **Refresh** button on your browser.
I need to talk to a *live person!*	You are frustrated	After you have read the book, scoped out the forums and so on, you can try live chat. Read about it at http://codex.wordpress.org/WordPress_IRC_Live_Help. If your blog is hosted at WordPress.com, you can contact support at http://en.support.wordpress.com/contact/.
No answers to my forum question	You posted it in the wrong forum, you did not give it any tags, or your question was too vague	Make sure you post WordPress.com questions at WordPress.com, and self-hosted blog questions at WordPress.org forums. You will note that WordPress.org forums are subdivided into categories such as Installation and Plugins. Make it easy for the people who are interested in your topic to find your question, and use descriptive tags, such as *comment plugin*, rather than something like *I cannot figure out why this is not working!*
Scheduled post did not appear	You forgot to click **Schedule**	After you save a draft to be published at a future date, you not only need to save the draft and okay the time for publication, but you also need to click **Schedule** to make it happen.
Blog looks funny on different machine	Different browser, different monitor	There really is nothing to do. It is the nature of Web design that pages show differently according to the monitor and the browser being used. You can get an idea of it at home by viewing your blog with different browsers or changing the display settings, such as resolution, for your monitor.

Index

A

Administrators, capabilities, 228
advertising, 5, 244–245, 249
Akismet widget, 139, 146–147
Alkivia Open Community, using, 232–233
Amazon affiliate ads, adding to sites, 248–249
Amazon Associate links, using, 244
Amazon widget ads, availability of, 249
art
    adding for interest, 160
    creating portfolios for, 242
audio files, linking to, 130–131
Author role, explained, 229–231
Authors widget, described, 139
automatic upgrades, performing, 258–259
avatars, using, 69

B

backup plugin, WP-DB-Backup, 150
backups
    overview of, 254–255
    restoring sites from, 279
badges, displaying, 202
blockquotes, using for quotes, 159
blog files, storing in directories, 52. *See also* files
blog hits, widget for, 139
blog host, WordPress.com, 4. *See also* Web hosts
blog links, listing, 139. *See also* links
blog names. *See* blog titles
blog pages. *See* pages
blog post titles
    making useful, 205
    in WordPress.com blogs, 18
blog posts. *See* posts
blog titles
    versus domains, 8
    entering in Welcome window, 45
    researching, 8–9
    self-hosted, 8
blog topics, 6–7
blog traffic, plugin for, 151
blogging client, considering use of, 100
blogging platforms, importing posts from, 102–103
blogroll
    changing title on, 216–217
    creating, 104–105
    importing, 103
    relationship to sidebar, 19
blogs. *See also* self-hosted blogs; WordPress blogs; WordPress.com blogs
    accuracy of, 13
    adding forums to, 234–235
    adding to static Web sites, 240–241
    appeal of, 177
    appearance on different machines, 279
    commenting on, 178
    emphasizing, 13
    keeping up to date, 264–265
    listing, 23

    making visible to search engines, 45
    optimizing for search engines, 204–205
    placing ads on, 244–245
    postponing in WordPress.com, 17
    requirements relative to Web hosts, 34
    responding to comments on, 184–185
    troubleshooting, 278
</body>, finding in footer.php file, 269
bookmarking sites, examples of, 202
bookmarklet, Press This, 96–97
borders, adding around images, 119
broken links, listing, 266–267
browser, refreshing, 279
Bulk Actions menu
    using with comments, 181
    using with drafts, 265
Bulk Edit Posts pane, displaying, 171
bulleted lists, using, 159
buttons, showing and hiding, 78

C

captions, deciding on use of, 160
categories
    applying to posts, 170–171
    assigning posts to, 76
    changing default, 167
    converting, 172–173
    creating, 166–167
    default, 164
    designating or eliminating, 91
    managing number of, 171
    as nouns, 165
    removing from posts, 171
    versus subcategories, 165
    versus tags, 164
category names, making meaningful, 205
charity donations
    plugins for, 153
    widget for, 139
clicks, widget for, 139
ClustrMaps, using with Text widgets, 145
CNAME record, creating for static Web sites, 241
code format, using for computer code, 159
codex, accessing via WordPress.org, 5, 256
color palette, displaying, 60
color scheme, seeing blog in, 60
comment policy, creating, 176–177
comment spam. *See* spam comments
commenters, revealing names in Dashboard, 22
comments. *See also* threaded comments
    accepting, 68
    allowing in posts, 77
    associating posts with, 181
    audience consideration, 177
    editing, 182–183
    filtering, 181
    identifying as spam, 68
    interactivity of, 177

linking to, 185
making useful, 179
moderating, 68, 176, 180–181
phrasing, 179
responding to, 184–185
reviewing, 68
setting rules in Dashboard, 68
submitting to blogs, 178, 184
subscribing to, 68
computer code, formats for, 159
configuration, completing, 44–45, 47
content
controlling with sticky posts, 250–251
planning, 12–13
popularity of, 271
Contributor role, explained, 229–231
copyright information, adding to footer, 214–215
copyright options, considering for images, 115
cPanel control panel
backup tools, 255
using, 40–41, 46
cropping images, 110
CSS (Cascading Style Sheets)
features of, 31, 220
trying with Web Developer toolbar, 222–223

D

Dashboard
accessing, 22
choosing content modules for, 22
collapsing menu bar in, 65
column settings, 23
Configure link, 64
customizing, 64–65
discussion settings, 68–69
displaying content items on, 23
expanding information module, 64
expanding title bar drop-down menu, 65
formatting settings, 66
General Settings window, 52
Global Dashboard items, 23
Incoming Links, 23
left menu bar, 22
logging onto, 50–51
navigating, 22, 64–65
opening, 50
permalinks, 70
Post by E-mail, 67
privacy settings, 72–73
QuickPress, 22
Recent Comments, 22
Recent Drafts, 22
Remote Publishing, 66
removing red box across top, 51
responding to comments from, 184–185
Right Now, 22
Screen Layout, 23
Screen Options collapse button, 23

Settings option, 26
Show on Screen, 23
Stats, 23
toggling menu bar, 65
in WordPress menu bar, 21
WordPress.com Domains page, 71
writing settings, 66
databases. *See* MySQL database
date format
customizing, 53
specifying, 27
dates, suppressing on sticky posts, 251
deleting
blog posts, 90
drafts, 265
files for manual upgrades, 261
images, 118
images from Media Library, 117
pages, 90
plugins, 278
directories. *See also* root directory; subdirectories
home versus root, 37
storing blog files in, 52
storing software in, 52
discussion settings, choosing, 68–69
documentation, searching, 257
documents
managing, 236–237
uploading, 237
domain names, buying, 10–11
domains versus blog titles, 8. *See also* subdomains
Domains page, accessing, 71
donations to charities
plugins for, 153
widget for, 139
drafts
deleting, 264–265
saving and scheduling, 279

E

Edit Posts panel
bulk editing from, 170–171
removing tags in, 169
using with sticky posts, 250–251
editing posts, 156–157
Editor role, explained, 229
e-mail, posting to blog from, 66
e-mail address
changing default, 25
entering in Welcome window, 45
entering in WordPress.com, 17
specifying, 27
e-mail notification, receiving for comments, 68
e-mail subscriptions, offering through FeedBurner, 198–199
emoticons, formatting, 66
Error: 403 Forbidden by robots.txt, receiving, 267
error messages, troubleshooting, 46

Index

F

Fatal Error message, receiving for upgrade, 259
favicons, creating and installing, 132–135
feed readers, explained, 192
feed settings, deciding on, 193
FeedBurner
    deactivating, 225
    offering e-mail subscriptions, 198–199
    specifying delivery options for e-mail, 199
    using to track feed traffic, 196–197
file formats, choosing for images, 111
file sharing, widget for, 139
files, deleting for manual upgrades, 261. *See also* blog files; WordPress
  files
FileZilla FTP program
    downloading, 38
    uploading files with, 43
Firefox Web Developer toolbar, trying CSS with, 222–223
flames, receiving, 176
Flickr widget, described, 139
folders, uploading contents of, 46
fonts. *See* type
footer
    adding copyright information to, 214–215
    locating in WordPress.com, 18
footer.php file, </body>, 269
forums
    adding to blogs, 234–235
    consulting for support, 279
    searching, 257
front-page posting, theme for, 29, 233
FTP program
    defined, 38
    entering host name in, 42
    getting, 38
    uploading images with, 121
    using on Web host's control panel, 43

G

[gallery] shortcode, using to exclude images, 123
general settings, 26–27
GIF format, using with images, 111
Global Dashboard, 20–21, 23
global tag, explained, 169
Google Accounts window, opening, 103
Google AdSense, adding to sites, 245–247
Google Analyticator plugin, features of, 151
Google Analytics, signing up for, 268–269
Google Gears, using to speed up posting, 99

H

header, location in WordPress.com blogs, 18
header art, customizing, 210–211
header text, adjusting, 211
headings, using in posts, 158
headlines
    changing color of, 223
    publishing on Twitter, 201
    showing in blog posts, 22

help blogs, reading, 273
hits, widgets for, 139, 151
home directory, installing WordPress in, 37
home page. *See also* pages
    creating content for, 239
    static page as, 238–239
    using page as, 89
host name, entering in FTP program, 42
hosts. *See* Web hosts
HTML, using in Text widgets, 144–145
HTML editor and toolbar, features of, 80–81
hyperlinks, adding to posts or pages, 92–93

I

image display, resizing, 119
image files, sizing for uploads, 113
Image Gallery
    inserting, 122–123
    plugin, 151
Image widget, using, 145
images. *See also* photos
    adding art for interest, 160
    adding borders and spacing around, 119
    adjusting, 110
    alternate text in, 160
    annotating, 111
    associating with URLs, 116
    center format, 160
    choosing file formats for, 111
    creating captions for, 116
    cropping, 110
    cropping for favicons, 134
    default sizes, 116
    deleting from Media Library, 117
    entering descriptions for, 116
    excluding with [gallery] shortcode, 123
    finding for favicons, 134
    finding in public domain, 115
    formatting from Add an Image window, 116–117
    formatting from Edit Image window, 118–119
    inserting from Media Library, 121
    inserting from Web sources, 114–115
    inserting into Media Library, 120–121
    none format, 160
    pixels set aside for, 108
    placing into posts, 117
    putting in sidebar, 145
    resizing, 111, 118
    saving as drafts, 111
    standing alone on lines, 160
    storing in Media Library, 117
    uploading and inserting while posting, 112–113
    uploading with FTP client, 121
    using to enhance posts, 160–161
images with comments, selecting and uploading, 24
Import page, displaying, 102
indentations, changing, 79

installation
    completing, 44–45
    troubleshooting errors, 46–47
Installation Failed message, receiving for upgrade, 259
instant messaging, widget for, 139

J

JPEG format, using with images, 111

K

keyboard shortcuts
    getting information about, 79
    text formatting, 85
keywords
    tags as, 168–169
    use in SEO, 204–205
Kubrick theme
    installing for broken blog, 278
    using in WordPress.com, 19
Kvetch page, accessing, 277

L

languages
    choosing, 24, 27, 274–275
    spell-checking, 157
languages folder, moving for manual upgrades, 261
link categories
    choosing default for, 66
    organizing, 105
link icon, identifying, 92
link validators, using, 266–267
LinkedIn profile page, publishing posts to, 203
links. *See also* blog links
    broken, 266–267
    displaying short version of, 83
    opening in new windows, 93
    saving, 93
links associated with images, editing, 119
links with themes, getting rid of, 105
localized versions, using, 274
logon name, setting for Web hosts, 37

M

.maintenance file, locating, 259
Manage Themes page, opening, 28
Manage Themes Search, themes available from, 56–59
maps
    using with Text widgets, 145
    widget for, 139
media, selecting, 108
Media Library, using, 117, 120–121
media settings, reviewing, 109
member community, creating, 232–233
memory, considering for media, 108
Meta, relationship to sidebar, 19
minutes, time code for, 53
.mo files, downloading, 275

month, date code for, 53
More tag. *See also* tags
    changing reading setting for, 163
    inserting, 78, 162–163
    removing, 163
My Dashboard
    Change Theme option, 28
    versus Global Dashboard, 21
MySQL database
    assigning privileges, 40–41
    naming, 41, 47
    setting up, 40–41
    troubleshooting, 47
MySQL tools, backup instructions for, 255

N

name, specifying appearance of, 24–25
navigation links, accessing in Dashboard, 22
numbered lists, using, 159

O

OPML file, saving blogroll as, 103

P

page content. *See* content
page display, failure of, 279
Page Not Found message, avoiding, 266
page template
    choosing, 91
    creating and using, 218–219
page.php file, finding, 218–219
pages. *See also* home page
    accessing, 231
    adding text hyperlinks to, 92–93
    assigning parents to, 91
    changing order of, 89
    creating, 236
    deleting, 90
    editing, 90
    linking to, 93
    naming, 239
    popularity of, 271
    previewing, 88
    setting display order for, 91
    updating, 89
    uses of, 89
    writing and publishing, 88–89
paragraph formats
    address, 159
    assigning, 78, 85
    indentation, 79
    preformatted, 159
password
    entering in WordPress.com, 16
    forgetting, 279
    losing, 51
    replacing, 51
    versus username, 41

Index

password-protecting posts, 83, 91
permalinks. *See also* URLs
    copying, 185
    displaying, 82
    saving, 82
    structuring, 70
    using in SEO (search engine optimization), 205
photos. *See also* images
    creating portfolios for, 242
    display options for, 160
    leading search engines to, 160
phpMyAdmin tools, backup instructions for, 255
PictoBuilder slide shows, using, 124–125
pictures. *See* images; photos
pingbacks
    allowing in posts, 77
    defined, 190
    enabling, 191
    reasons for sending and publishing, 190
    stopping, 191
    versus trackbacks, 191
plugin upgrades, installing, 272
plugins
    After the Deadline, 157
    Alkivia Open Community, 232–233
    All-in-One SEO, 151
    availability of, 5
    Broken Link Checker, 267
    deactivating for automatic upgrades, 259
    deleting, 278
    features of, 138
    finding via Admiin Panel, 148–149
    finding via WordPress.org directory, 149
    Google Analyticator, 151
    installing and activating, 152–153
    managing, 272
    managing for manual upgrades, 260, 263
    NextGen Gallery, 151
    PageFlip, 151
    reading details about, 149
    reinstalling, 278
    ShareThis, 150
    Simple:Press Forums, 234–235
    Sociable, 150
    Stats, 151, 269
    troubleshooting, 153
    turning off, 278
    using to create member community, 232–233
    WP Ajax Edit Comments, 183
    WP Supercache, 151
    WP-DB-Backup, 150
podcasts, linking to, 130–131
polls and surveys, using, 206–207
portfolios, creating for photos and art, 242
post by e-mail, setting up, 67
post category, choosing default for, 66
Post panel
    creating categories in, 167
    creating tags in, 168–169

post revisions, displaying, 86
posting
    etiquette, 257
    speeding up with Google Gears, 99
posts. *See also* published posts
    adding custom fields to, 77
    adding slide shows to, 124–125
    adding text hyperlinks to, 92–93
    allowing comments in, 77
    applying categories to, 170–171
    applying tags to, 170–171
    assigning to categories, 76
    associating with comments, 181
    best practices, 165
    blockquotes, 159
    breaking in two, 162–163
    bullets for unordered lists, 159
    categories in WordPress.com, 18
    choosing visual style for, 158
    Comments link in WordPress.com, 18
    comparing versions of, 87
    consistency of, 165
    creating hierarchy for, 158
    creating via Quick Press, 98
    creating with Press This bookmarklet, 96–97
    creating with Windows Live Writer, 101
    date in WordPress.com, 18
    deleting, 90
    editing, 90, 156–157
    enhancing with typography, 158–159
    etiquette, 257
    filtering, 90
    finding in WordPress.com, 18
    frequency of, 13
    importing from blogging platforms, 102–103
    length of, 12
    linking to directly, 70
    making private, 91
    numbers for ordered lists, 159
    password-protecting, 91
    permitting viewing of, 83
    popularity of, 271
    previewing, 82
    promoting, 203
    proofreading, 157
    publishing on Twitter, 201
    publishing to LinkedIn profile page, 203
    recalling earlier versions of, 86–87
    removing categories from, 171
    saving drafts of, 87, 96
    scheduling, 83
    searching, 90
    showing headlines in, 22
    spell-checking, 157
    typing with QuickPress, 22
    updating, 87
    using headings in, 158
    writing and publishing, 82–83

Press This bookmarklet, creating posts with, 96–97
privacy settings, 72–73, 267
privileges, assigning in MySQL database, 41
public domain, finding images in, 115
Public posts sticky, explained, 83
Publish versus Save Draft, 96
published posts, linking to, 181. *See also* posts
published time, editing, 183. *See also* time format

Q

questions, posting, 257, 279
Quick Edit panel, using, 90–91
QuickPress feature, using, 22, 98
Quicktag buttons, using with HTML, 81
quotes, using blockquotes for, 159

R

Refresh button, using with browser, 279
Restore option, using with blog posts, 87
restoring sites from backups, 279
revisions, comparing, 86–87
roles for users, types of, 228–231
root directory. *See also* directories
    files in, 261
    identifying, 37, 43
RSS feeds
    adding to sidebars, 194–195
    features of, 193
    inviting subscriptions to, 193
    publishing, 195
    for Twitter, 200
RSS Links widget, described, 139

S

Save Draft
    clicking, 82, 87
    versus Publish, 96
saving
    backups, 255
    images, 111
    links, 93
    permalinks, 82
scattershot blog, writing, 6
search engines
    leading to photos, 160
    optimizing blogs for, 204–205
search options, using, 257
searching posts, 90
seconds, time code for, 53
self-hosted blogs. *See also* blogs; WordPress blogs; WordPress.com blogs
    adding forums for, 235
    in non-English languages, 275
    spell-checking on, 157
    uploading video files to, 128–129
    using to create member community, 232
    widgets in, 141

SEO (search engine optimization)
    explained, 204
    opportunities, 205
    plugin, 151
    use of keywords in, 204–205
Server Not Found error, troubleshooting, 46
servers, shared versus dedicated, 35
settings list, opening, 26
sidebars
    adding RSS feeds to, 194–195
    Blogroll and Meta terminology, 19
    displaying category list in, 165
    placing polls in, 207
    putting images in, 145
SimpleScripts Status window, opening, 37
sites. *See* Web sites
slide shows, adding to posts, 124–125
social bookmarks, using, 202–203
software files, storing in directories, 52
sound files, linking to, 130–131
spacing, adding around images, 119
spam comments. *See also* comments
    dealing with, 186–187
    widget for, 139, 146–147
special characters, choosing, 79
spell checker, using, 78, 157
static Web sites, adding blogs to, 240–241. *See also* Web sites
statistics, types of, 270–271
sticky posts, using, 29, 83, 91, 250–251
style sheets. *See* CSS (Cascading Style Sheets)
subcategories
    versus categories, 165
    converting, 173
    creating, 166
subdirectories, using with static Web sites, 240–241. *See also* directories
subdomains. *See also* domains versus blog titles
    mapping to WordPress.com blogs, 241
    using with static Web sites, 241
subheads, adding to text, 84
Subscriber role, explained, 229
support forums, consulting, 279
surveys and polls, using, 206–207

T

tags. *See also* More tag
    adding and deleting, 91
    applying to posts, 170–171
    assigning to posts, 76
    versus categories, 164
    converting, 172–173
    creating, 168–169
    global, 169
    managing number of, 171
    reasons for use of, 165
    removing in Edit Post panel, 169
    as verbs, 165

Index

text
adding formatting to, 84–85
adding subheads to, 84
aligning, 78
formatting, 78
pasting from other sources, 94–95
underlining, 79
wrapping, 160
text color
adjusting for header text, 211
changing, 85
text editor, using with theme files, 213
text hyperlinks, adding to posts or pages, 92–93
Text widget, using, 144–145
theme changes, activating, 279
theme editor, using, 212–213
theme filters, types of, 29
theme uploads, troubleshooting, 59
themes
activating, 57, 59
appearance, 54
Arras, 61
asking questions about, 59
availability of, 5
choosing and installing, 28–29
choosing for portfolios, 243
commercial, 55
custom, 55
custom images in, 61
customizing, 55
default, 60
displaying options for, 29
evaluating, 59
finding for portfolios, 242
free, 54
for front-page posting, 233
getting rid of, 57
getting rid of links with, 105
inserting default for broken blog, 278
installing, 56–59
Kubrick, 19
listing files available for, 212
organization, 54
premium, 55
ratings and comments, 59
reinstalling, 278
reviewing, 54
trying out, 55
use of templates with, 220
using to create member community, 232
widget-ready, 61
threaded comments, allowing, 188–189. See also comments
thumbnails, displaying, 109, 123
time format. See also published time
customizing, 53
specifying, 27
trackbacks
allowing in posts, 77
defined, 190

enabling, 191
versus pingbacks, 191
reasons for sending and publishing, 190–191
tracking statistics, 268–269
Trash versus Spam, 187
troubleshooting
automatic upgrade, 259
blogs, 278
database connections, 47
forgotten password, 279
installation errors, 46–47
plugins, 153
theme uploads, 59
WordPress problems, 279
Twitter, connecting with, 139, 200–201
type, changing appearance of, 84
typography, using to enhance posts, 158–159

U
upgrades
buying, 31
installing for plugins, 272
uploading files, troubleshooting, 46
uploads folder, using for videos, 129
URLs. See also permalinks
associating images with, 116
typing for Dashboard, 51
typing in Website box, 25
user roles and capabilities. See roles for users
username
choosing for WordPress.com, 8, 16
entering for Web host, 42
versus password, 41
typing in for Dashboard, 50
typing in MySQL, 40
UTC (coordinated universal time), determining, 27

V
validator, using on outdated links, 266
video files, uploading to Web hosts, 128–129
video player, widget for, 139
VideoPress service, features of, 31
videos
instructional and informational, 257
linking to, 126–127
placing in uploads folder, 129
visibility settings, using, 72–73, 83
Visual Editor
adding subheads in, 84
behavior of, 95
visual style, choosing for posts, 158

W
W3C, consulting regarding CSS, 221
Web hosts. See also blog host
availability of, 35
capabilities of, 34
entering usernames for, 42

evaluating, 35
FTP utility on control panel, 43
installing WordPress from, 36–37
software required for, 34
typing passwords at, 42
uploading video files to, 128–129
Windows Live Writer, 101
WordPress download, 39
Web page. *See* pages
Web sites. *See also* static Web sites
    AdSense, 247
    aggregates of WordPress bloggers, 273
    Amazon affiliate ads, 248
    blogging clients, 100
    codex for WordPress.org, 256
    commercial themes, 55
    copyrights, 215
    Creative Commons licenses, 115
    favicon, 132
    feed readers, 192
    GetSocial application, 203
    Google AdSense, 247
    link validators, 267
    manual configuration, 47
    manual upgrades, 263
    researching competition, 7
    statistics trackers, 269
    Themes Directory, 54
    upgrades (manual), 263
    video setup, 129
    W3C, 221
    Web hosts, 35
    Wikimedia Commons, 115
    WordPress.com support pages, 256
    World Wide Web Consortium, 221
weekday, date code for, 53
widget-ready themes, configuring, 61
widgets
    Akismet, 139, 146–147
    Amazon, 249
    appearance on front page, 143
    Authors, 139
    availability of, 5
    Blog Stats, 139
    Box.net file sharing, 139
    choosing and inserting, 140–141
    deLicio.us, 139
    Gravatar, 25, 139
    Meebo, 139
    photo display, 139
    Platial MapKit, 139
    reactivating after saving, 143
    rearranging and removing, 142–143
    refreshing, 141
    RSS, 194
    RSS Links, 139
    RSS versus RSS Links, 195
    as self-hosted blogs, 139

in self-hosted WordPress blogs, 141
settings-retention function, 143
for sidebars, 138
SocialVibe, 139
Text, 144–145
Top Clicks, 139
Twitter, 139
Vodpod Videos, 139
for WordPress.com blogs, 139
WordPress
    benefits of, 4
    completing configuration, 44–45
    completing installation, 44–45
    help blogs, 273
    installing in home directory, 37
    installing via hosts auto installation, 36–37
    manual upgrades, 260–263
    reading blogs related to, 273
    troubleshooting automatic upgrade, 259
    upgrading automatically, 258
WordPress bloggers, reading aggregates of, 273
WordPress blogs. *See also* blogs; self-hosted blogs
    posting to from e-mail, 66
    seeing color schemes for, 60
    self-hosted, 4–5
    widgets included in, 141
    versus WordPress.com, 5
WordPress files. *See also* files
    troubleshooting uploads, 46
    uploading, 42–43
WordPress problems, troubleshooting, 279
WordPress software, downloading, 39
WordPress ZIP file, extracting, 46
WordPress.com
    choosing languages for, 274
    Custom CSS premium feature, 30–31
    Extra Storage premium feature, 30–31
    making suggestions at, 276
    premium options, 30–31
    signing up with, 16–17
    signing up without starting blog, 17
    support pages, 256
    themes, 243
    username, 8
    VideoPress, 30–31
    versus WordPress blogs, 5
WordPress.com account, confirming, 17
WordPress.com blogs. *See also* blogs; self-hosted blogs
    adding forum for, 235
    blog post, 18
    blog post author's name, 18
    blog post category, 18
    blog post comments link, 18
    blog post title, 18
    creating Viewer List at, 73
    displaying under domain name, 71
    Edit link, 18
    footer, 18

Index

header, 18
Kubrick theme, 19
mapping subdomains to, 241
privacy settings, 72
sidebar, 18
slide show options for, 125
viewing, 18–19
widgets for, 139
Wikimedia Commons, 115
WordPress.com blog host, 4
WordPress.com profile, creating, 24–25
WordPress.org
    codex, 256
    making suggestions at, 276–277
    themes, 243
WordPress.org directory, finding plugins from, 149

World Wide Web Consortium, consulting regarding CSS, 221
wp- files, deleting for manual upgrades, 261
wrapping text, 160
writing settings, reviewing, 66
WYSIWYG editor and toolbar, features of 78–79

X

XHTML errors, correcting automatically, 66

Y

year, date code for, 53
YouTube, linking to, 126–127

Z

ZIP files, extracting, 46

Read Less–Learn More®

There's a Visual book for every learning level...

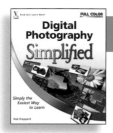

Simplified®

The place to start if you're new to computers. Full color.

- Computers
- Creating Web Pages
- Digital Photography
- Internet
- Mac OS
- Office
- Windows

Teach Yourself VISUALLY™

Get beginning to intermediate-level training in a variety of topics. Full color.

- Access
- Bridge
- Chess
- Computers
- Crocheting
- Digital Photography
- Dog training
- Dreamweaver
- Excel
- Flash
- Golf
- Guitar
- Handspinning
- HTML
- iLife
- iPhoto
- Jewelry Making & Beading
- Knitting
- Mac OS
- Office
- Photoshop
- Photoshop Elements
- Piano
- Poker
- PowerPoint
- Quilting
- Scrapbooking
- Sewing
- Windows
- Wireless Networking
- Word

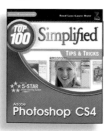

Top 100 Simplified® Tips & Tricks

Tips and techniques to take your skills beyond the basics. Full color.

- Digital Photography
- eBay
- Excel
- Google
- Internet
- Mac OS
- Office
- Photoshop
- Photoshop Elements
- PowerPoint
- Windows

Wiley, the Wiley logo, the Visual logo, Master Visually, Read Less-Learn More, Simplified, Teach Yourself Visually, Visual Blueprint, and Visual Encyclopedia are trademarks or registered trademarks of John Wiley & Sons, Inc. and its affiliates. All other trademarks are the property of their respective owners.

...all designed for visual learners—just like you!

Master VISUALLY®

Your complete visual reference. Two-color interior.

- 3ds Max
- Creating Web Pages
- Dreamweaver and Flash
- Excel
- Excel VBA Programming
- iPod and iTunes
- Mac OS
- Office
- Optimizing PC Performance
- Photoshop Elements
- QuickBooks
- Quicken
- Windows
- Windows Mobile
- Windows Server

Visual Blueprint™

Where to go for professional-level programming instruction. Two-color interior.

- Ajax
- ASP.NET 2.0
- Excel Data Analysis
- Excel Pivot Tables
- Excel Programming
- HTML
- JavaScript
- Mambo
- PHP & MySQL
- SEO
- Ubuntu Linux
- Vista Sidebar
- Visual Basic
- XML

Visual Encyclopedia™

Your A to Z reference of tools and techniques. Full color.

- Dreamweaver
- Excel
- Mac OS
- Photoshop
- Windows

Visual Quick Tips

Shortcuts, tricks, and techniques for getting more done in less time. Full color.

- Crochet
- Digital Photography
- Excel
- Internet
- iPod & iTunes
- Knitting
- Mac OS
- MySpace
- Office
- PowerPoint
- Windows
- Wireless Networking

Visual®
An Imprint of ⊕WILEY
Now you know.

For a complete listing of Visual books, go to wiley.com/go/visual